SUNLIGHT ON MY SHADOW

A Memoir

A Birth Mother's Journey from Secrecy to Renewal

Judy Liautaud

CITY CREEK PRESS, INC. ~ MINNEAPOLIS

This is a work of non-fiction. In all cases I have tried to be truthful and when necessary I have verified my recollections with others. Most names have been changed, except for the first names of close friends and family.

FIRST EDITION PRINTED 2013

Library of Congress Control Number: 2012916300

HTTP://SUNLIGHTONMYSHADOW.COM

ISBN: 978-1-883841-17-1

Published by:
City Creek Press
PO Box 8415
Minneapolis, MN 55408

CHAPTER 1
THE CABBAGE PATCH DOLL

The last time I played with a doll was over twenty years ago. I thought I was done with all that.

On a spring day in 1984 my two little girls, Kiona and Tessie, were at school. We were living in Cedar Fort, Utah, nestled on the edge of the Oquirrh Mountains, population 341. I was busy sewing hang-gliding harnesses for our flight school, Wasatch Wings, but couldn't find the scissors. Perhaps my kids were the culprits, so I went down to my girls' bedroom to take a look. There was the scissors lying on the floor next to one of their Cabbage Patch dolls. Alongside the doll were her adoption papers. You could fill these out, send them in, and get an official-looking birth certificate with your kid's name on it as the parent. The girls had made a little rag dress for the doll, using my scissors and sewing scraps. The doll looked like an orphan in need of some kind of comfort, so I picked it up. I didn't pick her up with the usual intention of cleaning a messy floor, but to cuddle her as if I were a child playing house. Nestling her head in the crook of my arm, I cradled her body close to me. I embarrassed myself, acting so childishly, and questioned my sanity. I was thirty-four years old, after all, and had two children of my own. Something urgent nudged me past my ill ease. I sat down on the edge of the twin bed and swayed back and forth while hugging the doll-baby. When I looked into her face, I saw sweet eyes and dark swirls of hair pasted to her head, reminding me of my baby, born seventeen years ago.

I wished I had held her back then. Her body close to mine felt delicious. I hugged tighter. Love pulsed through me with a soft electric hum. I started to cry and squeezed her body closer. I looked into her eyes and told her I was sorry. I was sorry I gave her away and I was sorry I punched my stomach when she was inside me. I was sorry I was missing her life and I was sorry I never held her. I sat there and rocked her while tears dripped down and slid their salty taste into my mouth.

I can't say how long I was there, sitting on the edge of the bed with the doll in my arms, but I stayed until I had said everything that had been knotted inside of me for the past seventeen years. When my words and tears dried up, I tucked the doll into the twin bed and pulled the covers to her chin. Grabbing the scissors from the floor, I went back upstairs and sat still at the sewing machine. I stared out the window and watched the newly budded leaves swaying on the trees. I felt crusty and smelly, as if I had been camping for a long time, and took a drenching, warm, cleansing shower. I found it strange how emotionally strong I felt, as though my body had been infused with a life force and a renewed capacity for joy, after doing something so insane.

It was then that I realized how much I had been holding inside and how much I was hurting, deep within the dark spaces of shame and regret. A bit of sunlight crept into my darkened heart.

The breakdown in the bedroom didn't come as a shock. I knew I was hurting. The ache was tangible, a shadowy lump in the left side of my body, inside my ribs. I had forgotten about the movie I had seen a year ago, which likely prompted my impulse to bond with the doll. I was with several midwives, labor coaches, and birth class instructors. It was about helping patients handle the grief of losing a baby in a more tender and caring way. The conventional method, whisking the stillborn away so the woman wasn't traumatized by a gray, lifeless child, turned out to be more harmful than helpful, the film said. The sweet women had felt their babies alive and well and had whispered to their little ones that they couldn't wait to welcome them into this world. Then, all of a sudden, there was nothing. No baby. Just silence after the birth. The women yearned to rub their hands over their baby, look at the tiny ears and toes. Well-meaning relatives and friends told the women it was pointless to have a funeral since the baby had never lived. Minimizing the loss made the women feel very alone in their sorrow. After months and years had passed, they wondered if something might be wrong with them because they couldn't get past their grief. They referred to themselves as emotional wrecks.

To help these women, health professionals were given tools to facilitate the process of grief. They gave the women dolls, proxy children, similar in weight to a newborn. They encouraged the women to role-play the rebirth of their babies, caress the dolls, and tell them how they were missed. Although they were initially fearful that they would crumble under the pain of loss, the women trusted the nurses and let their feelings and words flow. It was a heart-wrenching scene. In the end, the women said this exercise was extremely helpful. Almost all of them reported feeling at peace and lighter.

As I sat and watched the movie, a chord of familiarity resonated in my body. I thought the exercise might do me some good. I thought back to 1967, the last time I saw my baby. A junior in high school, I was one of those girls who got in trouble. I didn't think I fit the profile of these fallen girls. I came from a good, middle-class, Catholic family. I did my homework and got good grades. I used to grab my white leather missal and walk in the early morning darkness so I could ride the city bus to church. I attended Mass during Lent every day before school started. God had been good to me, answered my prayers. Somewhere along the line, I took a wrong turn. God wasn't going to get me out of this one, as I prayed rosary after rosary that my period would start.

In the 1950s and 60s, over one and a half million girls got pregnant out of wedlock, were sent away, and gave their babies up for adoption. We were liberating ourselves from the strict moral codes that our parents purportedly lived by, yet there was no readily available birth control, and nobody talked about it. Condoms were guarded behind the pharmacist's counter and remained there, unless you were 18 and could show an ID to make a purchase. It was before Roe v. Wade. The only abortions I heard of were from a movie I saw at school where desperate teens went for coat-hanger abortions performed by sleazy people who lived off alleyways; the girls escaped death by a thread.

The mothers and fathers of the girls who got in trouble concocted stories to explain their daughters' absences. School policy did not condone advertisement of this abhorrent behavior, so it was grounds for being expelled. Shunned by society, we were sent far from home to protect our secret. Many of us went away to Homes for Unwed Mothers. Some of these buildings were originally constructed to hospitalize the returning World War II veterans. Then, in the late 1940s, the hospital floors were converted into delivery rooms and maternity wards. Cots lined the walls for sleeping quarters and industrial-sized kitchens adjoined the dining hall. The home I stayed at was stark, yet efficient.

Fictitious names added dimension to our secret fantasy, as we were instructed to never, under any circumstances, give away our last names. We must, however, give away our babies. Our interlude with passion faded like a morning mist as we moped around the building, donning sack like blouses that camouflaged our protruding bellies. We were girls in waiting: waiting for our sentence to be carried out until the days of reckoning. Labor, birth, adoption. Clean and slick. Back home to resume life as usual, miraculously recovered from our alleged illness, instructed to never look back.

The master plan was to keep it a secret and all in my past. When it was over, I'd erase the memories like a swift punch of the delete key. When I was just sixteen, the carefully woven lie was a lifesaver. It would protect me from extra bullets of shame that already riddled my bones—the fear of what others would think if they knew I committed the mortal sin of sex before marriage. Shame sucked the breath out of me and lay tight on my throat and chest. If there was a way to get out of this predicament without being thought of as a slut for all eternity by my classmates at Regina Dominican High and the nuns and priests at Our Lady of Perpetual Help Church, I was eager to live the lie. I imagined if they found out, I would be a castaway, a leper, friendless, shunned and ignored, banned to a lifetime of lonely regret.

Giving my baby away was not easy to forget. As an adult, the resulting grief cloaked my spirit. When I saw a baby being born on TV, I cried. When I saw a mom at the mall carrying her newborn in a pack close to her chest, I was brought to tears. When my first child was born that was truly my own, I loved her so, yet sobbed for the one I had lost and began to wonder how I could have given away my own child to a stranger.

In writing the words of my story, I try to make sense of this traumatic childhood sorrow. It continues to be a dynamic process, like riding an escalator. Sometimes I climb up as the steps move, adding speed to my journey. In less productive times I shuffle backward, against the natural momentum, afraid to move ahead. This is when I stuff the rising emotions of sadness and regret, not allowing myself to feel, causing a flat numbness. During these times of procrastination I could spend hours writing early childhood anecdotes that really had nothing to do with my story; I was not yet ready to get to the heart of the matter. The upward part of the journey is when I write what matters and become reacquainted with my teenage self. During these times of grace I uncover compassion for the child in me and I find forgiveness. Regardless of my steps up or down, I continue my quest for the top in this, my sixtieth year of life.

When I first started writing, I navigated through a fog of lost memories, adept at having stuffed them away. But as the sun clears the morning fog, one by one the memories unfolded as I wrote, until the picture was repainted.

This one, an indelible part of me:

As we stood outside the Salvation Army Home for Unwed Mothers, with the trunk open and the items being gathered for my extended stay, my father took each of my books, including my cherished white leather prayer book, and, using his Parker fountain pen, scratched my last name from the inside covers of each one. I would be referred to as Judy L. during my stay. Then, my father gave his last bit of advice, "You'll forget about this, Judy, and you'll never have to speak of it to anyone again. Later, you may get married, but there's no reason to even mention this to your husband."

DAD FISHING - 1980

DAD, JEFF, JUDY, MOM 1956

CHAPTER 2
MY DAD, JOHN N.

Before anyone knew about my trouble, my dad was the person I most feared facing. I was scared of how it would disgrace our family, but mostly I was scared of his anger and what he would think of me because it crushed me when I got on the wrong side of Dad.

By the time I was a teen, I didn't particularly like hanging around home. Most kids are like that, but our house gradually took on an air of gloom after Mom got sick. She was in and out of the hospital with side effects from the drugs she took for her rheumatoid arthritis, and my brother Jeff had gone away to college. Sometimes it was just me and Dad at the dinner table. There was a code of acceptable conversation; if I had a good score on a test or got some kind of an award, that brought nods of enthusiastic approval, but if I was worried about a big paper coming up, or didn't feel so hot, or was sad, I would hold that to myself. I don't think Dad's radar picked up on emotional needs. If I accidentally steered the conversation in the direction of negative feelings, Dad's lips would get thin and I knew I had struck a wrong note.

Dad's emotional makeup had two extremes. On the one end, he was jovial and excited—the life of the party. If friends dropped by he would spurt with genuine exuberance and make a fuss, asking Mom to set an extra place at the table, saying how good it was to see you. He had a way of swelling you up like a puff bird.

On the other end, he had a fiery temper. When something set him off, his body stiffened and his face got red and rigid. His voice could shatter glass. I never knew what was coming when his anger flared, but to me, it had the ominous potential of a hairline crack in a river dam. When I was very small he took me over his knee and spanked my bareness. I don't know what nasty thing I did to invoke this treatment, but it might have been the time I pocketed some candy from the drugstore. He didn't hit me after I was school-aged, even though it was the "spare the rod, spoil the child era," and parents thought they should give us whippings to keep us in line. I tried fervently to refrain from invoking Dad's anger. The best way to do that was to do what I was told. During most of my young years I succeeded, but as a teen I veered off into combustible territory.

Mom and Dad had some explosive fights that shook the marrow in my bones. I still quiver inside when someone around me yells or spouts anger directed at me. My words get stuck in my throat. If I talk the tears flow, so I hold it in. Then my silence makes me feel invisible, insignificant. This happens infrequently nowadays because most of the people around me control their anger—or maybe it's because I've become less annoying.

My dad was over six feet tall and although he had a potbelly, his legs were quite thin, but you didn't see that because he wore khaki pants that hung tight at the waist and then loose from there on down. Also, the commonly seen rounded derriere that serves as a trouser stabilizer was absent in Dad. His body shape proved to be a hazard. I remember him working in the garage with both hands occupied when the pants would go. Like a roller coaster rounding the top, there was no turning back. He'd puff out, "Sonofabitch," stop what he was doing, and with disgust, yank the khakis back up to cover his exposed boxers and beanpole legs. In his later life, suspenders saved Dad from this pesky embarrassment.

The pants falling was a rare sign of Dad's vulnerability, because in most areas Dad dripped with dignity and charisma. He could light up any party with his joke telling: he was a Pied Piper of sorts. His charismatic skills led the way for his success in business, at social events, and on the lake. He could charm a northern pike right onto his hook while others in the same boat were just swatting flies.

Dad didn't like to leave the development of his prodigy to chance. His values were aptly conveyed: we should strive to be business owners because, if you work for somebody else, you'll never make any money; it's our duty as a family to stick together because if one is down, the others can help him back up; high grades in school are expected and praiseworthy.

Then there were the unwritten rules that I learned by example: Questioning laws or authority is commendable as long as you aren't hurting someone else; don't wait in a line if you can avoid it; and don't sit in a traffic jam if you can weasel your way around it. Thinking up ways to be efficient and save time are indications that you have a brain on your shoulders.

One time, shortly after I got my driver's license, Dad made an arrangement through his network. When I appeared in front of Judge So N So, I would be let off the hook for my recent speeding ticket. This scared me: would I have to lie? I stood in the courtroom and told the judge that I didn't *think* I was speeding. He ruled in the cop's favor and I got my deserved penalty. When I returned home and gave Dad the verdict, he spouted with disgust and said he'd have to talk to his contact to find out what went wrong. I could tell, though, that Dad thought I was the one who blew it.

Mom and Dad hosted Sunday Dinner for his five brothers at our house when I was young. It was a festive affair, with lots of business talk, gut-busting jokes, and booze flowing from the bottle to the glasses. The wives usually listened or talked amongst themselves while I sat unnoticed as I poked at my food, pretending I was still eating. No one said much to me except for the occasional comment from Uncle Phil, "You oughtta eat more 'cause if a big wind came up, you'd blow away." Hardy-har, they thought that was funny, but it made me cry inside because I hated being skinny and took it like a defect.

I may have been skinny, but I was strong. When I was in kindergarten, Dad held Poker Club at our house once a month. I remember when he'd give a yell upstairs to fetch me. The air was thick with cigar smoke and martini vapors; the men were gathered around green-felt-covered tables. They were usually sipping drinks, laughing and joking, with cards fanned out in their hefty hands when Dad would say, "Fellas, you have to take a look at Judy's muscles. Go ahead, Judy, show 'em what you got."

On cue, with pride, I pulled up my shirt sleeve and bent my arm in a tight vee. Each time—it amazed even me—a golf-ball-shaped muscle popped up from under my skin. It was like a magic trick because it wasn't something you would expect on a tender, string-bean arm. I thought I was akin to Popeye, the cartoon character who gulped cans of spinach, causing muscles to erupt on both arms. Dad didn't like the dainty, helpless, or weak type of woman, but admired strength and independence. My right bicep was unnaturally large from frequent flexing, but I was glad Dad never asked me to show the one on the left. It didn't seem to pop up properly.

I learned at an early age that my body shape, hair style, or clothes were an instigator of admiration or displeasure based on Dad's keen eye. I fell in line, brushing my teeth daily and washing behind my ears. When I started kindergarten, I'd have my school bag strapped over my shoulder, ready to walk out the door, when Dad would say, "Judy, wait just a minute. Come over here." Then he'd sit down on the couch and say, "Did you wash up? Lemme take a look." I'd put my book bag down and walk over to him.

Then he would pin me between his legs and squint.

"Smile. Let me see your teeth."

I'd bare my teeth.

"Now open up."

He'd put his hands on the sides of my cheeks, tilt my head back, and look inside—up, down, and all around. Then he would bend my ears back and look in the crease behind. He might say, "Very good, go on to school." Or, "There's sleep in your eyes, give it another once over. I want to see that face of yours shine." This was the routine, done in a matter-of-fact manner, like he was doing quality control on the assembly line at his factory.

When I was very little, Dad's compliments felt like fairy dust, swirling through me and lightening my spirit. A fond memory is the day I came home from first grade with straight A's: I thought Dad would take flight as he peered at my perfect report. I longed to repeat the performance, but the next year I got checkmarks for "lacks self-control"; I was prone to conversing with my neighbor.

Once I became a teen, the compliments from Dad were hard to come by and unpredictable, like a slot machine. I never quite knew when I would get the payoff, but I kept pulling the handle. I realize now that predicting how I could please Dad was a useless aspiration. He was like a sports coach, pointing out your weaknesses so you could improve. That was just his way of loving you and showing he cared about how you turned out. Sometimes he liked my outfit or new haircut, but I was often timid to show myself, especially when I had on my first pair of nylons or tiny high heels.

Dad was a master storyteller. My cousins and I would gather around for his stories of *The Snoose and the Snocker* ("POW," he'd yell as he pounded his fist into his other hand) or *The Three Billy Goats Gruff,* when Dad would sometimes stand up to impersonate the troll under the bridge who wanted to eat the tender little billy goats in one bite. I shook with fright and delight at these stories.

There was an obvious gap in the subject matter of Dad's stories, which was anything pertaining to family history. When I'd ask about our roots he'd say, "Better watch out, you might find out something you don't wanna know." I wondered if my great-grandpa was a thief or murderer.

As adults, we discovered Dad's family secret. My sister, Jackie, had told Dad about her desire to visit New Orleans to work on our genealogy. "Don't bother," he said. "The courthouse burned down years ago with all the records." Regardless of Dad's warning, Jackie visited the Big Easy and uncovered my grandfather's birth certificate with the race labeled "c," for colored. We, the Liautauds, thought we were Forever White, but this revelation necessitated a closer look. Could it be true? After all, we had full lips, curly hair, and darker skin that tanned and didn't burn.

Jackie came home, eager to see what Dad had to say about this discovery. Dad went off like a steam engine, sputtering and pointing his finger at the door. "Get out of my house," he said, "and don't you ever bring that subject up again." Months later, my brother Jim supplied Jackie with copies of family certificates, many stamped with the "c," confirming our black roots.

It was Uncle Phil who eventually filled us in on the details. In 1911, the social climate had changed for free men of color and their rights were being taken away. As Uncle Phil said, "They were

pinning crimes on us and hanging our friends." So, when Dad
was seven years old, his family bought a one-way ticket north. On
Friday they left their home in New Orleans, colored folk, unable
to vote, ride the bus, or drink from a public fountain. On Saturday
they stopped over in St. Louis, and boarded the front of the train.
When they got off in Chicago, they were white and free with all the
privileges of society's favored race. We were "passing" for white.

The Liautaud family made a pact to never speak of it again.
Uncle Phil told a story of Dad working as a bellboy at the same
hotel as his mother, who worked as a maid. They pretended they
didn't know each other because association with Mama might have
compromised Dad's employment. You had to be white to work as a
bellboy.

So when I got pregnant out of wedlock, it made perfect sense
that Dad would first react with a burst of anger and then concoct a
new story to protect our name. Judy would not bring shame to the
Liautaud family when we had fought so hard for the rights of the
privileged.

MOM AND DAD'S WEDDING 1929

CHAPTER 3
MY MOM, ETHEL MAY

Where Dad was hard to please, Mom was just the opposite and tossed compliments at every step and turn as I spun through life. When Mom heard about my teen pregnancy, she was painfully distraught and blamed herself for not being there to "mother" me. I felt horrible that I had let her down; I didn't think it was her fault that she was in and out of the hospital.

As a little girl, I could do no wrong and was often the center of attention. At first I didn't know what Mom meant when she called me her blessing in disguise, but I came to realize that the disguise was the unwanted pregnancy and the blessing was the baby she couldn't help loving. No one said it out loud to me, but I don't think Mom and Dad really wanted a fifth child. Everyone knows how life gets easier as the kids grow and become more independent. I remember Mom using a tone of exasperation when she talked about my birth, saying things like, "starting over at *my* age." Mom called me the baby of the family, which insulted me from the age of four clear on up to adulthood.

I know I slid in there under the wire, just before Mom hit menopause. Jeff, next up from me, was already seven and Jim and John were sprouting facial hair and liked girls. Jackie, the oldest of the family, would turn nineteen just before I was born and was in love with her soon-to-be husband. I was hitched on as the caboose after the family train had been chugging along for almost twenty years.

Mom was a good Catholic and used the only method of birth control the church allowed, the rhythm method. I guess she lost the beat.

Mom told this story about my birth:

"I was lying in the hospital bed with you nestled in my arms—you were just a few minutes old. I looked up at the ceiling of the hospital room and rose petals began to fall from above. The Virgin Mary stood by you as big as life. She put her hands out over you like they do in church to bless someone. When I looked down, there were crimson petals lying softly near your little body. As fast as the Virgin Mary came, she was gone, evaporating into thin air. It was like she came to visit you, to bless you with a greater purpose. I got the message. I would only be here to guide and nourish you, but your life would have some greater significance."

I always loved that story because it made me feel like I was a welcome and special addition to the family. I sometimes wondered if Mom took it to mean I was supposed to be a nun … Well, at any rate, that didn't happen.

In my early years, we lived in the city of Chicago in a neighborhood of mixed ethnicity on Fairfield Avenue. Mom used to flit around like a hummingbird: cleaning, rearranging furniture, and entertaining her bridge club ladies. She had lots of friends from the club and was also friends with the wives of Dad's fishermen friends. Mom was a loyal comrade, but if you ever said something derogatory about her kids or committed some other odious offense, she would drop you like a flash in the night.

People said Mom was a nice-looking woman. It wasn't so much that she was a natural beauty, but that she attended to the details of her appearance. Her ocean-blue eyes were her best physical asset, often twinkling with love diamonds when she cast her eyes upon her children.

Early on, Mom looked forward to her weekly visits to the beauty parlor and came home with cherry-red fingernails and a freshly curled hairdo she called a bustle. It was flat on the sides and held in place with two comb fasteners. The top and back of her head were full of puff, following the shape of a curly Mohawk. The bustle always looked best on the first day after the parlor visit, but it gradually flattened and frizzed out as the week wore on. Later on,

when the arthritis had a grip on her, she couldn't lift her arms high
enough to maintain the do, so she had it cut short. She said it was
easier to get a comb through it.

Mom often held a rosary to her chest, fingering the beads and
moving her lips: she found a respite from pain through prayer.
She cherished the Virgin Mary statue that sat on the dining room
shelf and the Sacred Heart of Jesus plaque that hung over the front
door. Virgin Mary wore a powder-blue hood with white tassels that
framed her porcelain face and a cape that draped over her shoulders.
Her fingers were delicate and graceful, about to be clasped in prayer.
The statue of the Virgin was only from the waist up.

The Sacred Heart of Jesus hung over the arched doorway. If
Mary was only from the waist up to save on raw materials, the
Sacred Heart of Jesus was super economical because it was just a
heart and no body. Thorns that looked like barbed wire, wrapped
around the bulging heart, and tears of blood dripped from the
wounds. I thought it was a little creepy, just a heart and no Jesus,
but Mom treated it like it was a sacred relic. She said it showed how
Jesus suffered for our sins and blessed everyone who entered our
home.

When I was nine we moved from our city bungalow on Fairfield
Avenue out to the fresh air of the suburbs. Glenview had some
older homes with stately trees and expansive yards, but we were in a
newer area with saplings and freshly laid sod struggling to take hold.
It was a trilevel house with three bedrooms upstairs: one for Jeff,
Mom and Dad in the middle, and one for me. We had all the new
conveniences, including a garbage disposal, push-button telephones,
and a garage door that opened with a remote control.

In our freshly built house, I was enamored with the French
Provincial decor. The sheer height of my headboard caused it to
wiggle whenever I plunked down. It was made of wrought iron filled
with cream-colored curlicues speckled with gold. The pink curtains
slid on gold rings that chimed when the wind blew in. When I
pressed the button in the middle of the dresser, the skirted arms
popped open to expose the drawers. It was fun when I was nine, but

by the time I was thirteen, I didn't bother closing the thing anymore. I just left it with the arms splayed out and stuff hanging out of the drawers like a cornucopia. The messy room was a bone of contention between Mom and me. She was forever nagging me to clean up after myself.

The best feature of my bedroom was the window that opened over the garage. On daring, starlit nights, if I had a friend sleep over, we'd stand on a chair and climb out the window, dragging our pillows and blankets behind. We had to be careful because there was a good pitch to the roof, but if we kept our legs bent and the soles of our feet on the shingles, we could keep from sliding. Once situated, we'd lie back, listen to the crickets, smell the freshly cut grass, and count the falling stars. We made sure to tiptoe and whisper so we didn't get busted. I thought it would be fun to smoke cigarettes up there, but since Mom quit smoking it was too risky. She was irritated by smoke and I was sure she would have been able to smell it right through the brick walls.

Around the time I was in fifth grade, Mom became incapacitated and we started having strangers live with us. Housekeepers, we called them. First it was an elderly, light-boned woman named Helen. She was from Hungary, cooked homemade spaetzle, and taught me how to knit. She brought her companion to live with us, a gentle but imposing black lab. The house took on a funny smell.

I had begged for a puppy when I was little, but Mom said she raised five kids and five dogs and that was enough. By the time I was born, canine number five was off to dog heaven. Jay Jay was a springer spaniel aptly named because the rest of the family were Jackie, Johnny, Jimmy, Jeffy, and Judy. My dad was John, so we joked that we should call Mom "J-Ethel."

The next housekeeper was Hugren, the Barbie-doll babe from Iceland. She had a cleavage that could dwarf the Grand Canyon, ice-blue eyes, and a white-blonde bouffant. She had an unsympathetic and cool style about her, maybe because her English was sketchy. I didn't really interact with Hugren, just offered a polite hello and good-bye as I came and went. When I was a teenager, I spent most of the time in my room lying on the bed, talking on my pink Princess telephone. When Hugren heard about my "secret pregnancy," she said she wasn't surprised because she had noticed, while doing the laundry, that my panties were suspiciously unsoiled. What the heck? Who would notice such a thing?

When I was ten, Mom contracted the illness that changed her life. She was helping Dad skin a deer in our bunkhouse cabin up at Bond Lake, and the next day she came down with shooting pains in her shoulders, hands, and legs. Six months later she was diagnosed with rheumatoid arthritis. She tried everything for pain relief, including aspirin, narcotics, and steroids.

At first Mom made incessant trips to the doctor for cortisone shots. When those quit working, she tried a "specialist" who worked out of his home in Mount Prospect. It was a long ride out there and the treatments took about an hour. Mr. Quigley plunked her into a straight-backed "miracle chair" and strapped electrode-studded cuffs to her wrists and ankles. The chair was attached to what looked like a car battery. Although Mom said she didn't feel anything after Mr. Quigley flipped the switch, he assured her that the treatment usually took a while to start working and it was the cumulative effect that would make the difference. Mom paid him a healthy sum, set up another appointment, and left feeling hopeful.

This just added to her long list of failed attempts at a cure for her pain. By the time I was in fifth grade, she spent most of her time in a motorized wheelchair, clipping corners and shaving the paint off the dining room wall. Dad hired house helpers to be Mom's kitchen hand. She'd direct the cook like a robot, giving explicit directions on the action of the knife, the size the pieces should be, or the consistency of the concoction. She didn't follow recipes but was a fabulous cook and had everything in her head, so it was particularly frustrating for her to communicate these artistic directives. She was crippled with aching stiffness that would flare up whenever a storm was looming. During high-pressure weather, her achy joints stayed at a constant painful hum. She used to say to me with a wistful look in her eye, "Oh, if only I could sweep the floor, or chop up some onions."

It was my job to answer the buzzer at night and take her to the bathroom. By day, I was often kept busy fetching this or that for her, opening jars, or handing her the telephone. When I brought her a drink of Squirt soda or emptied her piss pot, she would sigh and say, "You're my little blessing in disguise. I'm so thankful for you." It was sweet that she was appreciative, but oftentimes I resented being on call. Just when I was talking on the phone about some boy or doing homework, she would give a yell from her mechanical bed in the living room.

"Joooooody, come here, please."

The shrill sound grated on my nerves. Her retrieval voice had a falsetto tone that carried far and beyond. If I was in the middle of something, I might say, "What now?" Then, after the task was done, I'd feel remorse because I was thoughtless and selfish. I reminded myself that Mom couldn't help herself, but I was preoccupied with managing my adolescent social life. I prayed that there would be some miracle cure that would bring Mom back to the active, joyful homemaker she used to be.

I was proud of my mom when she was healthy and I was little, but as a teen, I am sad to say, I was embarrassed to bring friends over to my house. Besides for living in a motorized wheelchair or in bed, Mom had large bruises up and down her arms and legs from bumping into things. This bruising was a side effect of the prednisone, a steroid drug that she took for the pain. Her hands were swollen and her hair was now frizzy on the sides and flat in back from lying in bed and sweating. Despite my dread at the thought of introducing my mom, I still had friends over. But if they said something later, like "What's wrong with your mom's arms?" I'd cringe and feel protective of her, and get angry inside because it wasn't something I wanted to talk about. A lot of the time Mom wasn't home at all, because she had one illness after another that landed her in the hospital for weeks at a time.

The times I remember most are not when she got angry at me for not cleaning my room or when I disappointed her with my monster teen-pregnancy slipup; the memories I cherish are when she would joke and we would laugh together. One time, in the middle of the night, she grunted before I had the pot slid into the commode, pretending she was pooping on the bare carpet. I was horrified and didn't think it was particularly funny because I would have been the one to clean it up, but she thought it was hilarious.

Sometimes, when I would go see her in the hospital, she would pat the bed next to her and say, "Come and lay down next to me." So I'd crawl up there and have to lie on my side so I'd fit. Then she would clunk her arm on top of me and pat me and say with a sigh, "My little blessing." I could physically feel her love swirling around me in a warm glow.

Mom had good days and bad days. If it was a bad day and the phone rang, she'd lean over to grab it, wince with pain, and cry out at the sudden movement. She'd lift the receiver from the cradle and say calmly, "Oh, hello, Edith. I'm fine, just fine, how are you?"

Her cheery tone never faltered.

One time I asked, "Mom, why don't you tell people how you really feel?"

"People don't want to hear about your aches and pains. What can they do about it, anyway? Besides, I hate sympathy."

When Mom was in her mid-forties she accidentally got pregnant with me. Then, when I was a teen, I accidentally got pregnant. I regret to think that a baby in the womb might be able to sense how welcome they are. Perhaps I could feel the level of anticipation for my arrival by the way Mom rubbed her belly. And maybe I could feel the retching and discomfort of the nausea that filled our space. Maybe the haunting feeling I get now and again of "not belonging" is an echo from my time in utero.

When I think about how the mom and baby are connected in such an intimate way, I feel a profound sadness at how I acted when I was sixteen. I never thought of it as a real baby. I knew it intellectually, but I never touched my belly with any love or care. It was just a horrible growth attached to my insides, sucking the life out of me. All I could do was pray for a miscarriage. I heard that one in five pregnancies self-terminate because it is nature's way of taking care of imperfections. I never thought in terms of the precious life I was sheltering and nourishing within my womb. I hated everything about it. I was nauseated and then I was getting fat. It was an embodiment of my sinful nature and flagged my lack of self-control. It was a shame generator, spewing ugliness and self-loathing.

That is how I related to my pregnancy and all I could know during this dark time in my life.

JUDY 3 YEARS OLD

JUDY 7 YEARS OLD

BACKYARD OF 5806 N. FAIRFIELD
CHICAGO BUNGALOW

PART I - COMING OF AGE
CHAPTER 4
THE GOODNESS METER

I always thought of myself as a good girl, but I had my struggles. There was the time that my best friend Jane and I stole eggs from her family restaurant, stood on the patio rooftop, and pelted the customers' cars. It was fun hearing them crack and watching them explode in a yellowy burst on the windshields and car tops. It wasn't so fun when Jane's mom asked about it and Jane 'fessed up. She then banned Jane from playing with me. Several months later, when I started to come around Jane's house again, I cringed when I ran into her mom. I tried to forget about it, but since I didn't face Jane's mom and apologize, I stayed sick with regret. I was too ashamed to tell anyone about it, especially my parents, who wondered why I hadn't been playing with Jane lately.

I met Jane in third grade while at the school bus stop, shortly after we moved to Glenview. She pretty much ignored me at first while she played with her gaggle of brothers, sisters, and cousins. As we waited for the bus, I gawked as the kids balanced on the white rocks that bordered their restaurant driveway. They pretended they were suspended over the ocean and if they fell, sharks would eat them. I wanted desperately to play. I thought Jane was cute with her pixie haircut and navy-blue pea coat. I was envious when someone cracked a joke and laughter skipped through them like a stone on the water. How could I make friends? After standing on the sidelines for a few weeks, Jane asked me if I wanted to try it. Now the pressure was on. I was relieved when the bus pulled up and my performance was cut short. On the bus, I sat next to Jane. The ice was broken.

I came home from school skipping and singing. I made a friend, which I desperately needed since I was new to Our Lady of Perpetual Help School. In the following years, some of our favorite things to do were pretending we were Tom Sawyer and Huck Finn as we explored the river in the forest preserves across from Harms Road, or asking George the imaginary butler to fetch fancy shoes and dresses for Barbie's date with Ken.

"Good, I was good," I told myself, but what about the time I stole the gumdrops from the drugstore when I was five and Mom asked where I got the colorful candy? She marched me back into the store to apologize to the pharmacist. I was so disgraced that I made an inner plea to never, ever try that again.

And then, worst of all: the time I got caught playing doctor. I had met this kid, Julie, on our block and had invited her over to our house. When Mom finished her phone call she asked what we were doing in the bathroom with the door closed. When I said "playing doctor," Mom asked if we had our clothes on. When I said no, Mom told the little girl to go home and then gave me a lecture, saying proper girls don't act like that and I should never, ever play doctor. The shame from that episode stuck on me like a permanent wood tick.

Otherwise, I got good grades in school, did my homework, and never got in trouble with the cops, unlike my older brothers. I think Mom and Dad had big plans for me, because they bragged about any little skill I stumbled upon, to the point of embarrassment.

When I was thirteen, I had serious questions about my score on the goodness meter. I started liking boys and dreamed about doing things that I probably shouldn't. At first I omitted these embarrassing sins in the confessional, but then my conscience got the better of me, so I included the full spectrum of my offenses.

While kneeling in the dark with my head next to the wall, the shutter slid open and Father said, "You may start now."

I couldn't see anything, but I could tell the voice was Father Ryan's. I was glad it wasn't Father Monson, because he was the pastor of the church and recently preached about avoiding the kinds of sins I was about to confess.

"Bless me Father, for I have sinned. It has been about one week since my last confession."

"Go ahead, my child."

"I was unkind once. I didn't tell the truth once. And ..." *my voice lowers...* "I had six impure thoughts."

"Ask God's forgiveness, dear child, and say ten Hail Marys and fifteen Our Fathers. You have been forgiven. Go in peace."

"Thank you, Father."

The shutter slid shut. I felt relief for the quick ending.

I knew that if I was *really* bad, I would have gotten a lecture and a bigger assignment. The nuns taught us that of all the hundreds of religions in the world, Catholics were members of the one true religion. It was a sacred privilege to be able to have our sins forgiven in confession, because without it, you could end up in hell. If you had venial sins, like impure thoughts, then you went to purgatory and had a chance to work off the dirt, eventually making it to heaven. I wasn't sure what this work entailed; I pictured hundreds of disembodied souls swinging hammers, and then, one by one, after so much time, Jesus came down and handed them a pass to heaven.

But the most horrible circumstance was if you died with a mortal sin on your soul. You would go straight to hell with no chance to get out. These offenses might include murder, coveting another man's wife, and sex before marriage. In hell, you would burn for eternity. I pictured screaming souls, hands reaching upward for forgiveness, but God turning a deaf ear. I knew about burns. Back in the days when Mom was still able to fry chicken, I got too close. The grease splattered and seared my arm with eternal throbs of pain.

At this stage, my impure thoughts were about doing the wrong things with Bob Flannigan, a boy I knew in school who had a swanky way about him and wore his hair like Elvis. I dreamed of kissing him and falling into bed, like I saw in the movies, folding into a tight embrace, every part of our bodies touching. Then I'd get carried away and dream about taking our clothes off and feeling each other's body, skin on skin. The visions made me weak in the knees. I knew I would never actually do that; that was acting like a slut. That was being like Linda K. The boys at Our Lady of Perpetual

Help School giggled and whispered foul gossip that stunk up her reputation. I would never go that far; but still, I was a sinner. Father Monson said that thoughts precede actions, so any nasty thoughts were a sin.

I had a hard time keeping track of the exact number of impure thoughts I had between confessions and wondered how accurate I had to be to get wiped clean. What if I said six, but really had twelve? Is that the same as if I never went to confession at all? But for goodness' sake, it was impossible to keep *perfect* track of the number. What was I supposed to do? Carry a scratch pad along with me, counting the bad thoughts one by one? I could just hear my friend Annie asking me, "Why are you marking up that scratch pad?" And then I would say something like, "Oh, I'm checking off the times I think of God." Well, that was half the truth, because prayers often followed the impure thoughts. Prayers were supposed to cure us of our deviant ways, like dousing a campfire with water.

I always wanted to impress Annie and longed for us to be tighter friends. I remember the first time she invited me to sleep over in seventh grade. I was popping with good fortune, now that I was "in" with Annie, part of the popular crowd. She had tawny blonde hair, emerald-green eyes, and a swimming pool. She had a confident air about her; she never minced words but got straight to the point. This self-confidence was a rare commodity when most everyone else in my world worried about what others thought. Annie commanded a small army of boy admirers. Her soldiers were always the cutest and the coolest.

I hadn't really made out with a boy yet: the closest I got was in sixth grade. I spun the green 7-Up bottle and it pointed to Jimmy Bartlett. He had to kiss me. He grabbed my hand and led me to the make-out room. It was pitch black and a bit freaky, but in an effort to expedite the task, I closed my eyes and puckered my lips. He had his hands on my shoulders, but stood a foot away. Since he had little reference as to where my lips actually were, he planted a kiss on the side of my nose. We were both embarrassed by our juvenile attempt and quickly left the room, holding hands to make it look like we'd actually made out. I wouldn't admit it to anyone, but I thought he was kinda cute, even if he was a greaser. My friends and I didn't hang around with the greasers. They wore leather, tossed swear words around like confetti, and slicked their hair back with Brylcreem. I felt criminal for kissing in the dark like that.

I thought Bob Flannigan's kisses would be much different. We would actually hug before we started kissing, and it would transport me to some dreamy state, liquid with love. There I went again with my bad thinking. Tally one for the confessional.

In a halfhearted way, I really did try the praying, but it didn't work so well. I thought this was evidence that God was displeased with me and not really listening.

Confession was something I did because I had to. I never felt truly cleansed, because I didn't give any details about my impure thoughts. Eventually, I just came up with a template that included a sprinkling of each type of sin: lying, impure thoughts, disrespecting my parents. I could have gotten something out of confession if it had been more like a counseling session, discussing exact incidences with the priest and together coming up with a way to do better. But in reality, I didn't want to change my ways. So I just threw out a list of sins and thought that would probably cover it. At least I was fulfilling my confessional duty.

As a young child, sex was this gauzy apparition that slinked about our house, with no one mentioning its presence. At an early age, I got the impression that I shouldn't be touching myself in certain places. It came from getting caught playing doctor, but then it was probably earlier, when I was a toddler. Mom had disgust in her voice when she told me to get my hands out of my pants. The message was clear: anything having to do with the private parts was untouchable.

The real message could have been that sexual desire is natural and a sacred part of our humanness. Perhaps this attitude might have encouraged conversations about my budding sexuality, prying the dirt loose from my blackened soul, a much-needed shot of self-esteem.

I know the clergy's lessons were well intended and specifically aimed at girls like me, perhaps so I could avoid getting into trouble. But the mandates fell short because they were not accompanied by any explanation of why. The theory was simple; when you are tempted in the Garden of Eden, you just divert your eyes and think about cookies or milk or sunflowers. Switch the tracks of the mind, for it is a sin to have sexual thoughts. This goes against the grain of human nature and had us fighting a losing battle.

CHAPTER 5
HUMMINGBIRD NESTS

I was intrigued with the buzzing feelings I had when a boy paid attention to me, but there was always that taint of guilt that drizzled down on me. Although my friends and I spent the greater part of our time talking about the boys at school, I would never let my mom or dad know about any of the big things in my life, like the crush I had on Bob Flannigan. I couldn't wait to grow up. I already wore nylons with a garter belt and tiny elevated heels. When Dad first saw me in the grown-up garb he said, "What on earth's goin' on around here?" but Mom said it was okay because I was now a young lady. Dad just muttered something about me being too young for that sort of thing, shook his head, and dropped it. But more than the heels and nylons, I wanted a bra. I looked at ads in the Sears catalog and saw how perfectly they fit and helped shape your figure. They looked so feminine and substantial and womanly.

At seven or eight, when my new teeth came in, they were crooked and too big. When my breasts came in, they were tardy and too small. My friends were blossoming, but my body had no clue spring had sprung. They were whispering about what a pain it was having to use Kotex with the belt and how uncomfortable it was. I was thinking that I wouldn't mind. I would like it: it would mean I was a woman. Mom said I was immature for my age. What an insult! There's nothing worse than delayed development when you want to hurry up and grow up so you can get the attention of the boys.

I started anticipating some buds in fourth grade when Nancy Griffin showed up after summer vacation with a full figure. I didn't even know we were old enough for that sort of thing. The boys thought it was the funniest joke in the world, running past Nancy on the playground and calling out, "Where'd you get those jugs?" Nancy got the fly-by treatment until the leaves fell off the trees, and then I guess they got tired of it, since Nancy ignored them.

I wouldn't have wanted to be the first one at school to blossom, but it was worse to be the last. By sixth grade I was worried that something was wrong with me. I was still what we called "two raisins on a breadboard."

During a shopping spree at Marshall Field's with Mom just before sixth grade, I spotted something I wanted more than the pile of clothes stacked on the checkout counter.

There it was, under the glass counter, laid out on a royal-blue velvet cloth. It was snow white with pink lacy fringe and a tiny silk bow nestled between the cups of stretchy material. It was very petite, not like the large cups Mom wore with all the wire and padding. No, this one was for young ladies who were freshly budding like the leaves on the lilies of the valley at Easter time.

They called them training bras. I guess you were training your new developments to spend the rest of their lives inside cups that would forever hold them perky like when they were new. The bra followed the same principle as the stretch panel in maternity clothing. You could wear it a long time, even though your body was changing. That way you didn't have to run out and get a new bra every week or two. I thought it was very economical and clever. More than ever, I hated the ribbed cotton undershirt I wore. It was hot and hung on me like a gunnysack. People could probably see the telltale U-shaped neck that showed right through my chintzy uniform blouse.

The boys at school were curious about who wore a bra and who didn't, so they came up behind you and nonchalantly swiped a finger down your back to see if there was a telltale bra clasp under your shirt. Luckily, I was gifted with a super awareness of their intentions and was able to spin like a yo-yo if they were up to their tricks. The last thing I wanted was to publicize the fact that I wore an undershirt. If I wore a bra, I wouldn't have to worry about such things. In fact, I might even pretend I didn't see them coming and let them do their whammy snap.

Oh, how I wanted that bra in the display case. I could throw out my undershirts and start living like a real woman. I thought of putting the little cup holders around my would-be breasts and standing in front of the mirror. I would put one hand on my hip and one hand behind my head and push my hair up into a fountain of glamour. I would put the bra on first thing in the morning and no one would know I had it on, but I would feel it all the time, during class, during recess, clasped tight around my body, reminding me I was now a woman.

But how was I going to ask Mom for the stretchy-cupped bra? Mom was already highly invested with the pile of clothes on the counter. I was afraid she would think it was ridiculous because whenever she introduced me to people, she still called me the baby of the family. But I had to ask. I could come right out with it and say, "Mom, can I have that bra?" No. I didn't think the word "bra" was the right one. I never heard Mom use it. She always said something like, "Just a minute, I'll be right there after I put on my braazzzeeeerr." Brassiere? No, that word was for something much larger than the thing in the case. This wasn't a brassiere: it was a tiny set of hummingbird's nests. After I went back and forth, groping for the right terminology, I decided to avoid the dilemma altogether.

When Mom pulled out her wallet to pay for the clothes, I said, "Mom, come here. I want to show you something."

"What do you want to show me?" She already seemed impatient.

"Just come here." I curled my finger, beckoning her toward me. She pushed the carpet with her feet so she could back the wheelchair over to me. Her hands were too sore to work the wheels. My palms were sweaty and my voice was weak. I had a lot invested in this request.

"Mom?" I paused. "Can I have that?" I pointed down through the glass.

"What are you talking about?" she said, loud enough to make my ears curl.

"That," I said quietly, so the counter clerk didn't hear me. I pointed again.

"What is THAT?" Mom squinted her eyes.

Oh, geez, does Mom have to be so dumb? I thought.

"THAT," I said again, tapping the glass case right above the royal-blue velvet.

"That brazzzeeerrr?" she bellowed loud enough to wake the people of Kansas.

"Mmm-hmmm."

"Oh, for heaven's sake, you don't need THAT."

Then she opened her wallet and turned to the saleslady and said, "How much do I owe you?"

Shot down. I turned and walked away from the counter so Mom couldn't see the tears that spilled from my eyes. I sucked in my breath as I remembered the doctor-playing episode and thought the NO was another reprimand. Like I was veering into sexy territory and Mom had to put a stop to it. The tears just showed I was a baby and not mature enough for something so grown up. If my throat hadn't seized up from stuffing the tears, I could have said something like, "All the girls at school wear bras. Please, Mom." Mom thought she was doing me a great favor with the new clothes, but all I really wanted was the simple little bra. I felt misunderstood and insignificant. Anything having to do with my sexuality or impending womanhood twisted me with a nasty dose of shame.

It wasn't too long after the Marshall Field's debacle that I noticed I had something the size of lemon heads forming under my skin. I was finally blessed with two tiny drops to warrant my desire for a bra. It felt like semi-hardened fish eggs. You could move them around a little, but it hurt. Then my nipples puffed out like they were raisins soaked in rainwater. They were full and puffy but still sitting on a flat chest. I expected that once I started developing, I would soon be strutting around like Nancy Griffin from fourth grade. But the growth was retarded. Little by little my breasts formed until they were the size of kiwi fruit—and then they stopped as quickly as they had started. Even though Mom hadn't bought me the stretchy-cupped bra, Auntie Stell gave me a Christmas present that year that blew me away with delight. She must not have checked with Mom first. It was a powder-blue flowered bra and pantie set. It was too big at first; the cups sagged in a crease when I snapped it in back. Then, after I grew some more, I still needed a swipe of Kleenex to fill out the crease. I was hoping I was still growing. I waited and waited, but my cup never did runneth over.

CHAPTER 6
EIGHTH-GRADE SEX EDUCATION

I didn't get pregnant because I was ignorant. I knew full well how babies were made. I learned it from Mom before I was really ready and then again in eighth grade, when I was more eager. Eighth-graders attended a six-week class held in the basement of the church. The nuns walked us in single file at 8:45 am every Tuesday so we could be seated and attentive by 9:00 am. This was when Father Monson walked in the room to conduct The Class. The windowless basement had this musty smell like the bowels of the earth. Ghastly fluorescent lights made everything look flat, like a black-and-white drawing, but if you had a zit, that stuck out in perfect 3-D. They called the class Eighth Grade Preparation. I guess we were being prepared to fly off to high school, where we would meet all the challenges of boy–girl relationships. Preparation was a euphemism. The real name would have been "Sex: Stay Away or Go to Hell."

Father Monson asked, "Who can repeat the lesson we just learned?" He looked around, and when no one volunteered, he glanced over to the left of the lectern and then scanned my row.

My heart thumped as I prayed, "Not me, not me." His eyes stopped in front.

"You," he pointed. "Please come up here on stage and explain for the girls and boys the term "menstruation.""

"Me?" she asked.

"Yes, you."

Father coached her along, making sure she used the proper clinical terms. Her face was red and her voice soft. For the rest of the year, every time I ran into Carol Bromley, I could see her up there in front of one hundred eighth-graders, talking into the microphone and saying words like uterus and blood and vagina. Father made her say it.

When she tried to fudge, using more common words, he said, "Weren't you listening to the lesson, Miss Bromley? Use the correct terms."

Father Monson was the pastor at Our Lady of Perpetual Help Church and thought it was his duty to educate us in the proper moral direction. He said necking and petting were serious sins. He said sexual intercourse outside of marriage is the worst sin of all, a mortal sin.

The words "sexual intercourse" haunted me. I hadn't heard the term since Mom gave me the sex talk when I was nine. I don't think Mom was planning to tell me about the birds and the bees this particular day, but she was forced into it. My cousin Pamela was sleeping over at my house. In the morning Pamela went into the bathroom; a few seconds later she cracked open the door, poked her head out, and called, "Aunt Ethel, could you come in here?" She sounded like she was about to cry, like something was terribly wrong. I couldn't imagine what could be so bad that she needed my mom to come in the bathroom with her. I ran into the kitchen, where Mom was chopping up onions.

"Mom," I said, "Pamela's in the bathroom. She wants you."

Mom rinsed her hands and wiped them on the towel by the stove. She rushed into the bathroom with Pamela and closed the door behind her. I sat on the stairs and tried to listen. I heard Mom mumbling in a low tone, like she was teaching a serious lesson. She came out of the bathroom with a stern look on her face. She walked past me and went up to the second-floor bathroom. She came down with a blue-and-white box and went back inside the bathroom, closing the sliding door. I could hear Pamela sobbing.

When Mom came out I asked her, "Is something wrong with Pamela?"

"Oh, dear," Mom sighed. "She has her menstrual period."

I was scared to ask the next question. I was almost sure it had to do with Pamela's private parts, but I said it before I thought of the consequences.

"What's that?"

"Well," Mom said, "come into the living room. I want to talk to you about something."

She sat on the couch, patted the spot next to her, and said, "Sit down here, Judy." This was before Mom quit smoking, so she opened a fresh pack of Pall Malls and scooted back on the couch. She lit the cigarette. Mom was making a big production out of this. Maybe I shouldn't have asked. Her face was serious and I couldn't imagine what was coming next. Mom took a big puff and talked as smoke wafted out of her mouth.

"Auntie Stell hasn't had a chance to talk to Pamela. It's too bad because she got so scared. Poor thing, she thought she was bleeding to death."

"Why?" I asked.

"Oh, it was her period. Honey, when a girl goes into puberty, that's around twelve or so, she gets what's called a menstrual period. You ever heard a that?"

"Nope."

"It's bleeding from the vagina. It happens every month for a woman. It's a natural thing." Mom took another puff.

"Bleeding?" I said.

"Yes, from the vagina."

I choked down an inadvertent giggle. I squirmed and stared at the floor, afraid that Mom would see the smirk on my face. Did she have to keep saying the word "vagina"? I wished she could just say "down there."

"I want to tell you about this now so you won't be scared when it happens to you. You're getting to be a young lady now, you know. It's nothing to be afraid of. Okay, honey?"

"Okay."

Mom flicked her cigarette over the ashtray.

"It's just nature's way of getting the uterus ready for the time when you get pregnant and have a baby. The baby is kept inside the uterus. It's kind of like a basket that carries the baby while it's growing in you."

"A basket?"

"Yes, honey. You know, like a container that has food for the baby. During the month, if you don't get pregnant, the lining, which is the food, gets dumped out 'cause there is no baby. They call it the menstrual period. It's all very natural. It happens once a month."

This news didn't seem natural at all. Every month? Every woman? Just in case? It seemed like a whole lot of rigmarole for something that might not even happen, kind of like checking the mailbox on Sundays. Wasn't there some way to just turn off the fountain until you wanted to have a baby?

She scooted back on the couch and continued. "Now, there's more. I might as well tell you the whole story. I've been meaning to talk to you about this."

I was afraid of that.

"In order to get pregnant, you have sex."

At this point in my life, I thought that sex was some intense kind of kissing, but I wasn't exactly sure of the details. I couldn't get my head around what came next.

"The man places his penis in the woman's vagina. This is called sexual intercourse."

At nine years old, I did suspect there was some activity like this that adults engaged in, but I had no idea the man put his entire hot dog in the bun. When she said "places his penis," I imagined him taking the thing and carefully laying it inside the lady's lips. You know, lengthwise, like a hot dog in a bun. Whoa ... this put a whole new meaning on the word "sex." I thought it strange and wondered why he would want to do that.

"Do you have any questions?" Mom asked with a sigh that sounded like a period at the end of a sentence. I was too embarrassed to think.

"No, Mom," I whispered.

Mom took a big puff of the cigarette, let it out, and said, "Well, if you've got any questions, Judy, you just come and ask, okay?"

"Okay, Mom," I said.

But in my heart I knew there was no way I would be bringing

up this subject of my own accord.

Mom's explanation was thorough, except for the missing detail that there was a hole in the woman in which to place the hot dog. When Father Monson explained the mechanics of sexual intercourse with medical diagrams, I learned how the anatomy fit together: the man plugged into the woman like a toaster cord into the wall. The sex words startled my ears and brought embarrassment as I sat in close proximity to the popular boys in my eighth-grade class. I could hear myself breathing while Carol Bromley continued the explanation. As Father coached her along, not letting her gloss over the proper terms, my face got hot. I choked down a giggle.

We had been instructed by the nuns, before class, to refrain from laughing or talking. The nuns said the subject matter was "mature" and it wouldn't do to be snickering or giggling when we were talking about adult things. We obeyed and sat with our hands folded in our laps, staring at the floor, and then glancing at the clock, wishing Father would hurry and wrap up the lesson—before we got called on.

After I had settled down from the shock, I pondered Father's words. I thought his assessment was a little harsh and that if a boy wanted to hold my hand, I would go ahead and let him. Anyway, I had already committed that sin. By now I was also used to the impure thoughts and not all that convinced that they were serious sins. But I knew I would draw the line, somewhere after necking and before petting. I would never do that. Father Monson also had said that we should never kiss. Kissing was like a drug, he said: once you started it was too hard to stop, and it would lead to other things. I invented my own question on the SAT test. Marijuana is to heroin like kissing is to blank; the answer, of course, is the hot dog in the bun thing.

Punishment was not a good motivator for me, even if it was an eternity in hell. I tried to follow the advice of the good Father, but when I came up short, guilt and remorse were my constant companions, stalking me like an ominous ghost. I don't really know why I did exactly what Father Monson said NOT to do, and I had thought I wouldn't do it, but when I finally got to kissing Bob Flannigan later on in eighth grade, I let his hand wander to forbidden territory. Mom and Dad must have been out somewhere, and we ended up lying on the orange tweed couch down in our rec room. We kissed. He rubbed my back. We fell over like I imagined we would, so we were now lying side by side in a tight embrace. After a bit, his hand went under my shirt and rubbed my back, then it slowly migrated to the front. I didn't stop him. I thought it felt good, but at the same time I was surprised that I was letting him do this. I became self-conscious about the size of my niblets. Suddenly, he pulled his hand away and sat up. "I better get on home," he said. "It's getting late."

I felt uneasy and strange. I didn't see much harm in letting him cop a feel; I wouldn't have let him go further than that. Yet I felt misunderstood and wished there was some way to tell him I was just about to cut the advances. I wished I had been the one to draw the line. I wanted him to know I wasn't that kind of a girl.

He didn't call me again, so I felt even worse about what we did on the couch. I wondered if I was too easy, or if he didn't like what he felt, or if he was just testing me. I wished so bad I had never let him do it. I assumed he thought I lacked moral fiber and he didn't want a pushover for a girlfriend. The social convention in the 1960s was that a boy wasn't a man if he didn't try something, and the girl wasn't a lady if she didn't stop him. I guess I showed I wasn't a lady. I walked past him the next week at school and he just kept his head down, pretending he didn't see me. Later I found out he was back with Sally Stilleti. That broke my heart. He probably always liked her better and was just using me to make her jealous.

After the episode with Bob Flannigan, I didn't have a boyfriend for two more years.

CHAPTER 7
THE ROLLING STONE NIGHTCLUB

Most of the girls from Our Lady of Perpetual Help went to Regina Dominican High School and the boys went to Loyola. Since we couldn't meet boys in class, the Rolling Stone in Wilmette was a godsend. They converted the auto-body garage into a teen nightclub by painting the cement floor a woody color and suspending strobe lights and glistening mirror balls from the ceiling. The atmosphere gave me a comforting incognito feeling. The strobe lights made us look like Tin Men from the Wizard of Oz as we moved in jerky staccato. I felt unusually brave, alive, and excited to meet the boys. I didn't have to worry about whether my hair was parting to expose a bare scalp or if the Clearasil on my zit was still camouflaging the red.

The place had a musty smell mixed with wisps of Brut aftershave and Shalimar cologne. Sexy innuendos bounced off the walls, filling the air with pheromones and agitated sexual tension. For me, it coalesced and focused on a boy from Glenbrook South named Mick Romano. The guy was short as far as boys go, and I found that reassuring. My dad and brothers were over six feet tall, and their propensity for loudness and bouts of temper had me intimidated by large men. Mick was approachable and soft spoken. He had dark-brown eyes and a sinister little laugh that erupted from his innards, causing his eyes to squint in a way that melted me with rapt interest. He could dance too. A lot of the boys had bad rhythm or just stood on the sidelines talking to each other, but Mick broke the gaggle of Regina girls and approached me. Granted, his friend Kurt had already picked out Annie, so the competition was lessened. I felt like the golden girl, getting asked to dance by a boy who didn't even know me.

Ever since I was nine and my brother Jim taught me the cha-cha, I have been intoxicated by dancing. In eighth grade my partner and I took first place at a dance contest. Tonight I felt like a puppet being moved by the strings of the drum beat. The words to the song jazzed me up a notch. I felt free and uninhibited. It went something like this: You know she comes around here at just about midnight—She makes ya feel so good, Lord—She makes ya feel all right—And her name is G-L-O-R-I-A.

As Mick and I danced, I felt a surge of sexiness oozing out of my body. I wondered if he liked the way I was shaking my butt. My boldness shocked me. Eventually a slow dance came on. I could smell his spicy cologne and see the stubble on his clean-shaven face. They weren't those newly clipped peach-fuzz whiskers, but well established, like he'd been shaving for years. He was so manly. He put his hand on the small of my back and led me around like I'd sprouted wings. I skipped my ride home with Diane's mother and even though I wasn't allowed to go in a boy's car until I was sixteen, I let Mick drive me in his '62 white Chevy Biscayne. Not only was this guy cute—he had a car, and he knew how to drive it.

When we pulled into the driveway, he asked for my phone number. He didn't write it down. I was impressed that he could hold it in his head, but worried that he wasn't going to call. I skipped upstairs, giddy with the words to the song swirling in my head, "she comes 'round here, 'bout midnight." I couldn't believe that an upperclassman had noticed me. It was a miracle night. I knocked on Mom and Dad's bedroom door to tell them I was home. They didn't notice it was past eleven or that I had been delivered by a boy in his car. Luck was on my side. I wondered if Mick would call. He did ask for my phone number but what if he forgot it? Or maybe he didn't really care. Boys were like that. Sometimes they acted interested to be polite and then just disappeared.

I opened my window, then crawled in bed. There was a storm coming in and the curtains tossed and twisted, clanking the gold rings. Snow started to fall and blow in the window, so I got up and closed it. I fell into a fitful sleep too excited to really settle down.

Sure enough, the phone rang the next evening while I was in

the kitchen making popcorn. I turned the fire off, ran upstairs, closed my bedroom door and picked it up. It was him. "This is Mick, do you remember me from last night?" I was beside myself and all ears. I found out he had a dad who was Italian and that he lived in Glenview on the other side of town in a newer blue-collar neighborhood. He took calculus, no wonder he could remember my phone number; he was smart. He had one younger sister. His parents both worked. I thought it must be strange to come home from school to an empty house; so lonely and quiet. As we talked I could hear jets from the Glenview Naval Air Base flying over his house. He said he didn't get along with his dad so well. It didn't sound like he spent much time with his parents.

Mick asked if I'd like to go out Saturday night to a drive-in movie. I knew kids just sat in their cars and made out at these shows. I wasn't ready for that, but it would be fun to sit next to him, maybe I would scoot close, eat candy, sip a coke, and gawk over some romantic movie. But, what should I tell him? I wasn't allowed to go on dates. I had four months until I would turn sixteen. Then, I was supposedly old enough for dating and riding in boys' cars. Should I tell Mick I couldn't go? Should I tell him my Dad didn't allow it, but to meet me somewhere else secretly? Should I ask Dad about it again? Maybe he would ease up on the rules now that I actually had someone to go out with. I told Mick I'd have to see if I could go and could he call back tomorrow?

I approached Dad with the same assurance that I was going to finally find that horse in the back yard that I had been asking for ever since I was six. But I gave it a go. I told Dad I met this really nice, clean cut boy at the dance the other night and he asked to take me to a movie, "Could I go?"

Dad held up his hand and said, "Now, Judy, you know the rules. Not until you're sixteen. What's the hurry?" he said. "You have plenty of time ahead of you for that sort of thing." What sort of thing was he talking about? Talking to Dad was like a conversation with the tar baby from the Uncle Remus stories—it wasn't up for discussion. His lack of consideration made me angry. Plenty of time? Like Mick is going to sit around and wait for me? I was sure there were other girls who could go in his car that he could ask if I was out of the picture. This thing with Mick was not going to stay fresh forever.

I wasn't used to having the line drawn like this. Dad didn't prepare me for laying down the law because he had been lax in the past. For instance, he taught me how to drive when I was only thirteen and then he let me take the car all by myself. I was allowed free range within a five mile radius of the cabin– up to Heinz's grocery store to get candy or an ice-cream cone; that made me feel like I had arrived and I was ready for anything.

I could also take a sip of booze anytime I wanted. Dad offered it to me at a very young age. I remembered the adults laughing at the face I made when I tried it. Dad knew the strong taste would regulate my intake and letting me try it took away the mystique.

The point was Dad trusted me with adult-type responsibilities and Mom was the same way, so I didn't get why I couldn't go out with boys. When I asked Dad, Mom just sat there and said nothing, her silence showed she agreed with Dad's rule. The no dating thing seemed unusually strict and inflamed my sensitivities. I didn't like it.

I thought Dad was ridiculous and bullheaded. "It didn't matter what he thought," I told myself. I would just do it anyway. Mick and I could go places. Free as birds. Cool places, like McDonald's on Waukegan Road, the local hangout, or maybe even down to the beach at Lake Michigan to watch the waves come in. If Dad wouldn't budge on the rule, it was too bad. I just had to roll in that '62 Chevy. I told Mick I could go out Saturday night but he had to pick me up at my friend Jane's because my dad didn't allow me to date. Mick was okay with that.

JUDY IN HER SCHOOL
UNIFORM AGE 14

CHAPTER 8
ROUNDING THE BASES

The first kiss happened when we'd parked in the beach lot by Lake Michigan. We were watching the waves roll in and he leaned over and put his lips on mine. They felt soft and smooth and the stubble from his upper lip rubbed in a delightful way. It added manliness to the mix. And the smell of him; Oh that Brut men's cologne – just melted my raw edges until I felt like I was in a pool of liquid gold. I could smell a little bit of sweat mixed with the cologne. This drew me closer.

I liked kissing Mick, and I liked the warm, churning sensations that accompanied the kisses. When I heard the song "Puppy Love," I knew that wasn't me. This was deep. This was real. It wasn't "only" anything. I admired his intelligence and his dry sense of humor. We laughed and talked about things that mattered. He sometimes had a rocky relationship with his dad and when they had an argument, Mick got in a dark mood, his words full of anger. I didn't like seeing this side of him. He was too serious. But I always empathized and thought his dad was too hard on him. I loved Mick's straight white teeth and the way he looked at me longingly, with his eyelids at half-mast. His rapt attention started me thinking about letting love take us to the physical wonderland.

Since it was expected that I would keep my parents informed as to my whereabouts, each time I left home, I had to come up with a lie if I was meeting Mick. Jane lived across the empty field at the end of our street, so it was reasonable to say I was going over there and having somebody's mom pick us up to go roller skating, or shopping, or to a football game. The lies stabbed at my integrity and made me feel cheap, but I put a band-aid on the icky feeling by telling myself I wouldn't have to be lying if I had a reasonable father. If he wanted to treat me like a child, I would just break free. I was almost sixteen and fed up wih his old fashioned rules. And Father Monson telling us we shouldn't hold hands, we weren't robots. I was ready to skip the pursuit of purity. Mick was cute and cool and I just wanted to be with him as much as possible. If our lust carried us away, let the sails fill with the winds of love.

We continued our physical explorations, and even though I rationalized that confession was worthless and the church's stand on morality unrealistic, I had pangs of guilt that were hard to shake. I started to have this sick feeling that because I was letting Mick's hands wander while we kissed, he didn't respect me. Even though I'd heard that boys preferred girls that were virgins when they got married, I didn't think that was true. Would there be any virgins left by the time we all got married? But yet, the sliver of doubt wedged itself between my heady rush of sexiness and the thought that Mick might just be using me. But if he didn't really love me why did he want to hang out with me all the time. We did a lot of things together besides kissing. The realization that he got more interested after I started putting out frightened me. I rode my Catholic religion and my sexual desire like a see-saw, teetering between what I "should" do and what I "wanted" to do. It was so confusing. To stabilize the tug of war between my desires and my faith, I decided to throw out the religion. How could they co-habitate? I hated the guilt. The intensity of desire paled the doctrines of morality.

Intrigue and mystique filled my thoughts about sex with my love, this boy I idolized and respected for his intelligence and good looks. I wanted to be closer to him. I wanted to share everything with him. Messing around was enticing, so I figured the ultimate act of sex would be the perfect ending to a perfect day—starbursts and ecstasy. The heavens would open up and I would be transported like an angel to the beauty of true love. I eventually made the decision to follow my desire for love and throw away the doctrine, although I never was able to quiet my pesky conscience.

Mick would call to set up a time. I'd walk to the end of our street, cross the field, pass the two giant weeping willows, and there he would be, sitting in the restaurant parking lot with the car running. I'd hop in. Now the fear would ooze down and around me—the fear of getting caught.

As we approached a stoplight I would duck down in the car. Then Mick would peek at the nearby cars: if he didn't see a blue Lincoln Continental, like Dad's, he would declare the coast clear and I would pop back up. Then we would continue over to McDonald's. Sometimes we drove down to Lake Michigan, parked, and walked along the shoreline, holding hands. I felt pretty safe here because Dad and Mom never went down to the lake.

Not only was the car a means of getting around, it was also a means of hanging around. We spent as much time parked as we did driving. This saved on gas. We'd drift down residential streets until we found something deserted and dark. Then we'd park and make out. It was decadent to be using the car as a bedroom, just sitting there in the dark, kissing, and rounding the bases, practicing for a home run.

We were heavy into it one evening when a bright flash scanned our car. We zipped up and popped up as the officer walked over to the driver's side of the car and shone a flashlight on us. Mick rolled down the window.

"What are you kids up to?"

"Nothing, Officer. We just stopped to take a look at this map," Mick said as he grabbed one off the floor.

"Let me see your license."

The cop left for about five minutes, came back, and said, "Okay. Well, get along then. There's no parking along here."

My heart was exploding and my hands shook. When the cop walked away, my thumping heart eased as gratefulness washed over me. What if the cop had brought us to the station and I'd had to call Dad? The thought made me sick with fright. I wanted to say a thank you to God for the cop letting us go, but then I thought it wasn't God who helped me get away. God had probably disowned me by now because I hadn't been to confession in many months. First, in the dark booth, I skipped the impure thoughts because I had gone way beyond any of those innocuous sins. Then, I rationalized, what was the point of going to confession if I wasn't going to confess— especially if I wasn't sorry and had no intention of quitting my deviant behavior? I didn't do much praying, these days. Besides it seemed duplicitous to ask for stuff from God when I wasn't following his rules.

Mick and I agreed we had to find a better place for this sort of messing around.

CHAPTER 9
THREE STRIKES AND I'M BUSTED

It was one of the usual times when I had told Dad I was going over to hang out with Jane, and then set off to meet Mick. As I walked over to the end of Brook Lane and crossed the grassy field, the weeping willows reached toward the earth, their threadlike branches softly swaying in the breeze. Jane and I used to swing on the willows when we were little. The branches hung like ropes and we'd grab a bunch of four or five. While holding tight, we'd walk as far as we could without letting go. Soon the branches were bent like a bow, and it felt like we couldn't hold on. Then it was time to take a leaping run, pulling our feet off the ground and swinging like monkeys. The leaves came clean off the branches as our hands slipped, and our palms ended up green and sappy. I felt a longing for those carefree days. Now it was just a silhouette of brightness in the distant past. The branches were dangling there, but I had no desire to grab them and swing free: that was child's play. I had more important things to do. I was on my way to meet Mick. Mistake Number One.

While I was out, Dad could not find the credit card he had loaned me, because it was in my purse. He had let me use it to buy clothes and I had forgotten to give it back. Mistake Number Two. Dad called over to Jane's to see if I had the card. As fate would have it, I was nowhere to be found.

About three hours later, I walked in the house.

Dad was sitting in his chair by the window with a scotch and soda in his hand, reading the paper. He must have seen me walking down the street on my way home from Jane's. He turned his head the minute the front door creaked open.

"Judy, where were you?"

I could tell something was wrong the way Dad forced the words through tight lips.

"Over at Jane's?" I said it with a raised pitch like it was a question. I feigned innocence, but sensed its demise.

"Well, I called over there and Jane's mom said she hadn't seen you."

Sweat droplets collected on my sides. I was busted, in hot water, totally screwed. I scrambled for another answer to my whereabouts.

"Oh," I said. "I was going to go over there but I ran into my friend Mick in the parking lot and I was talking to him."

"He just happened to be there?"

That didn't seem feasible, so I said, "Well, no, I knew he would be there."

"And you were just sitting there in the lot for three hours?"

I considered expanding the lie, but it was useless. I could feel the corners of my mouth twitching into a smirk. I was a poor actress and a bad liar.

"Well, we went for a little ride; but it isn't fair, this rule about no dating."

Dad put his drink down and got up from his chair so he could face me.

"Went for a ride? What do you mean, not fair? You know the rules. You don't decide the rules."

I took a step away from him.

"But some of my friends can go in boys' cars. I don't see why you have to be so strict."

"I don't care WHAT your friends are doing. We have our own rules in this house."

His voice was getting louder and I started to shake. I knew when I should shut up and take the heat. I shouldn't push Dad any further if I knew what was good for me.

"Okay, that's enough. You've lied and broken the rules. I forbid you to ride in that boy's car or talk on the phone to him. I don't like the way you've been acting. That's it! No more of this bullshit, do ya hear me?"

"Yeah, I get it. Sorry," I said, with doubtful sincerity.

I went to my room, lay on the bed, and cried. I felt splattered in a million directions as the anger rose. It was so unfair that I had to lie about riding in Mick's car. My dad's stupid rules caused me to sneak around. Dad would never trust me again, but still there was no way I was going to give up Mick. Dad could spout all the rules he wanted, but I was in love and I wanted Mick. I hated this life Dad carved out for me. It was for babies. I was almost sixteen! It just wasn't fair.

I turned the ringer off my pink Princess phone, so that instead of the loud ka-diiiing, ka-diiing, it just made this soft ping when someone called. Sometime that night, after dark and after I had fallen asleep, I heard it ping. I thought of letting it go, but I had to tell Mick what happened. I knew it was him because he was the only one who called that late at night. It was quiet in the house, so I picked up.

"Oh, Mick, I'm in a boatload a trouble. My dad found out."

"Did he see us driving around?"

"No, he was looking for me and called over to Jane's. When I got home I had to tell him. He knew something was up."

"What happened?"

"It was awful. He blew up—said never to talk to you on the phone and to stay away from you."

"Your dad must hate me."

"He'd hate any boy I liked. He wants to keep me a baby for the rest of my life. I hate him. I gotta go, someone is up. Bye."

I hung up before Mick could say good-bye. I rolled over in bed and closed my eyes, but I was too worked up to sleep. I was so mad that now Dad said I couldn't even talk on the phone to Mick. What kinda life was this?

Around midnight, the phone pinged again. I heard Dad snoring in the room next to mine. Mom was in the hospital, so I didn't have to worry about her. I picked up. Mistake Number Three.

I lay in bed in the dark, talking, the receiver touching my lips.

"My dad's sleeping. I have to be really quiet. Mick, can I ask you a question?"

"Sure."

"Did you like me when you first met me at the Stone?"

"Yeah, I thought you were neat."

"You did?"

"Yeah, hey, do you want to go over to Lennie's tomorrow?"

"Oh, geez, I better cool it for a while."

"Just for an hour. He's havin' a little get-together."

"I'll think about it."

"Mick?"

"Yeah?"

"I was so excited when you first asked me to dance."

"You're a good dancer," Mick said. "I couldn't wait for a slow song to come on."

"Me too."

My bedroom door flew open.

"Who the hell are you talking to?"

I hung up.

I lay there, silent.

Dad knew who I was talking to.

"Didn't I tell you the phone is off-limits? What do I have to do to get you to listen? What's the matter with you?"

I started to cry. The fury in his voice made me scared of what might happen next.

"You wanna talk on the phone to that boy? I'll fix your talking on the phone."

He bolted over to the desk and grabbed the Princess phone with his big hands. He gave a yank to pull the cord from the wall. The phone was hard wired; when the cord didn't pull loose, he threw the phone on the floor and grabbed the wire closer to the wall. Using both hands, he pulled. Plaster and the phone plate flew, leaving a gaping hole.

"I guess that's what I have to do to get you to listen. Go to sleep now. I'm warning you. Don't you ever let me catch you talking to that idiot kid. Do I have to pull the phone out of the wall in the kitchen, too?"

"No, Dad. I'm sorry. I'm sorry," I said.

He slammed the door as he walked out.

I pulled the covers over my head and cried until my pillow was wet. I turned it over and wished I could talk to Mick more than ever. My dad was nuts, crazy, insane. All I wanted was to be in Mick's arms.

CHAPTER 10
THE INTERVIEW

Two weeks after the bust, I could use the phone again. Dad didn't know who I was talking to because I did that in private, running up to my bedroom before I picked up. Mick and I made arrangements to meet elsewhere and I stayed out of his car, but even Dad couldn't legislate morality. Eventually, I hopped back in the white Chevy, resumed the ducking at stoplights, and lived with a sickening angst about lying and the sexual exploration. The feeling of doing wrong nagged at me and sooted my spirit even though I told myself that church stuff didn't matter anymore.

Finally, I turned sixteen and expected the dating ban to be lifted. I passed my driver's license test, and Dad let me use Mom's yellow Chevy because she couldn't drive on her own anymore. The new freedom made it easier to maneuver my whereabouts without having to come up with lies. Dad had cooled down and the phone in my bedroom was repaired. I mustered up the courage to point out that I was sixteen now and should be able to date. I added that I was still friends with Mick and wanted to go out with him. Dad said he'd consider it, but that he would like to talk to this boy first.

This worried me. Dad already had a bad impression of Mick because I had snuck around with him. I was pretty sure Dad wouldn't like him. But it would be good to get the task done. Mick came over.

"Hello, young man. I hear you want to take my daughter out on a date."

"Well, yes, Mr. Liautaud."

"And where do you live?"

"Over on the west side of Glenview, kind of near the Naval Air Base." I could sense Dad's mind working overtime to size up this kid—it was already clouded with negativity.

"And what does your father do?"

"He's in the tool and die business." Mick was standing next to my dad's chair as he talked to him. I thought he looked like a tin soldier, short and stiff.

"I see. Do you have any brothers or sisters?"

"One sister, Mr. Liautaud."

Dad took a sip of his drink. "You go to school, I take it?"

"Yes, sir. Glenbrook South." I was embarrassed that Mick was calling my dad "sir." Dad thought that was an unnecessary formality. It occurs to me now that perhaps this reminded Dad of where he came from, and the days in New Orleans when the family was always saying "Yes, sir," and "Yes, ma'am."

"What grade?"

"I'm a senior."

"Going to college?"

"I haven't decided yet." Dad's face fell. Dad thought college was a given for young people.

I offered a consoling tidbit. "Mick takes calculus, Dad."

"I see," was all he said. I didn't like the way Dad glossed over that fact. It was hard to get into calculus and most kids didn't take it until they got to college. He should know Mick was smart.

"Now you know Judy has a curfew at 11:00; I expect you to get her home by then. Is that understood?"

"Yes, Mr. Liautaud. I need to be home a little after that anyway, so it won't be any problem." Bonus point for Mick. He added a few words to his response, letting Dad know that he had good parents who also set a curfew.

Dad turned to pick up the newspaper, opened it, and said, "Okay, you're free to go. Be sure to be home on time."

After Dad's interview, my impression of Mick lowered a notch. He stood up too straight, like he was trying to be taller than his true five feet, six inches. He didn't talk enough—just gave one-word responses. Dad dispensed disapproval, and at the end he had that look that seemed to say, "Okay, I'm done with you, get along." My dad's opinion mattered to me more than I wanted to admit.

Still, I was relieved that Dad finally met Mick and had waived the Cars with Boys Prohibition. After that, when Mick came over to get me, he would pull into the driveway and honk. I'd run out lickety split before Dad said anything. Once in a while he'd say, "Tell that boy to come in here. I want to talk to him."

And then I would run out and tell Mick to come in. We'd answer a few questions and then be dismissed, Dad saying, "Okay, you're free to leave." We loved getting out of the house then, relieved that we passed inspection. I finally had Dad's blessing to drive in Mick's car. Well, I wouldn't call it a blessing, but Dad was reluctantly allowing it.

Mick and I weren't comfortable hanging around at Mick's house, either. When I met his parents, I acted the same way; I couldn't think of anything to say. I didn't think they liked me. Later I learned that they said to Mick, "She's awfully young, isn't she?" Mick was only one year older than I was. But it was true that people were often shocked when they heard I was sixteen. They said I looked like I was thirteen. This was highly insulting and I heard it often, but I remember Mom saying that it was a good thing and I would come to relish it later on in life.

I don't remember my mom being there when Dad met Mick. I think she must have been in the hospital. She was in and out often. One time she contracted a staph infection and we thought we would lose her. We had to visit the hospital with masks on our faces and couldn't touch her. Then when she got better and came home, she was pretty sick and had to have an around-the-clock nurse. Thelma was hired and turned out to be an angel, staying at Mom's side, giving her back rubs and sponge baths, and putting lotion on Mom's fragile skin. Mom loved Thelma. Her skin was black as night and she had large teeth that took up a third of her face when she smiled. She had an infectious laugh and was sweet as caramel. When Thelma came on the scene, it freed me up from my nightly duties.

CHAPTER 11
CROSSING THE CAVERN

Parking on the end of a dark street was good for first and second base, but it wasn't conducive to a home run. One day, Mick suggested we go over to his friend Kurt's house. It was a school holiday. We sat downstairs and watched TV with Kurt, then went up to the kitchen to get a Coke.

I was a bit nervous and thirsty, so I chugged my drink. Mick grabbed my hand and said, "Come on, let's check out the upstairs." My innards tightened with fright and excitement. He walked me up the carpeted steps to the bedroom. Soft light seeped through the drawn curtains. The double bed loomed like a drug dealer in a school yard, advertising its goods. It was dressed in navy-blue fringe pillows and a powder-blue spread. Mick quietly closed the door behind us, turned to me, and started kissing my lips and neck. His kisses lessened my anxiety and brought me to a dreamy place void of coherent brain function. I kissed back. He pulled back the covers and we fell on the bed. He undid my bra. His hands on my bare body felt cold at first but warmed with the excitement of his touch.

He unbuckled his pants. When they slid down he kicked them off. It seemed too fast that we were already naked. I could hear the wind whistling through the window frames, making it cool and drafty in our dark space. We got under the covers. We continued kissing until my should-list went up in smoke with the fire that was gaining momentum.

He got on top of me and took it in his hand to point it toward my opening. The tip was all that seemed to fit. What on earth? How did this work? I had put Tampax inside that hole, but this cylinder was worth a dozen of those, kind of like the wicked stepsister forcing her foot into Cinderella's shoe. He pushed harder. I was frazzled with sensation, scared now because the stretching burned. Then I heard someone come in the front door.

"Who's here?" I asked.

"Kurt's sister."

"Are you sure?"

"I'm sure. His parents are at work."

"We should get up," I said.

"She doesn't care."

"What if she tells her parents?"

"She won't."

We started kissing again and he pushed harder now. It felt like something was tearing in my tender area. It went all the way in. I wanted it back out of there, but I wasn't going to make him do that now.

"How do I keep from getting pregnant?"

"I'll pull it out just before."

"Can you do that?"

"Yep."

"You sure?"

"Yep."

"Won't some get in?"

"No, I'll pull it out."

"Don't forget."

"I won't."

It seemed strange to me, this in-out action like the dogs I'd seen humping in the park. I felt numb and wooden as I lay there, wishing it would be over. All of a sudden he pulled out and lay facedown on the bed, still for a minute, and then he emptied his lungs with a heavy sigh.

He rolled over and said, "I told you I could do it."

I lay there in a smear of bloody fluid and dark feelings. So this was it. He had sexed me. I felt no love at this moment, just fright for how I let myself get carried away like a log in a river. I felt pain from the bruise between my legs. I felt remorse for my loss of virginity, the death of my innocence and purity.

"Let's get dressed before someone else comes home," I said.

"Good idea," he said in a dreamy, satisfied tone.

I didn't get what I expected. Sex didn't feel good. I wasn't expecting an orgasm, because I had never heard of it. I didn't know that was what made it so sparky and ecstatic. I didn't experience anything close to pleasure.

The next morning, I woke with a sick feeling of dread, like I had lost my head and murdered someone. It would have been different if it had felt good. All the lightness of heart, joy, and sweetness of my fresh youth were snuffed out of me at the moment of penetration. And the worst part was, there was no going back. If it really was a mortal sin, I had one on my soul. But there was no way I was going to tell this one in confession. My spirit felt limp and blackened. I didn't like the feeling of the sex, after all. It was harsh and it hurt.

I got my period that month, so I guessed his pulling out worked.

CHAPTER 12
THE NIGHT MY LIFE CHANGED FOREVER

The thing was, I didn't care so much about doing the wrong thing when I had the softening effects of alcohol in my bloodstream. Alcohol served as an effective off-switch to my annoying conscience. I was new to drinking. A few months ago, I'd been introduced to gin when, Lennie and Kurt, Mick's friends brought some spiked cokes to a Glenbrook South tailgate party.

At first the taste was gross. I sipped it slowly. By the time the bottle was half empty, it went down easier and my body felt like marshmallow. My words came easily and seemed enlightened, on the verge of genius. I was finally the person I always wanted to be: confident and self-assured. I had a couple more. It was all good until the next morning, when I suspected that my drunken happy was more of an obnoxious blunder. I cringed with embarrassment. Did I tell Mick I wanted to be his forever? Oh, geez.

We were all underage, but we could score booze by waiting in the liquor store parking lot for a likely prospect. We approached the weathered wino-men who looked like they needed a drink or the very young, hip, and cool looking types. Mostly we put Mick's friend Lennie up to it, because he was tall and looked the oldest. Lennie would do anything for a friend: he was a bit klutzy, hence the nickname from the character in *Of Mice and Men*. He was spontaneous, and a likeable guy.

Once I experienced the appeal of alcohol, it was cheaper and easier to lift it from my father's liquor cabinet, which was well stocked for his poker parties. I took a little of each type to fill my 7-Up bottle so the lowered levels would go unnoticed: an inch of gin, one of vermouth, and just a splash of scotch. Dad drank the scotch; if the bottle was noticeably empty, it would be a red flag. Then came some Jack Daniels, Kahlua, and, to top it off, Cointreau. It was a nasty concoction, but we called it "Love Potion No. 9."

If my line of morality was muddy, kissing and drinking were the combination that erased the line altogether. I walked out of my house on Friday evening with a freshly whipped-up bottle of The Potion.

My life would never be the same after this free-for-all open house party. It was September 30, 1966, uncommonly chilly and damp, like winter was in the wings. The parents were out of town, and there were beater cars lining the street. It was a teenaged free-for-all with no adults to keep us in line.

Mick and I started kissing on the couch and then he grabbed my hand and led me down a hallway. I was shy about anyone seeing us go into the bedroom, yet I was buzzed enough to ridicule myself for caring what other people might think and followed Mick to a room in the back of the house. Mick had gotten a condom from his friend John, so we wouldn't have to worry about the "pulling out" routine. After we kissed a bit, he took out the "gift" and put it on. Perhaps it was stale and stiff, purchased years ago, safely tucked into John's back pocket as it waited for its call to duty. Or maybe we didn't have it on right: leaving some looseness in the tip. At any rate, the condom lacked integrity. And, maybe, so did Mick. Maybe he felt it, maybe he didn't, but he failed to pause when the thing blew up inside me. I had no clue, but I thought it was awful wet down there if the rubber was supposed to be catching the fluids. I didn't feel it break.

With wide-eyed surprise, Mick popped up when he was done. He held the shredded rubber between his thumb and forefinger, waving it like a dead mouse held by the tail. "Jude, look what happened," he said.

After the party, I was morose and numbed by the alcohol as Mick drove the snowy roads back to my home. I stumbled into the house and knocked on Mom and Dad's bedroom door to say,

"I'm home." I opened the window in my room to let the winter
air freshen my drunken stupor, threw my clothes on the floor, and
crawled under the covers. The electric blanket felt warm on my skin,
but the inside of me felt like freezer meat.

Morning drifted in with a cloud of gloom. I could hear the tree
branches scraping on the roof shingles from the heavy winds. Each
time my heart pumped, I could feel it in the veins on the side of my
head. My mouth felt like powdery sand. An aching thirst wrapped
around my tongue and throat. Water, water, where was some water?
I reached over to my French desk and fumbled for the glass. It had
dust speckles floating on top, but I couldn't get up for a fresh refill or
I would puke. The more I drank, the thirstier I got. I might as well
have been gulping air. Then I remembered the night before.

I drank too much. I lost my mind. I lost my protection. Was it
true? Did it really happen like that? Did the rubber break? Even if
my mind was foggy, my gut told me the nightmare was real.

Icy air blew the curtains on my window. I reached over and
turned my electric blanket to high. I looked at the clock. It was
10:00 am. I hardly ever slept this late. I could hear Mom and Dad in
the kitchen. Dad was on the phone making plans for a fishing trip,
and Mom was wheeling around in her electric chair.

How could I face them ever again? The rubber shredded. How
could that have happened? "That was one big boo-boo," I thought.
I could cry and I'm using baby language. This is no joke. It's more
than a boo-boo. More like a natural disaster. It would have been
better if we used the pull-it-out routine. Sex felt a little better this
time; there was no bleeding. I still felt dark. I rolled over and tried to
go back to sleep.

The truth smothered me like a soggy blanket. I sighed. I yawned.
I couldn't get enough air or water. I took another drink. I wondered
how I could have let myself go along with the rubber idea. I screwed
up. I was screwed. I am screwed. If only I could erase the reality. If
only fairy tales were true. If only I could go back to sleep or back to
last night and do it differently.

The horrible part was the feeling of blackness and filth that came
with my lack of self-control. All the guilt I was squelching came

forth in relentless stabs. After the first time, I kept telling myself over and over, "I'm not a virgin anymore." My soul was blackened with mortal sin. I don't know why I expected to have self-control. I never set out telling myself I wouldn't do it. It just kind of happened. I didn't think ahead. But yet, I beat myself up with my lack of self-control. It started back in second grade when I got those black marks on my report card for "lacks self-control" because I was talking to my neighbor. It was a long-lasting character flaw, branded right into my heart.

Now the real arrow struck the center of my soul—what about the chance of being pregnant? Oh, God, I couldn't even go there. Another wave of nausea stabbed at my stomach.

I knew from the Maturation Booklet we got in seventh grade that on the fourteenth day after your period, you are fertile. When was my last period? I got out of bed and checked my notebook calendar where I marked my periods. They were always twenty-eight days apart, just like clockwork. The date circled was September fifteenth. Oh, God, NO. That was two weeks ago. I grabbed my feather pillow and stuffed it to my face so I could cry without Dad or Mom hearing me. I sobbed until the pillowcase had a puddle the size of a pancake, smeared with streaks of leftover black mascara.

"Judy, come on now," I told myself. "Pull yourself together. Don't jump to conclusions." Then I prayed, "Please, God, just this one time. I promise I won't ever do it again. Please let me off the hook on this one." I felt a sense of comfort and knew He would answer my prayers. Up to now, I had almost anything that I really wanted in my life. This would be no exception. I mustered up some faith and started to believe it would turn out okay. "Lots of people have sex and don't get pregnant," I thought. "It can't happen to me. If I get away with this, I will never, ever go there again. I promise, dear God, I will be pure until I get married someday."

I felt some hope after praying. I felt that God must love me because He had been good to me. I could have been killed the time I fell out of Jeff's Model T, but I survived with just some bruises. Even when I fell off the pier, Uncle Phil was watching and rescued me from the lake. God had been watching over me. I had been mostly a good girl too. I knew I had missed confession lately, but I would go back soon. What about those mornings when I got up in the dark, grabbed my white leather missal, and took the city bus into town so I could attend Mass before school started? I used to do that for weeks on end during Lent. God would remember that. I had some good deeds in my bank. I should be allowed a withdrawal. I rolled over and tried to go back to sleep. The inside of my head felt like there was a razor blade churning on the end of a drill.

I shivered from the open window's icy breeze as I got out from under the warm covers. I found my robe on the floor and shuffled to the bathroom to find some aspirin. I put two tablets in my mouth and leaned over the sink faucet to fill my mouth. I swallowed. I crawled back into bed. The wind was wailing and moaning, shaking the window-panes. I pulled the covers over my head to get out of the draft and snuggled into a fetal position. I lay there awake until the aspirin dissolved into my veins and quieted the throbbing in my head.

Still in bed at 3:00 pm., I noticed that my fancy dresser had the skirt popped open, clothes dripping from the drawers. I was such a slob. The phone rang.

"Hi, Goonsfield. How are you?" It was Mick. I was annoyed that he sounded so cheery, like nothing happened, and that he was calling me that name. It was his term of endearment for me.

"Not so good," I said. "I got the worst headache and I feel like I'm gonna puke."

"Oh, man, me too," he said. "I think we drank too much yesterday. That was a wild party."

"God, if my parents knew why I was sick today, they'd kill me," I said.

"Do they know you're sick?"

"Well, yeah. I've been in bed all day, told 'em I got the flu."

"Do you think your dad noticed some of his booze was gone?"

"Oh, I don't care about that. That's the least of my worries. I have a monster headache."

Then I started to worry about tonight when Dad went to pour himself the nightly scotch and soda. I didn't take very much scotch, did I? Well, even if he noticed his scotch was low, I didn't think he would suspect me. If he did, what would I say? It could have been someone else in the house who drank it, like Hugren, our housekeeper. But Dad knew she only drank beer. I just hoped he didn't notice. Dad trusted me and would never suspect that I would steal or abuse alcohol. That thought made me feel short of breath, queasy. He didn't trust me as far as boys went, but with booze he trusted me.

Mick didn't bring up the breaking-rubber incident, and I couldn't bear to go there.

"Do you want to go for a ride later?" he asked.

"No, Mick, I feel too rotten. I think I'll just stay in bed."

The rest of the evening I ached with the ominous feeling that something was terribly wrong. I knew what it was. I knew an impending disaster was on the crest. I rode the fear like a seesaw. My thoughts went from crushing worry to pleas to God that He would dispense my sins and make it so I got my period in two weeks. That was when I promised God I would say 500 rosaries the day my period started. Then I thought that wasn't good enough: I had to show my faith in His answer to my prayers and pray the 500 rosaries right now. I would start tomorrow and make a tally sheet. I even considered promising to join the convent. Then I wondered if that drastic a bargain was all that necessary and if it really would make any difference. Then I decided, no, I couldn't go that far: 500 rosaries, if that didn't work, the convent wouldn't work either. I would say 500 rosaries now, and if I got my period I would go to Mass every day for a year. I felt better, like I was doing what I could to make my period happen. I could hardly wait two weeks to get the good red news.

CHAPTER 13
BATHROOM JUNKIE

Three weeks later, I had become a bathroom junkie. My trips numbered up to ten a day. I didn't have diarrhea or a urinary tract infection. Those would have been simple to cure. I didn't go in there to smoke cigarettes or do drugs. I just went in to look. I looked for my salvation.

I knew I should pay attention in class, but the dates for history's milestones had no relevance to me. Perhaps I had a learning disability specific to American history. Sister Mary Joseph didn't pause to ask us questions, for that would be too engaging and interesting for her students. She was bent on sucking us into her gray and plain life, spewing mundane historical facts. Sister's voice droned into a solid hum. My eyes wandered and fixated on her pale lips; crusty deposits of spittle had accumulated in the corners of her mouth.

I had to flee. My mind returned to my looming problem. What if I was pregnant? My father would kill me. The kids at school would shun me. Nobody in my school had ever gotten pregnant. We just didn't do those things. I was a freak. I was preoccupied with my state of dryness down below. I wanted to feel a gush of red coming forth and didn't even care if it messed up my whole uniform and everyone saw. Oh, how I wanted those cramps. Now I noticed there was an ever so slight emerging wetness. I detected that old familiar cramp in my lower gut that always came with my "friend."

Hope pumped through my veins with adrenaline of impending relief. The moist feeling was like a lottery ticket with the first four numbers matching. I raised my hand. "Sister Mary Joseph, may I be excused?"

I quietly closed the door behind me and shuffled past a neat row of classroom doors. I liked the feeling down there; it was even a little cold from the wetness. I wallowed in gratitude. The rosaries had worked. This meant I would go to Mass every day for a year. I would do it with joy every day, recalling how I had escaped the holocaust of doom.

The Regina halls were painted white; the floor was shiny gray linoleum, smelling like freshly applied floor wax. It was silent and empty. Everyone would be in class for ten more minutes. I picked up my pace as I cut the corner by the library. A silver plaque with black letters read, "GIRLS." I leaned my shoulder into the swinging door. The familiar creak heightened my anticipation.

I chose the stall all the way at the end of the row. I closed the door and slid the metal latch into the slot. I lifted my pleated uniform skirt and sat down. With my underwear at my knees, I leaned over to take a look. It was dark in there. I squinted and saw a hint of pink there in the wetness. I moved my body to let more light shine in. Blessed day! Pink was the precursor to red. The sight made me giddy. Mass, here I come. Rosary beads—they'll be a permanent fixture between my fingers. I looked again. What was that squiggle shape to the pink? A simple pink clothing thread was responsible for the color that smeared the white wetness.

It had been ten days now that I had been coming in and out of this bathroom during every class change and even during class. Truth replaced my fervent wish with doom. My period was seven days late now and I had always been on time in the past. I couldn't kid myself. The worst possible nightmare was true. I was pregnant. My body bent in half as I muffled the sobs that erupted from my chest. I let the tears drip down until they fell and collected in a pool on my brown penny loafers.

A few weeks later, my breasts were sore. Then I remembered this is what happened just before I got my period. Like a one-armed man dangling from a cliff, I held on to the impossible. I prayed on my way to school, on my way home from school, before my nap, and at night when I went to bed. I prayed that my monthly friend would visit. I couldn't admit it, but with each passing day I came to know that the sore breasts really meant my body was preparing to nourish a baby.

Then the nausea set in. As I rode to school in a car full of Regina girls, I hung my head out the window, gasping for the fresh but frigid air. The cigarette smoke made my stomach turn. It would be too conspicuous to tell them to put out their foul-smelling sticks, so I hung my head out like a floppy-eared dog.

"Judy, close the window. It's freezing in here," Diane said.

"I can't. I feel like I'm gonna throw up."

"You should stay home then. Do you have the flu?"

"No I just kinda feel sick—it'll pass."

I crammed my body to the car door and pointed my nose farther out the window. My mouth tasted like metal and watered profusely. My stomach needed food, but I couldn't eat breakfast. Nothing tasted good. By lunchtime I managed some cracker and cheese packets from the vending machine, then washed it down with a Coke. This became my lunch routine.

By the time I got home from school, the nausea had eased and I was famished. I began a love affair with the round, red and white box: Quaker Oats. The gummy porridge soaked up the foul acids welling in my gut. It was my saving grace: creamy, gooey, glorious oatmeal, two heaping bowls.

After my tummy was full, I became unbearably tired and longed for a nap. Each step up the stairs was like walking through water; fatigue had its grip on my muscles. Sleep came fitfully, but as I finally slipped away, the black cloud lifted. Most of my dreams had to do with some sort of conflict I was frantically trying to solve, like finding my math homework when I knew I did it, or being called on in class and realizing I forgot to get dressed that morning and was horrified that I was naked.

When I first woke from a nap, I'd feel deliverance at the end of my fitful dream, but this was short-lived as the predicament of my waking life settled its darkness on my heart. Something was not right. I would ask myself just for an instant, "What was it?" Then I remembered—I'm pregnant—and the dread squeezed like man-hands on my throat.

Then my thoughts turned dark. What about that coat-hanger abortion I learned about in the movie at school? One girl was performing her own abortion and she ended up on the verge of death. Then I thought, "No, as much as I hate my life right now, I still don't want to die."

The debilitating shame froze all action as I waited for some miraculous turn of events. In the meantime, the baby continued to grow. When the period-producing prayers failed, I prayed for a miscarriage, but it seemed God had forsaken me.

CHAPTER 14
MICK, GUESS WHAT?

Mick picked me up at home, honking in the driveway. The car was still running when I hopped in. Sonny and Cher were singing "I Got You Babe" on the AM radio. That was our song.

"They say we're young and we don't know
We won't find out until we grow
Well I don't know if all that's true
'Cause you got me, and baby I got you
And when I'm sad, you're a clown
And if I get scared, you're always around
'Cause you got me, and baby I got you"

I loved to listen to this song while I was up at the cabin away from Mick, pining for his love and attention. Now it was a sham. So what if he had me and I had him. All that meant now was serious trouble.

Mick smelled like Brut, men's cologne. I usually liked it, but that day it smelled like he took a bath in it. The fumes provoked a wave of nausea. Instead of charming and attractive, he looked ordinary and a tad sinister. Maybe it was the overpowering sense of dread that made my body respond in this foreign manner.

Halloween was a few days off and the air was frigid; the trees were covered with frost crystals. We whizzed past the suburban houses that lined Glenview Road. Some of them were set back so you could gaze down the long driveways and dream about the castle like homes that lurked beyond. Glenview Road was pretty deserted this Sunday afternoon. The sky was gray and the air thick with fog. I stared out the window. There was a news show on the radio; Mick reached over and switched the channel.

I started mulling over the script. Adrenaline pumped through my veins. I rolled, hashed, and mashed the words in my mind. How should I put it to him?

"Uhh, Mick, guess what?"

"What?" he'd say.

"I'm pregnant."

No, that was too blunt.

How about, "Uh, Mick, I have to talk to you about something. I think I'm pregnant."

No, I can't say that. I don't think it. I know it.

How about, "Hey, Mick, my period is late and I'm worried." That might work. But there didn't seem to be a good way to say this. I thought, "What is wrong with me? I hate this indecision, wondering how to choke out a few dumb words."

How about, "I have some bad news." Maybe …

But what if he gets all mad or doesn't believe me? Worse yet, what if he denies it could be him that planted the seed? Impossible. He knows he is my one and only. But yet I could see how it could be tempting to deny the whole damn thing. The incurred responsibilities were daunting. His parents would freak out; maybe his dad would beat the crap out of him. I didn't know Mr. Romano that well, but I knew he and Mick had some run-ins.

Mick made a right turn off Glenview Road and onto Waukegan. We still sat in pregnant silence. The time was now, but the words stuck in my throat. I was scared of his reaction. I thought he might yell, freak out, deny it, or drop me.

He flipped the turn signal and we rolled into McDonald's. He parked in our usual spot in the back lot and turned off the key.

"Are you hungry?" he asked.

"Not really."

We hardly ever ate anything when we came to McDonald's. It was more like a place to be rather than a place to eat. Hot rods and old beaters filled the lot. The dam let loose; the words spilled out.

"Mick, uummm, I don't know how to say it, but I think I have some really bad news."

"What's that, Goonsfield?"

"Well, remember when the rubber broke?"

"Yeah …" he said, the word trailing off. His face got dark.

"Well, my period is two weeks late."

"Are … you … kidding … me?" He said it slowly.

"No, I'm just sure. I wouldn't kid about this."

"A lot of girls are late, though, aren't they?" he said.

"That'd be nice, but I'm scared shitless. I'm not the irregular kind."

Mick turned the radio down and said, "Oh, don't worry about it. You'll probably get your period tomorrow and know you're making a big deal out of nothing."

I stayed on my side of the car and could feel tears welling in my eyes. This wasn't going well. He didn't want to believe we were in hot water.

I placated him by saying, "I guess there's a chance I'm just late." My gut knew this was wrong. I was suddenly hot, and I rolled down my window.

"Why are you opening the window? It's cold out there."

"I need some air."

"Really, you haven't gotten a period since the party?" Finally he sounded concerned.

"Really," I said. I cranked the window back up but left it cracked.

There was a long pause and then, "Do … you … think … you … are ……?"

"Pregnant?" I said, filling in the blank.

"Yah, but you couldn't be," he said.

"Why not? All you need is one screw-up."

"Yeah, but that'd just be our luck. That idiot, John. Why'd he give me that defective piece a shit? It'd been better if we used nothing."

"Yeah, it's not good. My boobs are sore and I've been sickish. You know, like morning sickness?"

Mick shuffled in his seat and used his fingers to run his hair back. "Morning sickness? Oh, fuck. Great. This is just great."

"Don't get mad. That won't help."

"I can't believe that rubber broke. I never should have gotten that thing from John. He must have had it in his pocket forever. Some favor."

"Well, what happened, happened. We can't change that."

"What are you going to do?" he said.

"I don't know. Is there some way I can bring on a miscarriage?"

"I don't know," said Mick. "Maybe you could ask someone."

"Who?"

"A doctor?"

"Who'd I go to?"

"I don't know."

The wind was whistling through the cracked window. I was cold now, and rolled it shut.

"A doctor'd make me tell my parents. I can't do that."

"I don't know what to do."

"Maybe I'll have a miscarriage. I've been praying for that."

"That's a long shot, but worth a try, I guess. Do you think we should get married?" He asked it in a halfhearted, tenuous tone.

"I hadn't even thought of that," I said. "We're too young." That didn't seem like a good solution. The idea was suffocating.

"Oh, shit, this is awful," he said.

Mick stiffened his body and moved away. His eyes had a contemplative stare; his mouth was tight, stern. He seemed pissed off. I felt sorry for the worry on his face.

"Look," I said. "Lennie's pulling in."

"Who gives a fuck," Mick said. "My parents are gonna kill me."

"Well, don't worry about that now. We'll see what happens."

I tried to hold back the well of tears that were squeezing out; my throat was so tight that it ached. My organs shook inside their cavity.

Mick said, "We're in a mess. But don't worry about it now, Jude. You might still get your period. Straighten up, here comes Lennie."

I knew his words were empty. It wasn't going to turn out okay. I looked up and saw Lennie getting ready to knock on the window. Mick rolled it down.

"Hop in, Lennie. How's it goin'?"

We switched from life-threatening conversation to idle chitchat. My heart was still cold. I was surprised at how easily Mick could turn off the worry and switch to blasé chat.

After about thirty minutes, I said, "Mick, I better get home."

As Lennie got out, dread and worry returned with the silence. The wind had picked up and dried leaves were swirling around the parked cars. We pulled out and didn't talk much until we said good-bye when Mick dropped me off at home. I dragged my body out of the car.

I was a sickened and diseased soul. I had shared my burden with Mick, but it didn't seem to lighten the load. I had never felt so alone. I don't know what I thought Mick could do about it, but of course he had no solution because there was none. After telling him, I felt twice as bad—once for each of us. I wiped the tears from my face as I stepped into the house.

CHAPTER 15
CONSEQUENCES OF A SWOLLEN BELLY

If I carried any shred of hope that I was not pregnant, it was extinguished the night I lay in bed and ran my hand over my tummy, just above the pubic bone. I was shocked to feel a hard lump nestled deep inside, the size of a bird's egg. Then I knew this was my pregnancy and it was taking hold. I tried to move it around but it seemed glued in place. I had to get rid of it. It was just going to grow and get bigger, a freaky tumor taking possession of my body. I held my arm out straight and made a fist. Then I snapped my hand back to my belly and punched. It hurt. Had I gone insane, pounding my own body? I tried again and realized I had to try harder. So I punched again. And again. I waited.

I could hear myself breathing. Nothing seemed to happen. I wanted to feel cramps. Maybe I didn't try hard enough. I needed more force. I tried again. Arm straight: slam. It was difficult to get much power because my arms were too short. I tried again anyway. Tears spilled onto my cheeks. I'd had enough. It was hopeless. I hated myself and my growing belly with a newfound loathing. I settled down. I lay there. Was that a crimp in my belly? The start of cramps? I prayed again for God to bring the pains that would help me pass the lump. My arm ached from exhaustion and the skin on my belly was red. I cried, trapped. I rolled over and eventually drifted asleep.

The next night I tried again, but it was halfhearted. I suspected my efforts would be fruitless and it was just too nuts to be hurting myself like this. I was scared to use the force I thought was necessary and accepted defeat. The seed had taken purchase. It continued to expand, but still I told no one.

The weeks passed slowly until I was unable to button my uniform skirt. I couldn't get the waistband's button over to the hole, nor could I suck in my stomach enough to make it fit. It wouldn't suck. I knew this day was coming, so the previous week I had decided I needed more props to pull off my act. It was windy and about forty degrees in mid-February. I was now four and a half months along. I bundled up and drove Mom's car over to Edens Plaza. I went into the Ben Franklin Five and Dime and picked out the thickest and smallest girdle I could find. I knew it would look fishy if anyone I knew saw me buying a girdle—me, a skinny thing, except for the part no one could see. I plopped a bag of black licorice strings on top of the girdle when I got to the checkout counter to camouflage my purchase. I hoped I wouldn't run into someone I knew.

Today I was glad I had that fat compressor. I reached way back in the bottom drawer, and found it tucked under my pajamas. It was impossible trying to pull the thing over my belly, it was so teensy. I wiggled and pulled but my skin was sticky from the lotion I put on. I got some talcum powder from the bathroom and sprinkled that on me. Finally I got the elastic waist over my tummy and tried the skirt on again. My stomach was still big and hadn't compressed enough for the button to reach the hole. Now what? I only had two uniform skirts and they were both the same size.

While I was panicking over my predicament, I heard Dad's footsteps going up and down the stairs and then into the bathroom. I was afraid he would knock and want to come in. I had my robe lying on the chair so I could grab it fast to pull it over me. I didn't want him to see any shred of my body. I sat down on my overstuffed chair and put my face in my despairing hands. Dead end. What to do? "Come on, Jude," I told myself. "Pull yourself together. There must be a way." I wiped the tears with three fingers.

Then I had an idea. I threw on my robe and ran downstairs to the kitchen. I opened the drawer with the tin foil and grabbed an oversized rubber band from the corner of the drawer. It had been wrapped around the asparagus stalks. I scampered back upstairs. Dad was still in the bathroom. I went in my bedroom and shut the door, then I took the rubber band and folded it in half. I looped it around the button and then through the hole and back over to the button again. This gave me an extra two inches. It felt good. I left the girdle on, which seemed to help redistribute the bulge. I had a temporary fix for my expanding waist. For the first time, I was glad that we wore uniforms and that I had a blazer to hide my growing thickness.

The looping rubber band worked wonders, until one day at school my pen rolled off my desk. I bent down to pick it up and the rubber band snapped. It didn't make any noise, but my skirt started falling to my knees. I was mortified. While I was still hunched over, I held my arms around my middle and then walked to the bathroom. I was glad class hadn't started yet. I was also glad I had some change in my pocket. I put a nickel in the tampon dispensing machine and pressed "super." I went in the stall and tried to pull the cotton away from the string. It was sewn into the cotton cylinder and wouldn't come free, so I just looped the whole thing through the button hole and tied a knot around the button. I rolled my skirt up once so the tampon was hidden in the belt area of the skirt. It would get me through the day.

The stringed tampon didn't have any "give" like the rubber band, so my skirt kept trying to ride up to the thinner part above the protrusion, kind of like Gomer Pyle on *The Andy Griffith Show*, with his pants up to his ears. Besides, the girdle made the surface slippery. The rest of the day, I had to keep pulling the skirt down to keep it around the thickest part of my waist. I was never so happy to get home and change clothes. I put an extra couple of rubber bands in my purse in case of any more mishaps, sort of like an inhaler for a person with asthma.

This time when I carried the secret of my pregnancy, alone, was the darkest period of my life. I am sad for that lonely teenager who couldn't talk to anyone about her trouble. I could have saved myself some distress if I had faced the problem sooner and talked to an adult, but who would it have been? Dad would have had a solution. But telling Dad was too drastic, like jumping out of a plane. I couldn't do it until I absolutely had to. How could I not know that I would eventually have to come clean? I held on to the false hope that the pregnancy would expel itself. It was the weak straw that I grabbed, for I couldn't live without some shred of hope.

Not once did I think ahead of how it would all turn out. I never dreamed I would go away to a Home for Unwed Mothers or that I would give birth to a real baby. It was a time that I lived in absolute denial, an ostrich with its head in the sand. I lived each day in a shroud of fright that expanded with my belly. It was a life lesson for me.

As an adult, I try to address problems before they complicate themselves. I don't like living with the dread of the unknown. I feel a bit duped when someone confides in me and then follows their words with: "but don't tell anyone." I'd rather know up front so I can say something like, "that's ok, skip it," because I really don't like keeping secrets. They sit heavy on my heart.

CHAPTER 16
FRONT SEAT OR ELSE

About the time I was very large but still in hiding, my friends and I went out to the Pitt in Glenview for a dance night out. Diane was driving and there were eight or nine of us who needed a ride. This was before seat belts, so it was common to sit on each other's laps; sometimes we had six in the back seat. As we started to pile in, I panicked as I realized that if I sat on someone's lap they might reach around and be able to feel my thickness—or worse yet, if they sat on my lap, it would be stuck there like a sack of potatoes between us. Dread of the back seat made me weak. I couldn't risk being part of a double layer.

I crawled into the car, hoping I could keep my lap free, but then Jane started to crawl on top of me.

"No, Jane, get off. I'm claustrophobic."

"Jude, there's nowhere else to sit," Jane said.

"Too bad" I said. "I have claustrophobia and will pass out."

"When did this affliction appear?" Carol asked.

"Oh, I'm sure," Barb said. "Gimme a break. Close the damn door, it's freezing outside. Get in."

"I don't have anywhere to sit," Jane said.

"Sit on the floor," I said.

"Geez, Jude, don't have a cow," Jane said.

"I'm not having a cow; I just don't want anyone on top of me. We're packed in like sardines; I can't take it. Carol, will you trade places with me? Please. I can't breathe."

Carol had no sympathy. "Forget it," she said. "I get carsick. Besides, first come first served. I got dibs on the front seat."

"Please, I'm begging you. Really, I can't stand it back here."

"Close the damn door," Barb yelled again from the back. "Let's get going."

"Well, I'm not moving," Carol said.

Feeling backed into a corner, I made a hasty decision. "Then I'll walk," I said.

I closed the back door of the car and stomped across the street and headed north on Waukegan Road. The cars whizzed by, throwing spray on the sidewalk. Flakes of snow had gathered on the bordering grass.

I felt like such a baby. I hated how I acted. All I knew was there was no way I was going to sit in the back seat with all the girls. I was seething with anger at Carol. She was so selfish sometimes, but now I was scared. It was late February and one of those bone-chilling, damp Chicago nights. I had no hat or gloves. What was I thinking? How would I ever walk the five miles home at 10:00 at night? I didn't think I had a choice. Streams of anger came off me in waves. If only Carol let me sit in front.

I walked along, knowing that I had to make it home somehow. The snow was sloppy and stuck to my shoes; the moisture oozed through the soles. After a few blocks, Diane's car pulled up next to me. My fear eased. Carol rolled down the window and said, "Okay, get in. You're such a winner. I'll sit in back; get in." She opened the car door and walked around to the back seat. For us, a winner was a loser and although sometimes said in jest, this time it hurt. Carol got in back and sat on Jane's lap. I sheepishly crawled into the passenger seat. I hated that I acted so snippy because of my predicament. My friends must have thought I was self-centered—demanding the front seat when everyone else was cramped in the back. Even though I was ashamed of how I acted, I was mostly relieved to be back inside the warm car, speeding toward home. I sat in silence, while everyone in the back chattered away. Tears tried to form, but I held them back. A tight band squeezed my throat, like a nail was stuck in there sideways.

When Diane pulled up to my house, I hopped out and said, "Bye, thanks for the ride."

Carol said, "I hope you enjoyed the front seat."

"Yeah, it was great," I said and ran into the house. I suppose I could have at least thanked her for letting me sit in front, but I was way too angry to be kind. It wasn't like she gave it up willingly. I sighed with resolve as I walked in the front door of my house. "This is ridiculous," I thought. "I have to come clean about my condition. I just have to tell someone, but who?"

CHAPTER 17
MY SORRY LIFE

I tossed and turned most of those winter nights, waking and overcome by worry, then falling back into a fitful sleep. Five months into it and still nobody knew about my situation except Mick. The impending doom clouded my days with a sooty black. I knew I couldn't keep the secret much longer. My belly was full and swollen. I had been feeling the baby kick for several weeks now. At first they were butterfly flutters, but now they were definite rolls and punches. My stomach muscles were stiff and iron-like from all the practice at holding in my belly. I walked with a slight bend forward so my blazer would fall around the sides, concealing my thick middle. With the rubber band around the button hole to add space to the waistline, the pleats fell with a sloppy bend in the folds.

It was quiet in our house. Mom had been taking high dose steroids for her pain, and the side effects put her in and out of the hospital. When she was home she slept a lot. She had wounds on her legs from the slightest nicks. One time a whole flap of skin came off: the wound filled up with pus and wouldn't heal. With a compromised immune system, she caught illnesses easily. The worst episode was the staph infection that landed her in the hospital for several months, her life hanging by a thread, us visiting with masks tacked to our faces.

Hugren never could get the hang of making rice the way we liked it, so Dad did most of the cooking. His favorite meals included packaged sukiyaki with rice, T-bone steaks and rice, sukiyaki and rice. These were rotated on a weekly basis. As we sat across from each other at the glass table, Dad would look up from the newspaper and ask, "How was school today?" and I would say, "Fine." Then we'd resume eating. Shame filled my space as I gobbled my food so I could excuse myself and go off to my room and be alone. Like Bill Murray in the movie Groundhog Day, nothing ever changed. It was a gloomy atmosphere with a word or two wedged into the silence. Hugren ate on her own and didn't join us for dinner. The absence of Mom, who was in the hospital, and Jeff, who was away at college, left an uncomfortable emptiness. I was pretty much on my own those days; nobody paid much attention to where I was or what I was doing. I liked that part of it.

Mick and I had lost our romantic relationship. We were seeing each other occasionally, but there was such gloom wedged between us that the passion just slipped away. Our outings got fewer and farther between. After I was about four months into it, I heard through the grapevine that someone saw Mick at a Glenbrook basketball game, holding hands with some girl. My heart crumpled. How could he? I didn't want to believe it.

One of my lowest points that year was a day in theology class. Sister Rosa Marie was lecturing us on the pitfalls of dating. "Girls, the Lord wants us to be pure and clean. You must please the Lord and maintain proper conduct at all times around the opposite sex. Holding hands, although seemingly innocent, can lead to dangerous activities. Never, ever engage in kissing and necking."

While the words were coming out of her mouth, I could feel flutters and movement deep within my belly. If she knew how far away from the directive this young girl had gone, she would implode from the shock of it. Guilt and shame put a nasty green slime on my world. It felt like a moldy gunnysack was tied over my head: I couldn't get enough air and I couldn't see ahead. I longed for the innocent days when I went to Mass early in the mornings and just worried about telling Father in confession that I was thinking impure thoughts. If only I knew how good it was then. In the meantime, the baby that was hiding deep in there just kept on growing. I think it was around then that I put down the rosary before I completed my quota. What was the point? And, I never returned to confession. My sins were too monumental to divulge.

CHAPTER 18
BREAKING THE SILENCE

Memory works like Swiss cheese. There is the structure of the feelings and emotions and then the holes where the details should be. It amazes me that people who were present for the same event can remember entirely different details. As I gently plod along with the writing, all of a sudden I have a name, or a smell, or a scene from forty years ago distilling in my mind's eye.

It was about a week before Christmas, 2010, late and well after dinner. I was in Palm Beach, Florida, with my longtime friends, Annie and Jane. The weather was mild and warm as we gathered around the patio furniture with our glasses of wine. I read aloud from my backlit laptop as the thin, stiff leaves of the palms rustled with the breeze. It would be the first time they heard what I had written about my teen pregnancy in 1967. I felt vulnerable, like I was putting my words to the test for accuracy. I knew that my memory had some holes, and I was hoping they could shed some light on the subject. When I had finished reading, Annie said, "I distinctly remember we were under the bleachers at Glenbrook South at a football game and you lifted up your shirt to show us." This was contrary to what I had written. I thought we were in a hotel room or a sleepover and I was in my pajamas when I confided in them.

I didn't remember it happening the way Annie described it, but she seemed so sure about the details that I went to bed thinking, "Could it be?" Could that have been where I told the very first people about my secret, under the bleachers?

I rolled her words over in my mind. "We were under the bleachers at a Glenbrook South football game," she said. She painted a picture of us gathered in a huddle and me lifting my shirt to prove my predicament. As I thought about her words, a sickening feeling of fright, like something was very wrong came back to me as I remembered the dark, damp feeling of being under there with the butts and legs of people showing through the slits in the benches as we looked up. Like time-lapse photography, the image materialized in my mind, yet I didn't think I would be willing to divulge my secret in public or lift my shirt while I was outside and chilly. I remembered us gathered under there, but couldn't remember why. I suspected it was right after I had exposed my secret, and perhaps they all wanted another look.

Nevertheless, this is the story the way I remember it.

When March hit and the snow began to melt, we had a premature springy day of rain instead of snow. I had that nostalgic feeling about approaching spring. I felt the weight of my dark secret and remembered how carefree I was a year ago when my belly was flat and I was giddy and star struck, having just met Mick. I stood in front of the mirror and gazed at my shape with timid eyes. Without the girdle or clothes for a cover-up, my stomach relaxed into a small-sized basketball. My skin was dry and red from stretching to accommodate the growth inside. My breasts, which had been small and insignificant, now loomed large with the bottom surface resting on the skin below. Although I had longed for this fullness when I was fourteen, now it was freaky, unnatural. I was mortified at the extent of my disfiguration. I knew my reckoning day was coming soon. If I waited much longer, someone was bound to notice and call me on it. The secret was like a giant floating soap bubble, delicate and present, but tense with imminent destruction.

Annie, Jane, Carol, and I were at a sleepover. It felt like we were at a hotel. Could we have stayed at a Holiday Inn together for some reason or other? I don't know where we were, but the surroundings were not familiar, like my house or my friends' houses. I remember that I wasn't worried about someone overhearing us. It was just us. I was shaking in anticipation of spilling the news. I felt trapped and forced to tell. I couldn't hold the secret any longer. I was bursting at the seams.

They just couldn't believe it. After all, I hadn't even told them that Mick and I had sex. We never ventured into this topic. It was way too embarrassing and sensitive for me, and I was pretty sure none of them had done it. My friends were "good" girls. I wasn't going to offer the fact that I was no longer a virgin, because it was something I wasn't supposed to be doing. But now, I had to tell. I just had to tell someone.

I mustered up the courage and said the words I had been rehearsing for months. "I'm pregnant." I didn't give any details or lead up to it but just blurted it out, like diving into an icy pond so as not to prolong the misery by going in gradually.

A few summers before, we had read and passed around the Teen magazine issue with the cover story, "Pregnant and Still a Virgin." The girl seemed to have had a heavy make-out session, and the boy must have dripped enough so it could travel and get inside. This was great fiction, but how did we know? These magazines were like today's reality shows and we thought they were based on true stories. We took it as a warning to stay away from heavy petting.

Since all of us had read this magazine story, I was quizzed as to whether I actually "did" it. There were questions like, "How do you know for sure?" I told them we really did do it; I was no virgin.

When there were still questions, I told them I could feel the baby kick. I thought that would convince them. But then someone said maybe it was just gas.

"No, no," I said, and finally lifted my shirt. "See?"

Then, I think it was Carol who said, "You're just sticking it out." Carol had an amazing talent and could pooch her belly out on demand so she looked like a little monkey. It was the funniest thing. So perhaps they thought I had learned Carol's trick. I told them if they put their hand on my belly, they could feel it kick.

"That's creepy," someone said. Then they saw my belly roll and change shape, and they knew it was no joke.

Annie, who has always been good at offering solutions, said I should tell our local priest. This advice horrified me. Of all people, I couldn't bear the thought of going in front of a priest and confessing what I had done. I hadn't gone to confession in a long time, either.

Jane seemed sick with worry. "What are you going to do, Jude?"

They were all stunned, then concerned as they tried to help me come up with a plan.

By the end of the night, it was decided that my sister, Jackie, would be the best one to tell next. I felt very close to my friends and was confident that they would keep the secret, because I made each of them say, "Swear to God. Stick a needle in your eye. No peein' in the pot. No pickin' your snot. Swear to God." We used these words when it was really important that the secret be kept. Each repeated it, like a rite of passage. I was a member of a sacred group and reassured that my secret was safe.

Now I felt light and free, filled with a warm sense of release from the damned-up secret. With the confession, I was free from the lead anchor that was pulling me down. As horrible as I had felt for five long months, I now felt a glimmer of hope, like this would get worked out somehow. Now I would tell Jackie. I would get some help and this secret would be dealt with however it may.

ANNIE, JANE, AND JUDY 2011

CHAPTER 19
HYSTERICAL PREGNANCY

The next night I slept right through without lying awake with worry. In the morning I was ready for the next step. Even though I dreaded telling Jackie, I had cracked the shell of secrecy. It wasn't as bad as I thought. No one said, "How could you do it?" or "You're a slut." I loved my friends more than ever. I believed they would uphold our pact of silence.

If I had to tell someone, my sister, Jackie, was the least threatening in my circle of authority figures. She didn't reprimand me like she did her kids, but treated me like a sister. I always felt welcome at her house.

Since there were nineteen years between Jackie and me, she ended up being like a second mom. I stayed at her house whenever Mom and Dad went on trips. At first it was a culture shock, going from our silent, spotless house to the gaggle of spirited children bumping into each other and tripping over toys strewn on the floor. I didn't eat that much at home, but at Jackie's a strange impulse came over me. When a mass of fork-laden hands attacked the plate of pork chops, I found myself stabbing two for my plate. Never before in my life had I eaten two hunks of meat. We were praised for being members of the Clean Plate Club, so I managed to choke down the last bites.

Her kids tell stories of Jackie being so exhausted after birthing her tenth child in a span of thirteen years that she would lie on the couch and ping the rug rats with a fishing pole to keep them in line. Jackie was a baby-having expert. I remembered her words after coming from the hospital with one of her babies. "You aren't a real woman until you experience childbirth." I took that to mean it hurt a lot.

Sis gained a few pounds with each pregnancy, so by the time I was a teen, she was well padded. She was never stingy with her hugs and I craved them. Her welcoming arms swallowed you up like a mass of warm silly putty.

So the next day, after telling my friends, I picked up the phone and asked Jackie if I could come over to visit that afternoon. I told her I wanted to get her advice on something. It was set. I was committed. I was nervous now; I had five hours to wait until I could go over there. I went up to my bedroom and pulled out *Catcher in the Rye*. I got a glass of water, sat down, and started reading. After a few pages, I realized I hadn't absorbed any of it. My mind was arranging the words for my disclosure to Jackie and thinking about food.

Food was now high on my radar, strange for me, because during my childhood and teen life, I forced myself to eat. I hated being called skinny – it was another sign of my immaturity. Nobody was telling me that now, but my legs and arms were still quite thin.

I went downstairs and fixed a bowl of oatmeal, then another. There was some fruitcake with brandy sauce in the fridge. Mom baked it every Christmas and I wouldn't eat it unadorned, but the creamy, sugary brandy sauce made it delicious. That year, Mom had shown Hugren how to bake it, and we had some thawed out from the freezer. After the oatmeal, I had two pieces of fruitcake smeared with the thick sauce. My belly was packed until the skin was stretched tight. The jammed-in food made it hard to keep my breath.

With a full belly my mind went limp and there was only one option – take a nap. I woke just in time to get in the car and head over to Jackie's. She lived in Northbrook, a twenty-five-minute drive from our house in Glenview. There stood the familiar white-painted frame house with the enclosed front porch. As I pulled into her driveway, my heart started to clickety-clack, ka-boom ka-boom, like an out-of-balance Whirlpool washer. I knocked on the door, walked in, and called out, "Hi, Sis, I'm here."

Jackie responded from upstairs, "Hi, Jude, I'll be there in a minute."

I sat on the couch. "She has no idea what's coming," I thought. My palms were damp and I could feel drips of sweat falling down the sides of my chest. I wanted to flee but I stayed put, staring into space. Soon I heard her footsteps coming down the stairs. My nervousness elevated. She looked like she had just washed her hair: tight, dishwater-blonde ringlets covered her head.

"Hi, Pood," she said. "Let's go in the kitchen." Pood had been my nickname since I was a baby. Maybe it was because I pooed. Or maybe it was because some other baby couldn't say the "J" in "Jude."

We walked into the kitchen. "Sis, I have a bad problem and just don't know what to do or who to talk to," I said.

"Oh?" she questioned, the corners of her mouth turning down. Jackie closed the swinging door to the kitchen. "Let's sit down."

We sat across from each other at the oak table, big enough for the horde of kids.

"What's going on, Jude?"

I put my hand up to my chin and said it. "I think I'm pregnant."

I couldn't believe I blurted it out so quickly. Hearing the words out loud still shocked me, but it was a load-off to get it out.

"Oh. My. Why do you think so?"

"I haven't had a period in five months."

"Five months?"

"Yep."

"Judy, do you want a glass of water or something to drink?"

"No, thanks." Jackie got up and ran the faucet, filled a glass and sat back down.

"Oh, dear," she said. There was a long pause, as she tried to form a response. "Well, Judy, just because you missed your period doesn't mean you're pregnant."

Maybe Jackie knew something I didn't: after all, she birthed ten kids and should know about this pregnancy stuff. I wanted to believe. Oh, how I wanted to believe there could be a chance she was right.

Jackie's frown relaxed when a thought came to her. "Well, you know," she said, "there's something called a hysterical pregnancy. You can have all the symptoms but it's not really so."

My mind tried to grab on to her words. I wanted to be hysterical with relief.

"Really?" I said. "I never heard of that."

"Yes, it's the strangest thing. But it's a real thing. It's just like you're pregnant—you miss your period, get nauseated, and gain weight. The mind is a powerful thing."

I wondered if Jackie thought I was crazy enough to have a hysterical pregnancy. For an instant I wanted to jump in with both feet, believing this swollen belly was a figment of my imagination. But if it was true, that might be worse than the real thing, for what kind of crazy would I have to be to create all this just by the power of my mind? But yet, I so wanted to take the leap and grab on to the hope.

The lifeline snapped as truth set back in.

"Sis, I don't think so. I can feel it moving inside of me," I said.

"Really? Sometimes that can be gas."

"But I had morning sickness, too."

"Yes, that can be a part of the hysterical pregnancy too," she said.

"Really, it's a medical condition that exists. What we need to do is have you tested. You never know for sure."

"Hmmm," I said. "It could be, but I'm so scared." I started to cry.

"Well, we'll see, Jude. Don't get all worked up about it yet."

She put her arms around me.

"What we need to do is talk to Mom and Dad about this."

"We do? I was hoping we could keep them out of it."

"They need to know. You're their daughter."

"But, Sis," I said. "I just can't bear to tell Mom. She just got out of the hospital, and Dad will kill me. I'm too scared."

She took a sip of water and said, "Well, I can talk to Mom about it."

"That'd be good. I'm just so scared of what they're going to do. When will you tell her?"

"I'll arrange it. Maybe this evening, or I could go over there tomorrow morning. We can make a doctor's appointment so you can get tested."

"Thank you, Sis. I'm so glad I talked to you. I don't know what's gonna happen, but I have been keeping this secret for too long."

"You poor thing. We'll get it worked out."

I stood up and pushed in the chair. Jackie stood up, too.

"Come over here." She hugged me. "It's okay, Jude. It'll all be okay. We'll take care of this. Don't worry; we'll get to the bottom of this. The next step is to talk to Mom and Dad. I love you, Pood. Really, it's gonna be okay."

She gave me one of those enveloping hugs, slipping me into comfort like a warm tub of water. As she drew me close, for the first time since that fateful party, I felt like I could take a free breath. I started to cry. I was relieved there was no lecture or questions like, "How could you do it?" My sister was cool.

CHAPTER 20
COMING CLEAN TO MOM AND DAD

My mother pushed the joystick on her motorized wheelchair to get closer to the phone. Her finger joints were stiff and immobile, knotted with arthritis. She fumbled as she picked up the receiver and then used her index finger to punch the numbers on the phone. If we still had rotary dials, she wouldn't have been able to call because she had very little strength in her fingers. She was dialing Fendall, my dad's manufacturing plant.

Jackie and I sat on the blue satin couch. Jackie got up to reach the crystal candy dish. The unwrapping cellophane sounded like cracking thunder. I was so nervous.

"John Liautaud, please."

"His wife."

"It's urgent."

"John, I have some bad news but I'd like you to come home from work so I can talk to you about it."

"No, John, no one has died, but I don't think you'll be happy with the news. Please come home now."

"OK, bye."

Mom used her free arm to grab under her elbow for support. She leaned her body over to get closer to the tabletop and jerkily put the phone back in the cradle. Her aim was off-center, but she finally rocked it into place. Her eyes winced with the pain of movement.

"Is Dad coming?" I asked.

"Yes, he'll be here in half an hour."

"Oh, Judy, of all the things you could have done, this is the worst. Why didn't you come and talk to me sooner?" Mom asked.

Mom went on without waiting for me to come up with an

answer.

"Your father is going to be very upset."

Mom's eyes narrowed and her smooth, swollen face crinkled with her thoughts of angst.

"This is all my fault. I wasn't here for you during the most important years of your life," she sighed.

I wanted to protect her from the pain of what I had done, but there was no remedy for that. I felt sick at the hurt I had caused her.

Even though Mom was away from home, I didn't see how she could feel responsible for my condition. If she had been home, she wouldn't have been going out with me on dates.

"Oh, Mom, it isn't your fault," I said. "It wouldn't have made any difference if you were here; this still would've happened."

Of all people, I thought, Mom was the least to be blamed. Sometimes she had an overactive maternal instinct. Even though there was still Dad to deal with, I was relieved I was coming clean. Like a soldier to battle, I had my shield ready to fend off any punishment, including the angry words or freaked-out behavior that might emit from Dad.

"At least I would have noticed that you were gaining weight," Mom said. "Maybe I would have heard you getting sick in the morning. I could have done something for you."

"I doubt if you'd have noticed, Mom. No one knew, not even my best friends."

"But, Judy, you should have come to us right away and told us about this."

"Yeah, I got it," I thought. I not only got in trouble, but I didn't handle it very well, either. I acted like a zombie, stuffing the problem and ignoring its presence.

I didn't know how to explain myself, or if I even could. After a minute, I said, "Mom, I was too scared to tell anyone. Up until a few days ago, the only person who knew about it was Mick. I kept hoping for a miscarriage."

My defense sounded weak. My throat clenched and a sob creaked between the tightened strings of my vocal cords.

"I've really messed up. I know. I'm so sorry, Mom. I didn't mean for this to happen."

"How long has it been since you had a period?" Mom asked.

"Five months."

"Oh my God, you couldn't possibly be five months along. Why didn't you tell us sooner?"

She didn't believe it, but I knew I got pregnant the day the rubber broke at the party. But why would she think I knew anything when I had lost her trust?

"How did you manage to conceal it for that long?"

"I sucked my stomach in. I wore a girdle. My uniform blazer pretty much covered it up."

"Oh, Jesus, help us."

Now that I had told my mom and my sister and a few friends, I didn't want them to think I was a slut, which would be the obvious assumption considering my condition. I was surprised no one was asking me about any details. And I didn't know how to make myself look any better. Even if I said I only did it twice, it didn't seem to lessen my marred purity. I didn't know if I should offer the truth about the rubber breaking. I thought perhaps that would sound too "premeditated." I guess it was obvious. I did it at least once. That was bad enough. I sat in silence.

The front door flew open and in came Dad with a crease in his brow and fire in his eyes.

"OK, what's wrong, Ethel?"

"He knows," I thought. I could tell by the look in his eyes.

"Well, John, come sit down, now. Judy has gotten into some trouble."

"Trouble? What kinda trouble?"

Mom gave a sigh and said, "Now just be calm."

"Trouble! Don't tell me she's pregnant?" Dad asked.

"Yes, John, she is. She told Jackie about it yesterday."

"Oh ferchrissakes, are we sure about this?"

"She's missed several periods."

"Oh my God. Sonofabitch."

The veins on Dad's neck popped out and his voice began to rise with fury. Although the last time I got hit was a toddler spanking, I thought this might be the time he would do it again. His body was stiff, drenched with anxiety pulsing through his core. He paced back and forth on the living room floor like he was caught in a place he didn't want to be, like he was desperate for a way out.

My father seemed taller than usual. He had on his same old khaki pants and a white shirt. Maybe it was his head. It looked huge as I looked up at him from my lower position on the couch. Mom was tired of those khakis, said he should shop for new pants, but he always wore them. Today I hated those khakis too.

"Judy, how could you do this? Don't you know any better? Haven't we taught you anything?"

My tongue was frozen.

"Do you know who the father is?"

Dad's rage was mounting. My bones vibrated with fear.

"Of course I know who the father is," I said. My voice squeaked through my constricting throat. I was thoroughly insulted by his question. I tried to hold back the tears. He must have thought I was messing around with a bunch of guys and didn't even know who the father was. Anger radiated into my veins, but fright won over and I became meek. My throat felt like it was in a tightening vice.

"It's Mick, Dad. You know Mick," I whined.

"That son of a bitch!" Dad said. "Did he force you into it?"

"No. No, Dad. It's not Mick's fault. He didn't force me into anything." I wanted to protect Mick from the innate hatred my dad had for him. This definitely put the nail in the coffin for Mick.

"Do his parents know about this?"

"No. He hasn't told them."

"Good. Let's keep them out of it. There isn't any reason they have to get involved. We'll handle it."

I was surprised by this turn of events. I imagined our parents getting together and discussing the situation. I was relieved Dad wanted to keep them out of it and relieved for Mick.

Dad's lips stiffened and he said, "If that boy was any kind of a man he would be here right now, goddammit."

Mom fired up the wheelchair and rolled over to the window. She backed herself in so she was closer to my spot on the couch.

"Does anyone know about your condition?" Dad asked.

"Well, Mick knows, and I told Annie and Jane."

"You should not have done that, Judy," he said. "The fewer people involved in this, the better."

I knew in my heart that I wouldn't have been able to tell anyone if I hadn't first told my friends. They gave me the strength to move ahead with telling Jackie. I hoped they wouldn't tell anyone at school, but really, I wasn't even worried about that. I trusted their vow of secrecy.

"Well, I forbid you to ever see that boy again. Do you know the disgrace you are bringing upon the family?"

"I'm sorry, Dad."

"I'm extremely disappointed in you, Judy. I can't believe you've done this."

I sat silent, taking the heat. Then Dad's face relaxed a little, like he had an idea.

His next words shot me like an arrow in the gut.

"You'll have an abortion. That's the best solution. An abortion, that's all there is to it."

Dad didn't get it. I guess I hadn't told him that the baby was now a large moving mass in my belly. An abortion? Was it possible? I had been feeling my baby kick and roll within me for over a month. The skin on my stomach was stretched thin and substantially rounded. My lips quivered and my hands cooled to ice. The shakes started in my throat and settled to my gut. I was too scared to cry outwardly, but inside I was heaving.

Dad's anger had always made me want to run for cover, but the thought of an abortion sickened me. It was different when it was just an idea, but now I could feel it roll and kick. I wondered how I could do this to a live being inside of me. It was too late for an abortion, wasn't it? I knew it in my heart. But yet, I was too scared to protest. I said nothing. To think that it could all be over in a matter of hours with some kind of operation. Could it be possible? Oh, how could I let them do that to me?

"I'm going to call Dr. Keller," Dad said. Dr. Keller was Dad's fishing buddy and our family doctor. I had met him up at the cabin and always just said my hellos but never spent time around him. I hated the thought of Dad's friend knowing about me. I wished it was a stranger. I was relieved that my punishing lecture was brought to a halt by the phone call.

"Hello, Doctor, this is John. We have a problem here. Judy has gotten herself pregnant. Can you do something to fix this? Can she come in and see you today?"

Then Dad turned to me and said, "Judy, Dr. Keller is asking when you had your last period?"

"September fifteenth," I said. It was now the middle of March.

Dad relayed the date. He talked for a few more minutes and banged the phone back in the cradle.

"What'd the doctor say?" Mom asked.

"He said he doubts if Judy is that far along, because she would be showing. He'll give her a pregnancy test and examine her. We can get her in there in the morning."

"A pregnancy test, what a joke," I thought. These people think I'm imagining my condition.

As bad as it was telling my dad, it was a pain that felt good. It was the end to the unknown, the end of my silence, and I felt free. Free from the hiding. Done. Whatever happened to me now would be the penance that I was due. It would be nothing compared to the five months of secrecy and gloom that I had lived through. It was a great lesson to me of the added pain one encounters by procrastinating instead of resolving a problem.

Confiding in Dad during my five months of secrecy was just not something I even considered. I was afraid Dad would blow up into a crazy maniac. But why didn't I tell Mom sooner? When Mom was in the hospital, I thought she was too sick and fragile and feared the news might kill her. When she came home, I couldn't do it then, either. I just hoped my problem would disappear on its own, like the setting sun. I knew that if I told either of my parents, it would be like lighting the fuse to an explosion. Why would a sane person subject themselves to that kind of abuse? Mom and I started off on the wrong foot: first, when I was thoroughly embarrassed by our sex talk at nine years old and when I got caught playing doctor and then again when I couldn't tell her how much I wanted that bra.

I see now that if Mom and I had had a closer relationship when I was a teen, it might have filled some of the need I had to seek love at such a young age. Perhaps some mature input could have put some steadiness into my blundering steps into womanhood. Does anyone have that kind of relationship with their mom?

As a little girl I idolized Mom: I knew she was beautiful and smart and comforting in all aspects. She thought the same about me and believed I could do no wrong. I know I disappointed her horribly and was most sorry for how I had failed to live up to the woman she intended me to be. I am sure that Mom and Dad felt like they failed miserably in raising me, evidenced by the trouble I got in.

Chapter 21
A Visit to Dr. Keller

The next day Dad called Regina to tell them I had a doctor's appointment. This was the last truth he told those nuns at Regina Dominican. We took the thirty-minute drive to downtown Chicago via Edens Expressway riding in silence, except for the one question Dad asked when we got in the car.

"Judith Ann, how could you let this happen?"

"I don't know." Then the mind chatter gave me a beating. "I don't know? Oh, that was an intelligent and clever answer."

As I watched the rails of the expressway slide by, the posts one by one, I wondered how I could let it happen. What was I thinking? I obviously wasn't thinking. Well, it was a mistake. If the rubber hadn't broken, if the party wasn't held on the day I was spitting an egg, if I hadn't drunk Love Potion No. 9, if I hadn't met Mick…. I hated my weakness and lack of self-control. A wave of shame washed through me and tightened my breath.

I wondered if I really was on my way to getting an abortion. It sounded so violent. Deep inside, I felt the roll and kick. It's no lump; it's a baby. It was too big and too real to snuff away. I felt an urgent need to find a toilet.

We pulled into the underground parking on Wabash Avenue and took the elevator up to the fourteenth floor. I found a bathroom next to Dr. Keller's office and poured everything out of me. Once inside the examining room, the nurse instructed me to take off my clothes, handed me a folded white-and-blue striped gown, and left the room. I wondered if "take off my clothes" meant take off everything. It must. "I hate this," I thought. The gown had strings on the neck. I wondered if I should tie it in back or front. I tied it in back to cover the important parts in front. The back flap opening allowed cold air to waft around my bareness. Then I wondered if I was supposed to sit on the chair or the examining table. I stepped on the stool and scooted back on the crinkly white paper that covered the table. I sat upright with my legs dangling down. Steel stirrups protruded from the bottom corners of the table. I knew what they were for, and I didn't like it. Shaking from the draft that swirled around, I wrapped my arms around my body and noticed a chart on the wall. It was a side-cut view of a woman's belly with a baby curled inside. I wondered how the head ever squeezed through that tiny tube to make its way out.

The door swung open. It was Dr. Keller. "Hello, Judy. I'm sorry to hear about your situation. Let's take a look. Can you lie down?"

I lay back and let my legs hang over the table. I felt vulnerable and naked. Dr. Keller tapped on the pillow at the other end. "Judy, can you scoot your head up here?" I scooted up so that my legs were on the table. When he leaned over me, I could see the hairs in his nose. He had short brown hair, green eyes, and was of small stature. His expression was serious but soft with kindness. He put his hands on my bare belly and gently pushed the mass from side to side. He took out a tape measure and stretched it lengthwise across my belly. When he read the hatch mark, his eyebrows lowered and he shook his head.

He put his hand behind my neck and said, "You can sit up now, Judy."

I was relieved that I didn't have to put my feet in those steel things.

"Well, Judy, there's no sense doing a pregnancy test. You're well along, I can see that. Do you know when you had your last period?"

"I know when I conceived the baby, if that helps," I said. I was proud that I knew this. It obviously showed that I had only one boyfriend and we didn't just have sex all the time.

"Well, that won't be necessary; we go by the last period."

He reached into a drawer and pulled out a white cardboard wheel.

"Do you know when that was?"

"September fifteenth."

Dr. Keller spun the little cardboard wheel, read it, and recorded something on my chart.

"Judy—if, after all this over, you need some birth control pills, you can contact me."

"Oh, I won't need those," I said. "I'm not allowed to see my boyfriend."

"Well, that's fine and good, but maybe when you get to college or sometime later you might need them. I just want you to know that's available to you."

I was insulted by this. Didn't he know I learned my lesson? I wasn't ever going to have sex again until I was married. I was done with the black feelings of remorse and impurity. I thought his offer unnecessary.

How naive I was to think I would abstain from sex until marriage. Dr. Keller knew better. Several years later, it would be seeing Mick again that prompted me to take Dr. Keller up on his offer.

"Why don't you get dressed and then come into my office? We'll meet your father in there and talk about this."

The nurse led me into the office. The doctor's desk had pictures of his darling and innocent children. I thought they probably wouldn't be the type to screw up like I had. The nurse went to the waiting room to get Dad. He walked in, looking at the floor, and settled in the chair. I could see the last bit of hope lingering on his face.

Dr. Keller came in, shook Dad's hand, and said, "Hi, John. It's good to see you. I wish it was under better circumstances."

"Yeah, me too, Doc. What did you find out?"

Dr. Keller walked around the desk and sat behind it.

"John, I've examined your daughter. She is definitely pregnant and well along. I don't think it would be a good idea for her to have an abortion."

"Come on, Doc. If you can't do it is there someone else who can?"

"Oh, no, John. That's not the point. She measures twenty

centimeters, which means she is over five months along. It would be too dangerous for her. If she was under twelve weeks, it might be a different story, but at this point it would be very unwise." They were talking about me like I wasn't even there, which was fine with me. I wanted to pretend that too.

With the doctor's words, a quiet sigh released the knot in my gut. I knew I was too far gone. I couldn't bear an abortion after feeling the baby kick and move inside my belly. And yet I knew that I would have done whatever my father said. I felt like I forfeited my rights about the time I missed my first period. Dr. Keller was a good man and Dad trusted him.

"Well, what the hell do we do now?" Dad asked.

"Well, John, she'll just have to go ahead and have the baby."

"Holy Christ, that's a helluva note."

"John, there are homes for unwed mothers that might be able to take her. She could go away, have the baby, give it up for adoption, and then come home when it's all over. Nobody has to know anything about it."

"Where are these places? I never thought I'd be sending my child to a place like that."

"If you'd like, I can do some checking on it and get back to you. There are several homes in Illinois and Wisconsin."

"I'd appreciate your help on this, Doctor. Give me a call when you find something out."

Dad was deep in thought with one hand on the wheel and a scowl on his face. After we turned onto the expressway, Dad cleared his throat and said, "You know, Judy, if you'd come to us sooner we would've had some options."

"I was too scared to tell anyone."

"That was a mistake."

That was that. I regretted that I didn't tell Dad sooner. He would have helped me take care of this situation, but I kept holding out and praying that I would miscarry on my own. We drove the rest of the way in a crushing silence. I couldn't wait to get home and get out of the car. But yet, I was feeling relieved that the doctor visit was over and my secret was out. I was not going to have an abortion, and I was done keeping the lie for now.

My relief was short-lived as my mind took hold of a frightening thought.

What if my secret had slipped out and everyone at school now knew about me? How would I ever face my classmates? They'd be saying things like, "Did you hear about Judy Liautaud? She's pregnant. Oh my gawd, I can't believe it." The gossip would spread like flies on road kill. I would go down as the slut of the class of '68.

The next day, Dad had a plan that would protect me from the disapproval of my peers and the nuns at school. The plan would cover my ass and all the other asses that were related to me.

CHAPTER 22
GOOD-BYE, MICK

It stung my tender spot for Mick when Dad said, "If he was any kind of a man, he would be here." Maybe Mick was lily-livered. Yet I could understand Mick's reluctance to face my dad. If there was any way I could have skipped the Come-to-Jesus talk, I would have done it, too. With Dad's plan to keep his parents out of it, Mick could just stay hidden. I imagined him flirting with girls in his class, free as a bird as he flitted among the flock to find a new chick. Maybe he had one already. I imagined his parents thinking, "Ah, what a good boy we have, so responsible with his good grades," when in reality he had gotten some girl pregnant and off she went into the abyss.

As I built resentment toward Mick, my allegiance switched to my parents. I was giddy and light that I had come clean and my dad was going to find some kind of solution for me. I had hurt them enough. I would do whatever they wanted now. For the first time in a long time, I felt like everything was going to be okay. I couldn't wait to tell Mick he was off the hook. He would be happy about that.

That day at McDonald's when I first told Mick I was pregnant, I somehow expected him to fix it for me. Instead, he was quiet about it and didn't seem to want to talk about where we would go from there. At no point did he ever say, "Hey, we have to talk to someone about this. We have to figure this out." Instead, we just let it sit there for five months like a festering wound right between us.

Our last conversation was a sorry good-bye …

I went up to my bedroom, closed the door, lay down on my bed, and called Mick.

"Guess what?" I said. "I finally told my parents about the whole thing. I'm so relieved."

"Already? What happened?" he asked.

"My dad freaked out. He wanted me to have an abortion, but the doc said I was too far along."

"So will you have the baby then?"

"Yeah, there isn't much else I can do."

"How'd your dad take it?"

"He thought it was the worst thing I could have done. It was really scary. But it's over now. I'm glad it's out in the open and I don't have to hide anymore."

I suddenly felt chilly and asked Mick to hang on. I leaned over the bed and switched the electric blanket to high.

"What did your dad say about me? He must think I'm a real schmuck."

"Yeah, he's mad. I think he blames you, but I told him you didn't force me into anything. It's my fault as much as yours."

"Is your dad going to contact my parents, then?"

"No, he wants to keep them out of it. He says the fewer people who know, the better."

"Really? You mean he's not even going to tell them?"

"Nope. He doesn't want you to tell them, either."

"Well, does your dad want me to do something?"

"Nope."

"I can't believe this. I thought he'd call us over there to talk about it."

"Nope. My dad just wants my family to handle it amongst ourselves."

"Man, this is awful. I don't know what to do."

I was surprised that Mick wasn't jumping out of his skin with relief that he had a one-way ticket out.

"What's so awful?"

"Well, keeping me out of this. I feel shut out."

"You could have come with me to talk to my dad."

"But I didn't even know you were going to tell him."

"You knew I had to tell him sometime, didn't you?"

I was starting to feel the heat radiate through the bedspread. I kicked off my shoes and crawled under the spread.

"I suppose. I wish I had someone to talk to," Mick said.

"About what?"

"Well, you know, someone to talk this over with."

Then I heard his voice all choked up, like he was starting to cry.

"Why do YOU need someone to talk to? It's all taken care of. You don't have to do anything."

"But you have your parents and I have no one."

Now I could definitely hear him crying. I was surprised by his reaction. I had never heard him like this before.

"Geez, Mick. What's the big deal? I thought you would be glad about not having to get yelled at by my dad or be forced to marry me or something worse."

"I just feel so alone. I wish I could talk to somebody," Mick said.

"You're talking to me."

"That's not what I mean."

More sobs. I thought he should be laughing, not crying. He was getting off scot-free. I held the phone away from my ear. I couldn't take it. I couldn't see how he could be crying when he could just turn the page and be done with all this. I put the phone back to my ear.

"Mick, I'm sorry you feel so alone, but this is just how it is. You're lucky you can just go on like nothing ever happened."

"Well, what about us?" he said.

"I think US is done for. My dad made me promise to never contact you again."

"He actually said that?"

"Well, yeah. He said, 'I forbid you to ever see that boy again.'"

"He called me a boy?"

"Yeah, he was just angry."

Through the phone, I could hear someone moving pots or dishes in their kitchen. I thought it must be Mick's sister, because he wouldn't be talking like this if it was his mom or dad. Besides, they would be at work now.

"Can I call you later, in a month or two?"

"No, Mick. I have to do what my dad said. I have already made my parents sick with worry."

"So, I guess this is the end," Mick said.

"Yeah, Mick. I'm sorry, but I'm tired of sneaking around. It could never be any good between us."

"I 'spose so," he said in a choked-up voice. "If you want it like this."

"It's not me who wants it. I'm just going along with the plan."

"I'm sorry it happened like this," Mick said.

"Me too. I better hang up now," I said.

"OK, but can't I call you just once?"

"No, Mick. Please don't try. I'll get into more trouble."

"OK, then. I guess it's good-bye," Mick said.

"Bye," I said. "Don't worry. I'll be okay. My dad and mom will be taking care of everything."

"Bye," he said, and waited for me to hang up.

I put the phone on the cradle.

I folded over and pulled the bedspread to my neck. My throat was tight with stabbing pain. I cried deep wet tears for the loss of Mick. I felt so sad for him: sad that he was ousted, and sad that he wasn't glad about being out of the picture. I really thought he would have felt released. Man, if I could have just walked away from this nightmare, I would have done it in a minute. I felt so sorry for our aloneness. I remembered the night we first met and how I wouldn't have thought in a million years that it would ever turn out like this. All I saw that night were starry bursts of rapture. I longed for the days when we were young and innocent and just in love. I rolled over and hugged myself into a little ball, wondering what was going to become of me—and knowing that whatever it was, I would do it alone.

PART II - GROWING UP BEFORE MY TIME

 ## CHAPTER 23
LEAVING HOME

After he got over the shock, Dad handled my pregnancy with resolve and a methodical approach. He called school again to say I was sick and took me over to Old Orchard Mall to visit a clothing shop called Motherhood.

Dad sat on a wire bench outside the store and waited for me while I went inside. I knew I looked like I was only fourteen even though I was sixteen, but that was still too young. Maybe the clerk thought I was shopping for my older sister or an aunt or something. I didn't try anything on, just selected some pants, shirts, underpants, and a dress. I was glad everyone I knew was in school today, so I wouldn't run into a familiar face. I went out to tell Dad I was ready to check out. He reached into his khakis and peeled a few twenties from his silver money clip. I went back inside the store, paid the lady, and walked out with a pink plastic sack labeled Motherhood. I turned it around so the bag's logo was next to my body. I gave Dad the change.

In the 1960s you never wore clothes tight enough to show your round belly. It stayed hidden under loose, hanging folds of material. When I got home, I tried on my new duds, looked at myself in the mirror, and was shocked by the size of my middle—but oh, how I could breathe. As I took air in, my lungs expanded down to my belly button and out to the moon. Such sweet relief.

The new clothes fit my funny-shaped body perfectly. No more cinching along the waistline—and with the stretch panel my belly was enveloped with smooth support. They were as comfortable as my jammies. I'd dump the rubber-band backups out of my purse. I felt fantastically free, yet alarmingly conspicuous.

Dressed in my new pregnant pants and lacy blouse, I bit my lip and went downstairs to get a glass of milk from the kitchen. Dad looked up from reading his paper, raised his eyebrows, and said, "Oh my God, you're showing."

"Mm-hmmm. I told you I was five months along."

No longer camouflaged by the girdle and uniform blazer, it must have seemed to Dad like I had jiffy-popped overnight.

If the nuns at Regina High School knew the real reason I was leaving school, they would have expelled me right then and there, but we collaborated in a lie that got me off the hook. "Judy will have to leave school," Dad said, "for an extended time because of a serious illness."

Dr. Keller helped Dad come up with a reasonable diagnosis: glomerulonephritis. Most common in children and young adults, this disease is caused by a bacterial infection that affects the kidneys. In some cases it can be contagious; since Mom's condition was so fragile, this was another good reason for me to have to go away. It also has a long and protracted recovery.

Dad held an emergency meeting with the immediate family and told them the news in a hush. My brothers and sister were instructed to keep a tight lip. "Don't even talk about it to your spouses," Dad said. If anyone asked about my whereabouts, they should say that Judy had to go away to convalesce from a serious kidney disease; the fewer people who knew, the better the chance of being able to keep the secret.

I wonder, now, who really believed this cockamamie story? It appeared reasonable to me, and if anyone suspected the truth, I was kept unaware. At the time, it seemed like a perfect answer to reverse my horrible trouble.

Then Dad told the nuns that I would be leaving school for at least a few months to be cared for by my Aunt Helen up in Wisconsin. The nuns agreed to send my assignments by mail each week to Dad, and he would forward them to me. I would send the package back with my completed lessons for grading. Dad had arranged all this so that I could finish my junior year and graduate the following year with my class.

We were all packed up and ready to go. It was late March, with no sign of spring. A cold wind came from the north, and freezing rain was coming in at a forty-five-degree angle. Just two weeks ago, no one knew about my horrible secret, and now my mom and dad not only knew but they had it all figured out for me. It felt so good to let out the secret—and especially good to let out my belly. I could breathe again.

Today, I was leaving my friends, my home, and my school. When I came back at the end of June, all this would be over. I would have turned seventeen and it would be summer, with green grass and hazy hot days—and I would be free. Dad drove; Mom was in the front seat, her wheelchair in the trunk, along with enough of my belongings for my extended stay.

I reviewed the items I'd packed, hoping I hadn't forgotten anything. Besides the new maternity clothes in my brown leather suitcase, I had a green cloth zipper bag with my schoolbooks, Trig and Algebra II, U.S. History, Civics, and French III; a ream of notebook paper; and a pink-vinyl-covered pencil case with a metal protractor. I had a slide rule, the mechanical precursor to the electronic calculator, and a new box of number two pencils. I had also packed my treasures in a purple velvet case: the oil paints and brushes I got from Aunt Stell last Christmas (she always gave good presents), my white leather Sunday missal, and a few books to read.

The ride through lower Wisconsin was boring. I put down the book I was still reading, *Catcher in the Rye*, and stared out the window. I was hungry by now and had car fever—I felt all cooped up. The view from the back-seat window offered nothing but a string of cow pastures and harvested fields, obscured by the sheets of rain.

I had plenty of time to think, since no one was talking. I was relieved the hiding from my parents was over, and that the plan for what would become of me was in place. As far as I was concerned, this couldn't have worked out any better. No one would know the real reason for my absence. I could enter school right after summer vacation, when, I hoped, the kids would have forgotten that I was missing at the end of the year. It was good I lived in disguise for five months. This meant I only missed those last two months of my junior year. I was comforted that my best friends, Annie, Jane, and Carol, had sworn my dilemma to secrecy, and I hoped no one would be asking them any questions. After the night I told them about the pregnancy, I called them to let them know about my kidney disease, and then I didn't speak to them again. My friends never knew where I went or how to contact me. It was all part of the plan to preserve the secret.

During the six-hour ride, Mom and Dad were silent, except when we'd pass a field of fresh cow pies. It shouldn't have surprised me—but it always did—when Mom got all weepy and delighted by the thick aroma that wafted through the front window vent. With a faraway look in her eye, she sighed, "Ah, that reminds me of the farm in Indiana! Oh, I love that smell." It smelled like cow poop to me, and I certainly wouldn't call it pleasing.

Mom had a difficult childhood: her mom was divorced and sent Mom and her brother to Indiana to be raised by the grandparents. As kids, they worked in the fields, walked miles to school in bad weather, and got whipped with a willow switch for eating peanut butter from the pantry. Still, Mom elicited fond feelings from the smell of farm crap. Funny, how the mind handles memories.

Mom remembered the farm and I remembered my condition. My breath shortened as I thought about my stay with Helen and Ed. I wondered what I would do each day, living in a farm town with none of my friends nearby. Would the townspeople stare at me in disgust if I wanted to go shopping? Would everyone know the real reason I was "visiting"? What would it be like living with two old fogies? These were solemn thoughts. I hardly even knew Helen and Ed; I vaguely remembered them from Dad's fishing trips to Winneconne and a long-ago bridge party when they lived in Chicago. I didn't think I ever said more than two words to them. Helen wasn't really my aunt, just a friend of my parents who happened to live far away and in a remote Wisconsin town called Waupaca. It seemed to be a million miles from home. It would be strange living there, just the three of us, for several weeks until I could transfer to the Home for Unwed Mothers near Milwaukee.

There were a few pregnant girl's prisons like this closer to home, but the object was to relocate me so I wouldn't be able to "run into" anyone I knew.

Before we arrived in Waupaca, Dad turned around in the front seat and said to me, "Judy, don't you worry about what people will think of you. For all they know, your husband is in Vietnam and you're just here to spend the time until he gets back."

That sounded reasonable to me and slightly eased my anxiety. I guess now that I was away from Regina I needed a different story. I hoped no one asked me why I was there. I always thought people could see right through me if I was making stuff up.

CHAPTER 24
HELEN'S WELCOME—WAUPACA, WI.

We arrived in Waupaca in the late afternoon. Main Street was lined with white-globed street lamps. Some of the stores on my side of the street were Ben Franklin's Five and Dime, Sew 'n Knit, and Walgreens Drug. A few teens in rain gear were huddled around a lamppost, smoking cigarettes. I envied their freedom and breezy demeanor. We continued past a line of bare-boned oaks, their spring leaves still dormant. Wooden barrels stood on each street corner waiting to be planted with spring flowers, I imagined.

Dad pulled into a gas station and called Helen from a phone booth to get the final directions. As we walked up the gravel pathway lined with a knee-high white picket fence, the front door swung open before we knocked.

"Hello, all. Welcome."

Helen held the door ajar, stepping off to the side so we could pass. She was a hefty woman with short brown wavy hair; she seemed countrified in her blue striped seersucker dress and brown oxfords. In a low voice I heard her say to my father, "You know, John, it's the good girls who get in trouble. The bad ones know how to avoid it." Now I was glad I hadn't told Mom and Dad the rubber broke—that would have tossed me into the "bad ones" category. I think Helen's greeting was her way of saying that I was welcome despite my carnal condition.

Ed seemed to take the back seat to Helen as he stood inside the foyer to greet us. Ed was much thinner than Helen; he was lanky, with a birdlike mouth and a pointy nose that completed his crane-like appearance. He welcomed us with a willowy handshake and invited us to sit down. There was a homey feeling from the smell of freshly fried chicken. I was ready to light into it, being queasy from an empty stomach. But then again, I was always hungry those days.

I sat down on the plaid couch, and Dad wheeled Mom near the fireplace and then settled on the other end of the couch. A draft that smelled of charred wood emitted from the white-brick fireplace. There were a pair of his and hers recliners, green and blue plaid, facing the TV; the walls were knotty pine. The room was dim. "Why didn't they have the curtains opened?" I thought. It could have brightened things up, even if it was a stormy, rainy day. I had a heartsick feeling and struggled with the mixture of hunger, the dark room, and the thought of staying here with virtual strangers in unfamiliar territory. We sat and talked about the storm that had a hold on the countryside clear from Chicago on up to Waupaca. Finally Helen said, "Are you hungry? Let's go eat."

Dad pushed Mom in her wheelchair and I followed behind as Helen led us into the kitchen. The smells made my mouth water and the bright kitchen brought a sense of hope; there was a sliding glass door by the kitchen table that looked out onto a wooden deck, which was littered with pine needles and cones. A chipmunk stopped munching on an acorn and scattered. It reminded me of our cabin at Bond Lake. I liked the pine-tree woods—alive with critters. It could be peaceful here, and a good place for me to hide. But, oh, I was so far from my friends. I wondered what they were doing now. They were probably finished with history class and Sister Mary Joseph. I didn't miss that, and I was glad my trips to the privy looking for the good red were in the past. The kitchen table was set for five with white, orange-edged CorningWare plates, orange tumblers, and red-and-pink floral paper napkins. A centerpiece of fake daisies punctuated the maple dinner table.

"Well, let's all sit down," Helen invited.

Helen, Ed, Mom, and Dad talked about President Lyndon Johnson's decision to escalate the Vietnam War and how the young people were getting killed at a horrifying rate. Mom said she was so thankful that Jim had already served in the military and that Jeff had a physical deferment. She called his accident a blessing in disguise because it probably saved his life by keeping him out of the war.

A few summers earlier, Jeff was operating a punch press at my father's factory. He had an accident that sliced off both his thumbs under the stamp of the press. Mom seemed to blame my dad for this, saying he should have had better safety precautions in place. We were all sick about it, realizing Jeff would be permanently impacted without his manual dexterity. About two months after the accident, Dr. Stromberg performed what he called an experimental procedure that surgically moved Jeff's index finger over to the thumb's location. This allowed Jeff to have an opposing digit so that he could pick things up and use his hands in a normal fashion. The other thumb was still half there, so a year after Jeff's accident he resumed normal function of his hands in spite of the deformity. It was a horrible time in our lives, full of regret and worry for Jeff. But Jeff accepted his injury as his cross to bear and didn't look back. He was like Mom that way, good at accepting what is and finding the positives in adversity.

It seemed to me that there was an elephant in the room, but everyone was just chattering on about politics and current affairs. The real topic was my condition and my stay here and what I would be doing. I was but a fly on the wall, chomping on the fried chicken and mashed potatoes. I was done before anyone else had finished their salads.

Finally, Ed turned to me and said, "And Judy, what grade are you in now? Or were you in, or I guess you still are." His face turned red.

"I'm a junior," I said.

"Will you be goin' to college?" he asked.

"Oh, yes. I want to go to college, but I'm not sure where yet."

"Well, you have plenty of time to decide on that," said Ed.

Now there was an uncomfortable pause in the conversation. I thought I was supposed to be saying something, but when I searched for verbiage, all I found was garbage: whipping thoughts about how dumb I was for being mute.

Dad finally eased the uncomfortable silence. "Say, I had a good fishing trip in Winneconne last spring. The fish were biting like they hadn't eaten all winter."

As long as they talked fishing and politics, the spotlight was off of me. I liked that I didn't have to think of anything to say for now. The conversation meandered like a lazy stream. I thought that was unusual. My dad was usually the life of the party, full of stories and good at keeping the company spellbound. Tonight his words were quiet and calculated. It was because of me. I thought he was probably embarrassed by me.

CHAPTER 25
MOTHBALLS

Dad said he hated to eat and run, but they had a long trip ahead of them. He thanked Helen and Ed for taking me in. Ed said, "Think nothing of it, John. It's our pleasure."

Then Ed turned to me and said, "We'll have a lot of fun, won't we, Judy?"

"Yep," I said, like a parrot trained to speak.

When I hugged Mom good-bye, she told me to be sure to help Helen around the house and to pick up after myself.

Of course I would do that. I might not do it at home, but I knew enough to do it here. My breath shortened when I said good-bye. I could feel the tears welling up so I said it quick, before I started blubbering like a baby. I was a grown girl now, wasn't I? I didn't like being left with strangers, but they weren't throwing off any disgusted glares at me or anything. They were nice and polite and pretended like they didn't even see that I was a young kid with a telling protrusion. I heard the car pull out of the driveway. It was still raining outside.

Helen pushed the chairs around the table and said, "Let me show you to your room, Judy."

We walked down the hallway lit by a light bulb hanging from a wire. I peeked in as we walked past their bedroom on the right. Under normal circumstances it would have inspired cheer, with the crocheted roses hanging from the yellow spread and the matching lace curtains. A photograph of their youthful days hung in the hallway. Ed looked even skinnier then, and Helen had a 1920s hairdo with spit curls pasted to her cheeks. They weren't smiling; they looked like airbrushed statues, serious and alert. Then we passed the bathroom, decorated in a muddy pink. A family of porcelain ducks lined the back of the gray speckled counter. A mauve shag rug was strapped to the toilet seat and its twin was set in a horseshoe embrace around the base of the stool.

"You can use this bathroom, Judy."

When we got to the end of the hall, Helen flipped the light on and extended her arm to point the way. "Just make yourself at home, and please help yourself to the refrigerator at any time. I emptied out the drawers and closet in here so you could have a place for your things. Go ahead and get settled in and let me know if you need anything, okay?"

I heard Helen's footsteps go back down the hall. I sat on the bed. So this was it: my home away from home. It was strikingly quiet here. I heard the heat kick on but it didn't seem to be blowing much warmth. The room wasn't exactly girly. There was a bass mounted on a pine board, his tail swished in a stiff position, and it was too shiny for him to look real. Why did they put that red-fly-hook in his mouth? To make him look like he was caught this morning? I had little appreciation for taxidermy art. I just couldn't look the fellow in the eye, afraid I might see the pain of him being ripped from the waters. The view out the window was more appealing. Jack pines and blue spruce as far as you could see; tufts of brown grass sprouted from the pine-needle floor. I thought I might see a deer if I stood still long enough.

The quiet felt good. I was relieved that I didn't have to put my brain in a cramp, scrambling for the right words to say. I felt like an eyesore those days, an imposter in my own body. Helen was cordial but businesslike. I wondered what they thought of this pregnant teenager who had been deposited into their living space.

I settled back on the bed and recalled the life I left behind. I was a Regina girl, one of the crowd. When the bell rang to change classes, we hustled to our lockers and waved hello to friends in the hall with a "How's it goin'?" This place was strikingly quiet: no hall chatter or hurry here, just the sound of the heat kicking on and an occasional scuttle from the woods. Squirrels maybe. I felt chilly and got up and wrapped Mom's old sheared raccoon coat around my body. The silk lining felt smooth on my skin and the fur soft, supple, and warm. It smelled like Mom's perfume, Channel Number 5. I inhaled to get her smell. The heat from my body swirled warmth within the fur. I moved my green school bag over by the desk and put the purple velvet case with my paints and projects on the floor by my bed.

The bifold closet doors squeaked, and a whiff of mothballs burned my nose. The smell reminded me of Nanny and Deds's place. Deds was my ancient godmother, who lived in an attic apartment above Uncle Clare's house. You got the fumes from the mothballs the moment they opened the door to let you in, and then you had to walk one foot in front of the other to weave around the chairs and tables so you could sit down. It was always very warm up there: comforting at first on winter days and then stifling as your body got used to it.

When I was little, Mom and Dad took me to visit. I would sit quietly on a tapestry footstool while they all talked, twitching with boredom because I had come to expect some kind of gift from Deds and hoped she would get to it. After I started sweating from the heat, Deds would get up and say, "Let me see what I can find here for you, my little Judy." And she would search around in her dresser drawers until she came up with a miniature bottle of perfume or a ruby-studded pin. If she couldn't find anything, she would give me a flowery greeting card with five bucks folded inside—a fortune!

I slid my brown leather suitcase over to the closet, opened it, and hung up my expectant clothes. The pregnant undies looked huge: no hip hugging briefs for me. I folded four pair and stashed them in a pile of strikingly clean whiteness inside the maple chest of drawers.

After the first week, I found a manila envelope on my bed from Regina Dominican, Wilmette, Illinois. I rubbed my hand over the return address, like I could be there for a minute. Just a few days ago this envelope was sitting on some teacher's desk at my school. I smelled it, hoping for a whiff of the cafeteria or the newly waxed floors in the hallway, but there were no trailing smells, just the generic smell of office paper.

Right now my friends would be eating lunch, talking and acting things out, like how Sister used her pointer to tap the geometry theorem on the board, or gossiping about the crazy way Sally Short wore her hair. Like sap from a maple, pangs of longing dripped the life out of me. To be with a friend or two, how glorious! To laugh with them: food for my starving soul.

At Regina we were served cafeteria style, grabbing a tray and sliding it along the silver rails until we reached the main-course section. You told the cafeteria ladies what meal you wanted and they dished it out in uniform portions. You couldn't mix and match. For instance, you couldn't have lasagna with carrots, because carrots only came with the roast beef and mashed potatoes.

They only offered milk to drink, but you could buy a Coke in the vending machine in the hall. Before I got pregnant, the food tasted tinny; then, when I was nauseated, it tasted like cardboard. When I got over that, it tasted hearty, warm, and uncommonly delicious. Lunchtime was my favorite part of the school day. We all sat together, Annie, Jane, Carol, and I. On a good day, I cracked a joke that made everyone laugh. I suppose that was why I liked my friends: they laughed at my jokes.

I felt sorry for the girls who ate alone or changed seating locations with every meal: they were the unpopular ones. We called them queer, which just meant any kind of different. I was glad I had my spot and knew where I fit in. I hoped it would still be there when I returned in the fall. I had a lot ahead of me before I got back to the Black and White, aka Regina. Rah rah the Black and White! These were our school colors and heavily fortified because our nun teachers wore the Black and White on a daily basis.

After I had developed my "problem," I had a hard time concentrating on schoolwork. My grades went from Bs to Cs. At test time, I couldn't remember the lessons. School was just a foggy mess riddled with fear.

Even so, I took the ACT for college in March. I didn't seem to have enough time to finish the reading portion, so I left a lot of it blank. On math I forgot some important formulas and blanked out in my panic of forgetfulness. Then I had to go pee in the middle of the test, but they wouldn't let you escape. Not for a minute. Did they think you would find the answers in the privy?

I sat on the bed and opened the Regina envelope. "Well, kid, the fun is over," I said to the corduroy spread, as I spilled the packet onto the bed. There were some algebra worksheets, a paper I had to write for civics, and some reading assignments in French. I wondered if the nuns really believed Dad as they gathered my assignments for the week. What if they knew the real story and were just playing along?

I couldn't take it just now. I set the schoolwork aside, lay down on the bed, and closed my eyes. Sleep would let me escape the worry of whether I could figure out how to do my homework without being in class, and the worry of what they knew about me back at school.

I fell asleep and slipped into a familiar dream.

I was behind the wheel and following the road signs. It was urgent that I waste no time in getting there. Where? I don't know. But the task was to be on time. Wind from the left side of the car buffeted the wheels, so I had to correct the steering to stay on track. I came to a T in the road. I tried to go left, but the wheel spun like toy and the car kept going straight. I pulled the wheel frantically right, then left, just trying to get it to go either way, until I glided off the road. I put the car in reverse to get back on the road, but my eyes saw black. I kept blinking to focus. I drove backward, looking into space like a blind person until I felt the gravel under the wheels and knew I was back on the road. I powered the car slowly forward, and came to a junction. I pressed the brakes to slow the car, but they were soupy mush. I pressed harder, pumping the brakes, but the car just kept on rolling ahead.

I woke up frazzled and tired. The sun was setting and an orange glow lit the pines in the yard. I rolled over in the bed. My back felt like knives were pinging across my backbone. The skin on my tummy was dry and itchy and stretching thin. Well, I supposed I would start the homework tomorrow. Then I heard Helen call out from the hallway, "Judy, dinner is ready." It smelled like she had made fried chicken again.

Now I was going out, like people do. Helen's blue Buick steered weird in reverse, so I got a little close to the edge of the gravel driveway as I backed it out. It was refreshing to be free. I had my purple velvet case with my paints and thought maybe I could find a lake scene to inspire a Renoir. If I could transfer the beauty of the sun glistening off the waves or the birds swooping onto my canvas, I could feel nature, be closer to it. I meandered past a farm. Mom would have loved it … cow poop galore. I turned down a gravel road that ended in an empty lot on the side of a lake. The wind was causing white caps on the lake and foam settled on the shore. I parked, propped the canvas on my belly, and gazed at the lake. I set the paints on the passenger seat and dabbled for a couple of hours. I was looking for that burnt sienna I saw in the crayon box, or that bright and vivid fuchsia, but my colors were muddy and drab and the lake looked like a cutout that I had pasted on the canvas. I gave up in disgust and headed home for dinner.

My painting was a perfect reflection of my mood and the mess I had made of my life. How could I project clarity and serenity when I was all jumbled up inside with shame, lack of confidence, and fear of what the next days would bring?

After dinner, I lay in bed and read my Sunday missal. I loved the feel of the soft leather cover and the gold glisten on the page edges. I read the Latin responses to the Mass and remembered how back home I usually couldn't wait for the service to be over so I could get back home to call someone to do something. Even so, I missed going to Mass; I missed the sweet smell of incense and the people rustling in their seats. I turned the delicate pages of my missal softly and I found comfort as I mumbled the words. I didn't know what they meant, but to me they meant familiarity and the things we said in God's house.

CHAPTER 26
SELF-IMPOSED BOOT CAMP

I questioned my ability to maintain self-control and believed I was seriously lacking in that department. It started back in second grade when Sister gave me a black mark for "maintains self-control." I guess I couldn't keep my mouth shut. If this personality flaw reared its ugly head when I was seven, it was a six-headed monster by the time I turned sixteen and got myself pregnant. I busted right through the façade of self-control, leaving in my wake tiny pieces of rubble, strewn about like shrapnel.

For redemption, I decided to follow a scheduled regimen. This included a daily low-calorie menu, homework, and a nap, all to be followed at specific times of the day, just like class changes at school.

The Diet: Dr. Keller said I should be very careful about eating so that I didn't gain too much weight. If I did, he said, I would never get it off again. I weighed 105 pounds until I was inflicted with the expanding belly. I knew if I came home fat, people would think that I looked too healthy and plump to have had a serious illness like nephritis. So I set myself on a diet. I had coffee and oatmeal for breakfast. From about 10:30 till noon, I looked at the clock every ten minutes to see if it was time for lunch yet. At 12:00 sharp, I put a pot of water on the stove and sat there watching, waiting for the bubbles to break loose from the bottom of the pot. Once they rose, I plopped one—oh, how I wanted two—measly hot dog in the water and let it roll for a drawn-out five minutes. I had my plate ready, loaded with a healthy squirt of ketchup. Once out of the pot and on my plate, I cut the dog into tiny pieces so I could get the maximum ketchup-dipping action. For an afternoon snack, I had a half cup of cottage cheese; for dinner, it was one tiny helping of each thing that

Helen cooked. I'd refuse the offers for creamy Wisconsin ice cream. The only time during the day that I wasn't ravenous was the hour that followed eating.

After a week of my gourmet hot dog lunches, Helen became alarmed.

"Judy, you need to eat something more. How about some potato soup or some mac and cheese?"

"No, thank you."

The following day, Helen glanced at my empty plate with the left-over smear of ketchup and said, "How about some of these delicious, fresh cheese curds and some saltine crackers?"

"Thanks, but I already ate and I'm full."

The next day, when she offered me her homemade chocolate-chip cookies, I had to halt the advances, so I said, "No, thanks. The doctor said I should watch it so I don't gain too much weight."

"Oh, I see," said Helen.

The day after that Helen must have forgotten: she offered me some butter brickle ice cream after I had inhaled my hot dog. I didn't have to answer this time: Ed came to my defense.

"Fergodsakes, Helen, leave her alone. She's following the doctor's orders." Ed had a way with Helen. That put a stop to the offerings. I followed the starvation diet religiously. My secret depended on it.

The Homework: I always did that from 12:30 to 3:30. I read and reread the assigned chapter in Algebra II, but they always stuck some questions in from another part of the book and I couldn't figure out how to do those. I knew I was winging it, but I sent my lessons back to Regina once a week and hoped they would have mercy on me. It took a couple weeks to get anything returned, and by then I had forgotten the lesson and didn't feel like going over the red corrections.

The Naps: 3:30 was my favorite time of day. Once my head was on the pillow, I slipped into a free world: free of the nagging dread, no matter that I replayed trauma in my dreams. It still was a relief from having to engage socially with Helen and Ed and having to figure out my crappy homework. I didn't feel guilty about napping. It was something Dad relished and did when he could. I took it that

napping was not a sign of laziness, but rather a time to replenish
the soul and a privilege. Later in life, spouses would coin the term
"Afflicted with LSD," Liautaud Sleep Disorder, because napping is a
family tradition.

The days in the country whizzed by like time in a dentist's chair.
The purple pasque flowers came into bloom and now lined the
backyard deck. My soul filled with that springtime longing for the
lazy, hazy days of summer. I ached for the time when I could leave
this prison my body had put me in. I flashed back to last summer:
waking up drowsy and thinking I had to get up and get ready
for school and then, like a warm liquid, the reality of the start of
summer vacation erupted through my body and I knew I could lie
there as long as my heart desired. I'd watch the wind blow on the
trees outside my window and the puffy clouds drift by. How I loved
summer! I felt the warm breeze on my face from the open window,
smelled the newly mown grass. The curtain rings tinkled with the
breeze like bell chimes.

Then I'd roll over and go back to sleep and dream about Jim
Bowley or Mark Edwards or some other popular boy who didn't
notice me in my waking hours. When I awoke, I'd call Jane or Annie
and find out what's up. Sometimes we would take a trip to Old
Orchard Mall or just hang out at McDonald's or drive over to the
Valley Lo Country Club and go swimming. I was usually only home
a week or so before we would all head up to spend the rest of the
summer at Bond Lake, but those few days at home with my friends
were golden.

One day I was lying on my bed getting ready to take a nap when
I overheard Helen talking on the phone. "Judy is a sweet girl, but
she hardly ever says a word, unless you ask her a question. I hope
she isn't too lonely. I suppose she misses her friends. She just doesn't
eat enough. One hot dog is not enough to support a growing baby.
I worry about her." I was mortified that Helen thought I was too
quiet. I was hoping she didn't notice, but the shame of my condition
paralyzed me and I knew that anything I had to say was irrelevant.

I've never been in jail, but I can imagine the similarities. Unlike jail, the conditions here were comfortable. I had a nice room, a clean bathroom, and fresh air at my disposal. But similar to jail, I was on a schedule and I couldn't be with my friends. I wanted to know who was going out with whom and what events were going on at Regina. I didn't have anyone my age to talk to, and it seemed that these were the only people who brought out my real self. These days I was just a shell of a girl trying to pass the time without death by boredom.

CHAPTER 27
BRING ON THE SUNSETS

Each day, when the horizon darkened, I made a mental note that another day was done. I spent a good amount of time in my room, yet I longed to escape the evil eye of the stuffed fish. Eventually the cabin fever got worse than the fear of facing my shame. I ventured out to the town of Waupaca, imagining the thoughts of the townspeople. "That young child had sex?" "What's wrong with her?" Ugh. Dad had sent me some spending money, so I thought I might get a project in town, perhaps knit something.

As I drove down Main Street I remembered the day we arrived. A lot had happened since then. My belly had doubled in size and I was walking with a slight backward tilt. The barrels on the corner were now planted with red- and yellow-headed petunias. There weren't any kids hanging around the lampposts; it was 10:00 am and I was sure they were in school. I found Sew 'n Knit and pulled into an empty slot right in front, where there were plenty of parking choices.

The clerk said "Good afternoon," and asked if she could help me find something.

"I'm just looking."

I didn't like it when salespeople hovered while I was trying to make a purchasing decision. I peeked down the aisles and found the knitting section. I picked up a skein and squeezed it, then brushed it against my face to assess the softness. I wondered what color would look good on Mom. With her dark hair and blue eyes, she always looked good in yellow. The clerk moseyed over and planted herself a few feet away. She pretended to rearrange the spools of thread, but I thought she was probably just spying on me.

"Are you finding everything you need?" she asked.

"Yes, thank you." I wished she'd just bug off.

I picked out some creamy yellow skeins of soft angora and a pair of shiny blue aluminum needles. Mom would probably like a scarf for Mother's Day. It had been a few years since I knitted and hoped I remembered the knit and perl. I loved the sound of the needles clicking as I wove the loose yarn into a solid piece. Our housekeeper, Helen from Hungary, had taught me to knit the European way, which was faster and more efficient than the way most Americans did it. I liked it.

I brought my knitting things to the front of the store. The clerk followed and then got behind the cash register.

"That will be $6.97," she said. I reached into my wallet.

"I haven't seen you 'round before. You new to town?"

"Yes, I'm visiting."

"You gonna be 'round awhile?"

"Oh, I'm not sure how long." I turned to look at something behind me.

She probably sensed my discomfort with her nosy chatter and didn't press for more. "Oh, geez," I thought. "She knows. She knows I'm an unwed mother in hiding. Why else would I be so young, pregnant, and visiting Waupaca, Wisconsin?" I took out a ten-dollar bill and handed it to her, anxious to be on my way.

The summer heat felt good on my skin after the store's air-conditioned coolness. These trips to town were infrequent, but they were the highlight of my stay in the country. It was good to feel the breeze on my cheeks, smell the pines, and warm my cheeks with the sun on my skin. None of the townspeople asked me any more questions. I made it a point to keep my eyes otherwise occupied so as not to appear friendly. I was getting good at hiding.

It took a few rows, but soon my knitting stitches were uniform. I was a little disappointed that one edge was slightly longer than the other, but Mom always loved anything I made by hand, no matter how imperfect. I designed a card out of notebook paper and colored the punches with squirrely circles to make the holes look like they were part of the design. I used my paints to color the words

"Happy Mother's Day," and then the scissors to scallop the edges. I mailed the package. I thought that next year at this time I would be a mother myself, even though I had no child, so it wouldn't really count. I was the farthest thing from a mother.

A few weeks after Mother's Day, I got a call from Dad telling me that there was now a spot for me at the Home for Unwed Mothers and that he and Jackie would come to pick me up on Saturday. Mom was healthy enough now to be up at the cabin with Thelma, her nurse, and Hugren. She was getting things ready for their summer stay.

Although I dreaded seeing Dad in my enlarged condition, I was looking forward to a change in my living arrangements. I was glad Jackie was coming along. She was the equalizer and took the spotlight off me. I didn't love being alone with Dad. Our conversation was stilted, and I never quite knew how to answer his questions. He seemed to ask them in a leading fashion, like he was baiting me for the right answer. It was like he used his interrogation as a way to teach me something. Pressure to speak boiled inside me. This was my shame speaking.

I never knew what kind of arrangement Dad had with Helen and Ed, or if he paid them for my room and board. I am sure he did. They were retired, and I thought they could probably use the money. Besides, Dad didn't like to take things from people or owe them anything. He was stubborn about that to a fault: he was good at giving but not receiving.

Helen and Ed had tolerated my presence, letting me be, and they went about their daily business. I didn't play my part in Ed's prediction that we would have a lot of fun, because I stayed in my room most of the time. They didn't have any visitors at the house during my eight-week stay. The best times were when they went out and left me in the house alone. I liked the quiet feeling with no pressure to interact. I imagine they were relieved that their boarding duties were coming to an end and they could have their place back to themselves.

I mailed in my last batch of assignments; school would soon be out for the summer. I wondered if Annie and Jane thought about where I went and what I was doing. Oh, how I missed them! If I looked at my watch and it was 3:00, I would think, "School is out. They are probably getting in their car to drive home, chattering about the silly nuns or a test they bombed." I wondered if anybody had a new boyfriend and if they had any new meal selections in the cafeteria. I missed the roast beef and giggles for lunch.

I thought about the home. It would be refreshing to be with girls my own age, even if they might be the "less" desirable types. Maybe their hair was all ratted up into piles on their heads. Maybe they were all greasers with low-cut blouses and tight skirts above the knees. Maybe they were all painted up with white lipstick, red nail polish, and black mascara. There couldn't possibly be any "good" girls, like me. I didn't care, though. Just being around people closer to my age would add intrigue to my jail sentence.

On Saturday, the sun was streaming through the pines outside my window. I woke with a remote feeling of excitement. What was it? Oh, yes! I remembered. Today, I would be leaving Waw-lacka, aka Waupaca, and embarking into the next chapter of life as an outcast. They even had a special place for people like me, and I was going there. I looked forward to fitting in. My flashing belly would blend in with all the others: all in the same boat, even if it was sinking.

I got up, gathered my clothes, and went into the bathroom to take a shower. Before I stepped under the sprinkling shower head, I looked at my naked silhouette in the mirror. Many moons ago, my belly was tight to my backbone, flat and smooth. Now, it was swollen and heavy. The weight of the baby caused the skin to fold into a crease at the bottom. Sweat collected there and caused an unbearable itching. Tiny red bumps dotted the crease and spread out from it. The pesky itch was a constant reminder of my discomfort. The only time it stopped was when I was in the shower and for a few minutes afterward. I was amazed at the size of my breasts. I had always been so small. Now they were full and turgid. My nipples had turned from pink to brown. They looked ancient.

I barely used to fill a cup size AA, and now I had cleavage.
I guess that's what happens when you get knocked up—you get
knockers. As much as I wanted a full figure a few years ago, it was
now something I tried to hide. But I would feel differently about it
when the belly was gone. I had hopes that the chest enhancement
would be a permanent condition. Little did I know that months
after I had given birth, the fullness would deflate like an old balloon
and I would be left with a couple of dollar-sized pancakes of
stretched-out skin and dried-up milk.

I heard a car pull up in the driveway. I answered the door to let
Jackie and Dad inside.

I led Dad back to my room to grab my brown suitcase, book
bag, and velvet case.

"Wow, you sure had a nice pad while you were living here, didn't
you?"

"Sure. I miss home, though."

Dad glanced down at my middle and his eyes lingered. I hated
my body.

My pregnant body was me and with me, yet I felt that I was
wearing a costume. I was stuck in a mother's body while in my mind
I was a flat-bellied, slim and spunky teen. My body was mortifying,
inconvenient, and uncomfortable. Only a little over a month and I
would be free.

It is incredible what sacrifices must be made to keep a lousy
secret. Was it worth all this? How can shame and maintaining a
reputation be a motivator for such unnatural gyrations? I don't
remember watching TV at Helen and Ed's except in the late
evenings. I suppose I could have turned it on during the day, but
I thought watching TV was a lazy thing to do and it wasn't on my
schedule. I don't remember listening to music. I had no radio. I
don't remember reading much, except I finished *Catcher in the Rye*
and opened my missal once or twice. I brought some other reading
material but fell asleep or got bored when I tried to read. So what

did I do? Just school work, paint, knit, drive to town a few times, and look forward to meals, naps, and sunsets.

CHAPTER 28
LEAVING WAUPACA

We meandered through county roads lined with red barns and white-painted farmhouses, slowing through the middle of towns only because the person driving in front of us slowed. The towns were deserted and lonely. It seemed like every other building was abandoned, although they looked as if, once upon a time, they had been thriving. Once out of town, Dad would step on it until we were speeding along at an alarming pace. He would often pass with no safety margin, getting back in his lane just before the approaching car passed us. The blaring honk from the oncoming car never seemed to faze Dad. He was often in a hurry and always seemed to know where he was going.

When we got to Milwaukee, Dad exited at Glenview Road. The name made me homesick as I thought about what it was like back home right now. We entered a residential neighborhood in Wauwatosa. There were signs of decoration and activity about the houses: a dragon-shaped windsock was stationed off the porch, and a toddler's Big Wheel sat on the grass on the front lawn. Piles of brush and leaves were neatly stacked on the curb in front of each house; perhaps it was spring cleanup day when the city's garbage trucks picked up organic debris. The brick bungalows were shaded by leafy elm trees that lined the street in a perfect row. The neighborhood felt organized and well thought out, unlike my life. I wondered how on earth I got into such a predicament and how it would all turn out.

Summer was in the air. Now that we were moving slowly, I rolled down the car window and felt the fresh air blow across my face. It was tinged with the scent of lilacs and tickled my hair. I felt free and light for a second. I wished we could just keep driving for the rest of the afternoon, so I could gaze inside the cozy homes and dream about life in the real world, and watch the neighbors going about their simple, everyday lives.

My nose was extremely sensitive. Now I could smell something like rotten oranges. What happened to the lilacs? I feared we were nearing the HOME. My sightseeing cruise would come to an end. Who would I meet? What would it be like? My heart quickened as I thought of meeting the girls. What if they were hoodlums and mean and stole and stuff like that? What if they swore all the time and didn't care about life, or anyone?

Dad pulled over to the curb at 6306 Cedar Street. There was a small bronze sign by the walkway that read: Booth Memorial Hospital–Salvation Army. But by convention it was known as the "Martha Washington Home for Unwed Mothers." It was both a home and a hospital, convenient for the attendees.

It didn't look much like a home but more like county offices or a big old school. It was red brick and built in 1893. Long cement steps led up the hill to the double front doors. I had heard it started out as a hospital and then a place for recovering soldiers during WW II, and in the 40s it was changed to house "unwed mothers."

I wondered what would be in store for me and how I would feel in a month or so when I walked back down the steps, free to leave because I had delivered my baby.

Dad turned off the ignition and got out. I followed him to the back of the car to gather my things. He unlocked the trunk. He set my things on the curb. A few books had slid out of my book bag and were lying on the floor of the trunk. Dad opened my Algebra II textbook and saw that my name was signed on the inside cover. He took out his Parker pen, which he always kept in his front shirt pocket, and in the place where it said "This book belongs to Judy Liautaud," he scratched out the Liautaud part. I watched his scribbles and started to simmer. I didn't like that he was wrecking my books. I kept quiet as he inspected the inside covers in earnest. He went through them all, scratching out the identifying letters, my— our—last name. It was out of character for Dad to be crossing words out with his pen. I was always taught that you rewrite something and never scratch it out. Dad had beautiful penmanship and I never saw him scribble or mar any papers that passed his hands. Dad must have been aware of me looking over his shoulder. He explained himself.

"While you're here, you'll be Judy L. This is the policy of the home. It's to protect your identity. There's no reason you'd ever give your last name to anyone. The girls here go by their last initial. Be sure to adhere to this, Judy."

OK, so at least there was good reason for vandalizing my books. He sure was thorough about it. I wondered what would happen if someone found out I was his child. My gut squeezed with shame. I figured he was doing what was expected, but when it came to my white leather prayer book, I found his diligence over the top. I loved my missal. It was my sacred channel to God. It was a special-order item, placed through the church, and a gift for my first communion when I was eight years old. I loved its soft, white leather cover, embossed with gold leaf trim. When the book was shut, the tissue pages glistened with their golden edges. The book was my constant companion at Sunday Mass ever since third grade. God himself lived within the pages. When I opened that book, a peace and serenity came over me. I thought back to those winter days when I walked to the city bus stop with my white leather missal clutched in my hand, feeling reverent and good, on my way to daily Mass in the morning darkness so I could praise the Lord before my first class of the day.

The sharp wet point of his pen sheared the fragile page and the blue ink bled to the page behind. I couldn't take it anymore.

"Watch out, Dad," I said, "you're ruining my missal." My voice quivered as I held back the tears. The sound of the page ripping was the final straw. I loved that white leather book and he was crucifying it.

Dad closed the cover and put it back into my book bag. "You know, we have to take care of this before you get inside." There were only two more books. He opened them but didn't see my name, so he shut them back up and was done with the Liautaud-name massacre.

So now I would be Judy L. No identity, no history, no family, just a belly with arms and legs waiting until the time was ripe to give birth. Then I would resume life with a first and last name, just like nothing happened. I saw the disgrace in Dad's eyes. I knew he didn't want anyone around here to know that I was his daughter.

Before we picked up my bags and started up the cement steps, Dad gave his final words of advice.

"You'll forget about this, Judy, and you'll never have to speak of it to anyone again. Later, you may get married, and there's no reason to even mention this to your husband."

His plan sounded like the only reasonable one. I would just slice this whole nightmare from my mind. I wouldn't have to think of it again. It would just be some bad dream I had back when I was sixteen. I was still angry about my books and couldn't wait for him to drive off and leave me here.

Dad was following policy by scratching out my last name, but the action coincided with Dad's desire to protect the Liautaud name. My dad always signed John N. Liautaud, and when people asked what the "N" stood for, he said it didn't matter what it stood for, it was just "N." When it was suggested that the middle name of one of the grandkids be Numa, Dad was not flattered; instead, he said, "Don't you dare." I never learned the significance of the name Numa, but I suspect it was tied to the secret he was holding about

us passing for white in the early 1900s. Thirty years later, Dad was still fighting for the protection of our reputation as he scratched out our last name from my books.

HOME FOR UNWED MOTHERS — ORIGINALLY BUILT TO CARE FOR RETURNING WWII VETERANS

CHAPTER 29
THE HOME FOR UNWED MOTHERS

We were greeted by the head lady of the house, who was small and official looking in her navy uniform with the upside-down, canoe-shaped hat. She seemed to be expecting us. She led us to the front office so I could register and sign in. While she was explaining my duties, Jackie asked if the home provided any counseling for the girls. I was insulted by Jackie's assumption that I needed psychological help. I prided myself on how strong I was and how good I was at handling all this. Jackie hadn't been with me the last few months, so how could she know? But I knew. I barely ever cried. I got my schoolwork done. I didn't eat too much. I was a pillar of stone: why did Jackie think I was going to crumble?

I was too proud to see it then, but today I realize that her question was a good one. Jackie, having birthed ten children, knew what I was up against, and of course she also foresaw the heartrending task of giving up a baby for adoption. The head lady said they didn't have any special counseling and that if Judy needed it, it would be up to us to provide it.

If I needed it: was I some special case, fragile and on the verge of a breakdown? Each resident was provided with a social worker, she said, who would guide us through the adoption process. Dad said, "Judy'll be fine," and that was the end of it. After my admission papers were signed and we got a brief tour of the common areas, I gave a hug and kiss to Dad and Jackie. Again, I choked back a tear, but never let it fall. I told myself I was glad they were leaving because I didn't like being seen in this body of mine.

My room was on the third floor. I walked over to the window

and peered below. There was the back parking lot and, off to the side, a tall brick wall. I could see over it and into the yard. There they were: a gaggle of girls, all pregnant, sitting on lawn chairs. A few were smoking cigarettes. A few looked like they were sleeping, and a few were chatting in a heated discussion. They didn't look as rough as I had imagined—they could even have been Regina girls. Only a couple of them looked like greasers, their hair all poofed up and back combed. I turned away from the window, hoping I would find a friend or two in the bunch.

I sat on the bed and opened my green book bag. I reached into the bottom to find the missal. The inside page was just as Dad had left it, my last name scratched out so you couldn't decipher any of the letters. It looked ugly to me, all ripped up and smeared with the ink. I tore out the page to get rid of it. After I did that, the back page, which was printed on the same sheet as the front page, fell out. It made my heart sick. I stuffed the loose page back in and shut the missal. Maybe I could get another one when I got home. But they probably didn't make them like that anymore, and besides, it wasn't just any missal. This was my own personal heirloom.

I tightened with anger as I thought about Dad and the trunk episode. He was irreverent and didn't care about anyone but himself. All he cared about was how we looked to other people. He didn't care that he had ruined my sacred book. I felt helpless in my desire to tell him what I thought; he was spinning down the highway toward home by now. I probably wouldn't tell him off anyway. I stuffed my anger and disappointment and told myself, "No use crying over spilt milk." I rubbed my hand over the blessed cover and put the missal back into my book bag. Then I reached into the bottom of the bag and fished out my Regina Dominican High School calendar. I sat on the bed and flipped it to May. All the school events were listed.

I would miss the junior prom next week. I wondered if I would have gone. If I did, I would have asked Mick. What shoes would I have worn? My little heels would have made me taller than he was. I was kind of glad I couldn't go. It was dumb, anyway, because in our all-girls school we had to ask the boys to the prom. That was just wrong and unnatural.

It was almost summertime now and Annie and Jane were probably getting new bathing suits for their trips to the beach at the Valley Lo Country Club. I had also missed the spring Choral Concert. Jane sang in it, so I would have liked to go. What was I doing that day? Probably sitting in Helen's car trying to paint the lake scene in Waupaca. That was a disastrous day. My palette blended into the color of mud. I remembered sitting behind the steering wheel with the canvas in my hand. My belly was smaller then.

The title for the concert was probably something like, "Songs for New Beginnings." That sounded like springtime. Baby animals were born, tulips popped out of the ground, and the air changed from harsh to welcoming. The whole world was your home when spring came. You didn't have to stay in the cabin or the house to be warm. You had the whole great outdoors. It made me want to just burst out of my skin like the flowers that popped from the ground. I wished this birth could have happened in spring. All of this would be over and I would be starting a new beginning. But then again, the timing was perfect, because I was able to go to school for most of the year. I did my lessons, so I was able to finish my junior year and stay with the rest of my class. By the time we got back to school in the fall, everyone would probably have forgotten that I was missing the last few months of junior year.

Nostalgia for school days rippled through me, leaving me weak and hopeless. I pulled myself together again. "It's okay," I told myself. "I will like it here. It's not long till all this will be over." I was relieved that I didn't have to pretend anymore. Everyone here had my same trouble. This place would be the home of my deliverance. In four to six weeks, when I walked out, I would be a changed woman, having birthed a child and returned to my free status, just like the slaves after the Civil War.

I flipped the calendar page to June and circled the twenty-first: that was my due date. I didn't think that date was right because the doctor didn't want to know the day I conceived, even though I offered it. If it takes nine months to ripen a baby, then that would mean my due date should be June thirtieth. So I was wary of his calculation. But perhaps babies didn't take exactly nine months. Maybe the twenty-first was right; of course, the sooner the better.

I counted the numbered squares on my paper calendar. Today was May twentieth; I had about thirty days until I could escape from this place. I would be washed clean of all the remorse and have my life back. I wondered what the birth would be like. I remembered when Jackie told me, "You aren't a real woman until you experience what it's like to have a baby." I had asked her if it hurt a lot. She didn't mince words. "Yes, it's one of the worst pains, but the blessing is, you don't remember. That's why people have baby after baby."

I wondered, though: if she can't remember, how does she know it's one of the worst pains? Her words were not comforting. I was scared, but I knew I was strong and I was sure I could handle it. I had been through some pain in my life and I always made a conscious effort to be boy-tough and not cry whenever I got hurt. I thought: "I am strong and I can take whatever comes my way."

I did remember crying like a baby once, but then again, I was only six. I lost my footing while climbing up a rusty, nail-studded pine tree. When I started to slip, I hugged the tree to break the momentum; the nails zipped down my stomach and chest, ripping the skin. My summer blouse was torn, and a river of blood dripped from the raw flesh. I ran into the cabin, wailing. Mom stopped making pie crust and painted my sores with red Mercurochrome; monkey blood, some called it. This made me cry even harder, but then she covered the sores with gauze and fastened it with adhesive tape. She drew me up into her lap and said, "There, there, now, Judy, you're going to be okay." I melted with her attention and comfort.

By the time I was nine, I was beyond all that crying stuff. I wanted to be tough like the boys, to prove I was worthy of their company. Jeff and his friend Jigs from across the lake were in the cab of Jeff's Model T. We were driving down Smith Bridge Road and Bobby Leslie and I were in the back of the truck. Bobby was sitting in the bed and I was standing on the ridge, holding on to the cab's smooth roof and facing forward. I felt like I was flying as we whipped down the road—me face-first into the wind, peering over

the truck's roof. Suddenly, Jeff hit a pile of sand and swerved with a
jerk. Or maybe he was just screwing around, driving crazy, but I lost
my hold on the cab and was tossed face-first out of the truck, onto
the road, and knocked unconscious.

When I opened my eyes, Jeff, Bobby, and Jigs were bent over
me. When I saw the look in their eyes, it scared me. I knew it must
be bad.

"Judy, are you okay? Are you okay?"

I couldn't find air to form words. I had a mouthful of sand
tucked under my lips and tongue. I grunted an "Uh-huh" … and
tried to spit the sand out of my mouth, but the dryness made it
stick. My knee ached like it was smashed in two. But the good thing
was, I was alive. And I wasn't spitting up blood or anything. My
body still had its arms and legs attached. The boys helped me up and
carried me into the truck. I was too shocked to cry, I suppose.

Jeff said, "You are really tough, Jude. Are you okay?"

"Yes, I'm okay," I said. I loved it that Jeff said I was tough. I was
proud to be one of the guys. If there was anything I wanted to be,
it was tough, especially in the eyes of my brother. I thought if I was
tough, like them, they would let me hang out. There were seven
years between Jeff and me, so he didn't always love having me tag
along. I always wished I had friends my own age at the cabin so I
didn't have to pester Jeff.

Yes, I had been through enough to know I was tough and
could handle the worst. I was sure I would sail right through this
childbirth thing. I had a plan to help the time pass. Each night
before I went to sleep, I would open that door to my closet and cross
off the waning day. I would write the new amount of remaining days
on the calendar.

How innocent, young, and naive I was! No one can know what
having a baby is like until you have done it. Even the movies and
the childbirth classes don't prepare you for the building pain of
contractions and the striking fear that visits a woman as she wonders
if something is wrong because the pain is so intense. It came down
on me like a surprise hurricane. Afterward, I thought, "Does every

woman really experience this?" It just didn't seem feasible that every woman on the planet who had given birth had lived through such horrific pain. And the Indian squaws who went off to labor alone: was that for real? The evidence made it so.

CHAPTER 30
THEY CALLED ME JUDY L.

The home reminded me of something out of Oliver Twist.
Each room had four single beds with wire mesh springs. Along the
hallway, there were several numbered doors leading to other girls'
rooms. The pine floor creaked on the east side of the room. The
windows slid on ropes with lead counterbalances that clanged; they
almost opened themselves once you got them sliding. The summer
breeze felt delightful in the afternoons when the temperature rose.
I had a secret battle going on with one of my roommates who liked
to close the curtains at night. I would wake in the dark to go pee.
When I came back to the room, I'd walk over to the window and
slide the curtains open. I loved waking up to the sun casting shadows
on the wood floor as it shone through the trees.

We shared a bathroom down the hall. It was like school, with a
row of stalls, but around the side there was also a row of showers. We
took care to never undress until we were inside of the stall, bringing
our clothes with us so we could be fully clothed as we walked out
from the shower.

They gave us classes on how we were to handle ourselves while
we were residents at the home. We were not to answer questions
about where we came from. We were forbidden to give out our last
name or strike up friendships that would last beyond our stay. This
was supposed to be just a short time in our lives that we would
forget about, and we shouldn't linger on any details or memories of
our stay here. We were allowed to go out once a week, a free day to
walk to the nearby town or go to the park, but we had to travel in
groups of at least three. Each girl was assigned a chore to help with
the housekeeping. We were supposed to do our work in a timely

fashion without complaint. Guests were allowed in the lobby/living room area but were never to be taken into the home proper.

Absolutely no one except maternity patients was allowed on floor two, the hospital floor. During my stay, I had no visitors. I think it was to keep the secret safe. Jackie later told me she wanted to visit, but Mom advised against it. Anyway, I didn't think I wanted visitors. I looked like a freak. It's one thing to be mature and pregnant, but I was so young. I probably looked as strange as those little people who age really fast and look like elderly children.

I was assigned to kitchen duty: pots and pans, to be specific. I didn't like it much. I couldn't get close enough to the sink to reach down into the industrial-sized pots unless I stood sideways, and this twisting lean hurt my back. Most of the girls went upstairs after dinner but I was stuck in the kitchen with the cook, scrubbing until the pots were clean, dried, and put away. After a few weeks, the cook said I was strong and a hard worker, so I liked her and then I tried even harder to do a good job. I remembered my first-grade teacher telling Dad that I took pride in my work. I asked Dad, "What does pride mean?" He said it means you take care to do it right. I never forgot that and liked to remind myself to do things the "right" way. It seemed I didn't mind the pot cleaning as much after the cook said I did a good job.

Every week or two, depending on how far along we were in our pregnancy, we piled into a van to attend our prenatal appointments. I loved this escape from the home, riding along and watching the houses and stores whiz by, breathing in the city air, even if it was tinged with exhaust fumes. We were deposited at a clinic on the other side of town, while the driver sat in the van and waited for us in the parking lot.

We must have been a spectacle to behold as four to six of us walked into the clinic. I didn't look up to see, but I was sure people were gawking at the girls who came from "The Home for Unwed Mothers." We sat down and waited as we were called one by one to the back clinic for our doctor's appointment. The visits were quick, matter of fact, and devoid of discussion. I peed in a cup, got my belly measured, had my blood pressure taken. Then the nurse wrote down the numbers and the doctor said, "Very good. Any questions?" I never had any. I dreaded an internal exam each visit. But, lucky for me, my pregnancy was normal and that wasn't part of the routine until the end. Then, when they checked for dilation, I hoped they'd reach in there and say, "Oh my goodness, this baby is coming very soon!" But they never offered any predictions, just did their business and sent me on my way.

I didn't really make friends like I'd hoped, but I took a liking to a girl named Linda P. She seemed like she could be my older sister. She was about twenty-two, which seemed very adult to me. She had brown hair, cut in swirls around her face, soft blue eyes, and a bounce in her step. I wondered why she was even here, when she could just be out in society with age on her side. Linda told me her boyfriend was drafted and would be leaving for Vietnam. He didn't want to get married, so she was giving the baby up for adoption. She seemed sad about that, like she would have married him. I knew she came from the good side of town because she had crisp, clean, fashionable clothes.

On sunny days, we liked to hang out in the back yard. Over by the large oak tree were several Adirondack slatted chairs. It was serene out there; nobody from the street could see us because of the height of the brick wall. The yard was dotted with a few stately oak trees and the grass was lumpy, but green. Lilac bushes lined the building and were in full bloom when I arrived. The scent of the lilacs brought a fresh longing for the days when we lived in the city

Mom loved lilacs. When I was little, she would cut a fresh bouquet from the bushes in our back yard and arrange them in a tall drinking glass on the kitchen table. They filled the house with their luscious scent. I'd put my nose right into the blooms and give a good sniff. I marveled at the fluted horn blossoms that dotted each branch. I could never inhale enough of their sweetness.

Before we moved out to Glenview and lived in our Chicago bungalow on Fairfield Avenue, we had lilacs and grapes along the fence and lilies of the valley along the back-yard sidewalk that led to the alley. Oh, how I missed that yard in the city! You could pick the grapes right off the vine and pop them into your mouth whenever you had a hankering for some fresh fruit. I thought it was glorious to have a fresh supply offered right from nature. I remembered how they popped and squished making purple stains on the sidewalk when you stepped on them. We also had lavender irises that got full of ants when they were budding. I guessed they were just too sweet.

The days at the home stretched like the horizon over the desert. There was little to do. We all wore our cloak of shame. It showed in how we shuffled in the halls, slow and mopey. Laughter was hard to come by, and for the most part, the words that passed between us had to do with the tasks at hand or the weather, rarely anything interesting or personal in nature. The somber mood prevailed like a funeral home, each of us waiting until we could get out and go back home to our real life. Although we were all in the same boat, I still felt alone and quite different. I thought I was the one good girl who accidentally got in trouble.

Spring was past and summer was here. The night before, I'd written the number fourteen to show how many days were left on my calendar. The leaves were fully unfolded, dressing the trees in lime and grassy colors. I decided to go outside and do some sewing. I found a seat on a worn wooden chair: only half of the white paint remained, with the residual chips curling on the edges. I was making a pink dress for my little niece Mimi. She was the youngest girl of Jackie's family of ten – an even five boys and five girls, her last baby, Pete, just born the previous October. Mimi had turned three while I was gone—oh, how I missed hearing her talk, the way she put together sentences. She had a doll-face and a head full of blonde curls.

There were three girls in a row next to me, facing the sun. They had on shorts and sleeveless shirts and smelled like coconut oil. They became quiet when I plopped myself next to them. "Uh-oh, should I have done that?" I wondered. "Was I intruding?" I pulled out my thread and needle and started sewing the white lace on the hem.

"Are you making that for your baby?" the girl next to me asked.

"Oh, no," I said. "I'm giving this to my niece. I won't be keeping my baby."

"Well, I'm not either, but I'm making a blanket for my baby."

"That's nice," I said.

But, really, I didn't think that was so nice. I thought she should get over it and not pine and linger about this baby she was giving away. I thought preparing a gift was dwelling on the impossible. Why get attached to something you can't have? I thought my child wouldn't want a gift from me, because I wasn't supposed to exist. Her new parents wouldn't appreciate it either.

We sat in silence for about an hour until I finished the lacy hem and started in on the two puffy sleeves. I couldn't wait to surprise little Mimi with the pink flower-print dress that I had sewn by hand. When the sun became too hot, I got up and went to my room and took a nap. That night I ticked off another day and marked thirteen days left on my calendar.

I really didn't know what to do with myself. When I was at Helen and Ed's, I had imagined that I would have a social life here, but that didn't happen. I think we were all too sad to be able to strike up friendships. And since our time here was short, it didn't make sense to make a friend when you would be saying good-bye in a few weeks. It seemed that some of the girls who were closer to delivery had friends, because they had been here longer. I was a shy kid and not so good at making new friends. When Linda P. started talking to me, I was flattered, but I was surprised because usually the older ones like my brother and Jane's sisters didn't pay much attention to me. But then I realized there weren't any girls her age, so she might as well pick me. Overall I was quiet and kept mainly to myself.

CHAPTER 31
VISITS WITH MY SOCIAL WORKER

Catherine Cavanaugh was assigned to my case. She picked me up from the home in her red Buick and took me out to lunch at Denny's. I pictured an older woman for my social worker, matronly and caring, but she was very young, and looked like she wasn't much older than I was. She had fiery red hair, cut fashionably short. I knew I was doing fine and didn't need any counseling so what was the point of the visit? What could she say that would help me with this? My situation was hopeless.

As we sat eating our cheeseburger, fries, and chocolate shake, the conversation was strained. What was my favorite subject in school? What sort of things did I like to do? Then she got to the point. "What are you going to do when the baby is born?" she asked.

"I'm giving it up for adoption."

"Have you thought about other options?"

"Like what?" I asked.

I was insulted. I thought that by this point I should know what I was doing. Anyway there weren't any other options. After spending many weeks at Helen and Ed's and telling everyone I was sick, I was sure I wouldn't be changing my mind. There were no other options but give the baby up and go back home like nothing ever happened.

"Like, keeping the baby," she said.

"Oh, I couldn't do that. That's not what my parents want me to do."

"That might be fine for your parents, but have you thought about what *you* want to do?" she asked.

"Doesn't matter what I want. I screwed up and now I pay the

price, besides I agree that adoption is best."

"Well, Judy, you really do have a choice, you know. Is there a guy in the picture? Did you consider getting married?"

"There's a guy, obviously—but oh, no, we didn't think that was a good idea. We're too young," I said.

Each of her questions burned like a razor cut. Didn't she know I had already thought about all this? It was a little late to be bringing up options and alternatives. If we got married and kept the baby, everyone would know the real truth. That was not an option. I couldn't imagine quitting school and marrying Mick when I was only seventeen. The thought was suffocating. How would we support ourselves? Mick hadn't worked a day in his life and he was just graduating from high school.

I steamed with anger at being forced to talk about useless things and having to justify my decision to this stranger.

"Well," she said, "if you're sure you want to give up your baby, I'll bring the papers for you to sign the next time I see you. I just want to make sure that adoption is what you want. Once you sign the papers, the baby will be placed. I want you to be sure you know what you're doing."

"Oh, yes," I said. "I thought plenty about it. I definitely want to give up the baby. I think it'll be the best for the baby."

"It shouldn't be because your parents want it, Judy. You have a choice too."

"I know. This is what I want."

"OK, it seems like you've already decided."

"This lady is swift," I thought.

I couldn't imagine what it must have been like for Catherine Cavanaugh to have to handle this girl: a girl who didn't want to learn anything new or talk about the heavy decision that she had made. It was an impossible task and I know she meant well, but I guess I needed to have built some trust with her first before I could even hear what she had to say. She was too abrupt and probably new at her job, but had the prescribed points that she had to cover to do her social-service duty. I was ashamed of my condition and defensive.

My mind was closed and made up, kind of like Dad's was before he met Mick. I just wanted the lunch to be over. I was trying to prove to her that I didn't need this counseling. I was strong and I wanted to show her how tough I was. She was a little late on the scene.

"OK, then we can talk about the adoption," she said. "Do you have any requests about the adoption process?"

"Not really," I said as I sipped my milkshake. The straw flung a bit of frozen slush as it pinged out of my mouth.

"What about the adoptive parents? Do you have any desires about who will get your baby?"

"Well, a good person would be nice." I took another sip of my shake.

"Oh, all the adoptive parents are carefully screened; your baby will go to a good person. What I meant was … well … I see that you're Catholic. Do you want the baby to go to Catholic parents?"

I pictured the people in the pews next to me when I attended Mass. They seemed like a good bunch.

"Yeah, that'd be good," I said.

"OK, I'll get the papers together for Catholic Charities and they will do the placing. Maybe at our next visit, we can go over the papers."

What was there to go over? I thought I already said I wanted to do this. I scooted my chair away from the table so I was sitting sideways. Catherine asked for the check. I was ready to bug out of this place.

Two weeks later, Catherine arrived in her red Buick again but we stayed at the home and went into the library to talk. Catherine had the papers.

"I'll tell you what the fine print says and then you can sign," she said.

"I want you to know that signing here means you'll be giving up all your rights to the child."

I put my hand to my chin and leaned over. "Yes, that makes sense," I said.

"The adoptive parents will have sole custody of the baby."

"Didn't she already say that?" I thought.

"Once the baby is placed, you're not to try to contact the parents. By signing, you agree that you relinquish all rights as the mother of the child."

She didn't really have to be telling me all this. What did she think I was going to do? Stalk the new parents? I knew what adoption meant and I knew what I was doing by signing the paper.

"You'll have a ten day grace period after the birth of the baby to change your mind, but once that time is elapsed, everything is final. Do you understand?"

I was surprised to hear about the grace period. I couldn't imagine someone changing their mind during that time and snatching the baby away from the new parents. That would be horrific. Anyway, I knew I wouldn't be changing my mind.

"OK, I understand," I said. "I'm ready to sign."

It was a warm day. The window was open and the curtains rustled with a swirl of wind. Thunder clouds were building in the sky.

She pointed to the line on the bottom of the page. I signed, Judith Ann Liautaud, and dated it, June 7, 1967.

"Judy, can you also fill out the info for the birth certificate?" she asked as she handed me another paper.

I filled out the name of the mother, Judith Ann Liautaud, but when it asked for the name of the father I didn't know what to do. A loud clap of thunder rattled the open window.

"I know the name of the father; should I put it on here?"

"That's up to you," she said.

"Will he be contacted by anyone? His parents don't know a thing about this." Rain started to fall and blow inside. Catherine got up and closed the window.

"The father wouldn't be contacted unless there was some sort of medical emergency and the biological parents had to be contacted. But otherwise, these papers are strictly confidential. The adoptive parents will not know the names of the birth parents."

I worried that somehow Mick would get into trouble and that

this would be like ratting on Mick. I decided to leave "name of father" blank. Then it asked for the name of the child.

"Am I supposed to name the baby?" I asked.

"Well, you can if you want."

"Why didn't she just tell me what to do?" I thought.

"The adoptive parents usually give the baby their own name, but your baby will have the name you give it until the new parents receive the child."

I wrote Helen or Edward for the baby's name.

"Helen is the name of the lady I stayed with before I came here," I said.

"I'm sure she would be very honored," Catherine said.

It was easy to sign the papers while the baby was still inside of me. I had no attachment and I was just waiting for all this to be over and done. I knew as sure as the night is black that I wouldn't change my mind about giving away the baby, and I knew I would have no reason to contact the child after she was gone from my body. I couldn't know how giving birth would change these feelings, and I couldn't know how differently I would feel once I saw the baby and heard her cry. I was in for a shock. I was sure I knew it all— and I knew nothing. Such a child I was. Just like the song "Unwed Fathers," by John Prine; "Someone's children out havin' children in a brownstone buildin' and all alone"

CHAPTER 32
WAKE-UP CALL AT WAKING OWL BOOKS

Even though we could go out on Thursdays, it took me a few weeks before I got the courage to leave the safety of our prison. After we walked down the front steps, I felt like I had busted out of jail. I held my arms out and spun around so I could feel the summer air swirling on my skin, wet and dewy with humidity. I loved walking down the tree-lined streets and looking at the homes. Sometimes I could see people moving about through their front windows and I wondered what their life was like, these people who lived free. I imagined them sitting down to dinner and telling each other about their day at school or work. I was sure their lives were carefree episodes of joy.

Our favorite destinations were shopping at the Village of Wauwatosa or eating ice cream at the town park. Of course, going out made us subject to public scrutiny. Everyone in town knew about The Home on Cedar Street. I was sure people were secretly pointing, staring, and laughing at us during these outings. I kept my eyes on the ground, afraid to see them gawking. On these trips, I liked to stock up on the stretch-mark preventer, Mother's Friend, or buy a magazine or a Butterfinger candy bar. Just one. Just once in a while.

It was warm and humid, near ninety degrees. I was getting hot and tired from the eight blocks we had covered. We walked past a quaint little bookstore with posters in the window advertising the new arrivals: *Games People Play* and *Rosemary's Baby*. Hmm, *Games People Play*, that sounded like a good book. I asked the girls if we could pop in.

The door chimed as we closed it behind us. Hair blew in my face as a cool blast of air showered us from the vent above the door. It was a welcome reprieve to be out of the hot sun. The air smelled delicious, like newsprint. It reminded me of the first days of school when I had all my new textbooks. I'd rub my hands over the covers and then flip through the pages and sniff. The fruity smell that lingered from the printing press always brought a wave of nostalgia and desire to learn everything that the books held in their pages. At the start of the school year, I was excited to meet new friends and wear my fresh, new school uniform.

There were only a few people in the small store. Our presence was bold, doubling the occupancy. I was self-conscious at being part of this pregnant group. Linda P. walked over to the turnstile and started looking at the greeting cards. The rest of us followed. I picked up a card, read the inside, and giggled. I handed it over to Linda. "Check this out," I said. Then I looked up. There was a middle-aged, balding man standing stiffly. He had his arms folded. In a voice loud enough for all of us to hear, he said, "We don't patronize your kind."

What was he saying? I wasn't exactly sure of the meaning of patronize. His motive was so far from anything I could imagine that my mind fumbled for meaning. Does he mean they don't have the sort of things we would be interested in? Was he trying to save us time? No—his demeanor and tone of disgust clarified the meaning. It was a command to leave the store.

Apparently, Linda P. got it. Without saying a word, she put the card back on the rack and turned to walk out. The rest of us followed. As we got near the door, he clarified his intent. "You're not welcome in this store," he said, "so go back to the home where you belong." We didn't say a word or look back. The spring-loaded arm shut the door behind us. The chimed alert rang good riddance.

After we were outside, Linda said, "Did that really happen?"

"We just got kicked out."

"I can't believe it."

"That guy is such a moron."

"Let's head back," Linda said.

"I hate this town," I said.

So instead of continuing on, we turned left to return to the home.

The humid summer air warmed the skin on my cheeks, and the sun beat hot, but nothing daunted the chill in my bones. My heart ached with the injustice. Frozen shards of shame pierced my innocence. "That man is an idiot and doesn't know shit," I told myself. "Forget about him, he is inconsequential." These words shouted inside of me as my throat constricted, trying to contain the deep hurt and anger that was boiling upward. We walked back to the home like zombies, in dead silence.

Being raised in an all-white neighborhood, I didn't have any experience with blatant prejudice. I hadn't done anything to harm the bookstore man, yet he lashed out at us. It shocked me and felt entirely unjust. I remembered the scowl of disapproval on his face. By the time we got back to the home, the four of us went our separate ways. It felt safe to be back inside these oppressive walls. Everyone here looked like me and the help were used to us. I went up to my room. I was relieved nobody else was there. I lay on my bed and let the boiling inside take over as I sobbed. I hated the know-it-all man. I felt so misunderstood. I wanted to go back to the store and yell at him, "What do you mean, 'patronize your kind'? What KIND am I? I'm not a whore or a slut; I'm an innocent girl from a good home. My father owns a business. I'm from the suburbs and a good Catholic school."

As fast as the anger balloon inflated, it hissed to flatness. "Yeah, right," I thought. I knew I would never give him a piece of my mind. My condition spoke for itself. He was just saying what everyone else wanted to say. I wanted to punch his face in and mash it between my fingers like crunchy goo. I thought about the song we used to sing, "Sticks and stones can break my bones, but names can never hurt me." "What a joke," I thought. "Dream on, baby-cakes." I was so naive, such a child. The bookstore owner validated my worst fears. I was so bad that I wasn't allowed to frequent a public store. The anger sat trapped in me, with no way to express it. I bought into the humiliation and owned it. People did think I was slime. It confirmed what I already knew.

After the bookstore incident, I stayed clear of the Waking Owl and made my town visits quick and to the point. I had been educated. I now knew what it was like to be on the targeted end of prejudice.

I had learned in school that babies in orphanages could die merely from the lack of human touch and love. It was called "failure to thrive." Belonging and feeling wanted is crucial to our survival. Adults need it too. Being shunned causes a severe psychological pain. And unlike a broken bone, you don't have the sense that you will heal. It just seems to simmer there in recurring pain, because you have no way to get back at the perpetrator or to set them straight. You are stuck with the humiliation and the rejection. I felt like Hester Prynne, who wore the scarlet letter "A" to mark her disrepute. With the scarlet letter, townspeople could stay clear of the girl who bore a child out of wedlock. That story was written in 1850. Here we were, in the twentieth century, and not much had changed.

How ironic that I was experiencing the same sort of prejudice my family in New Orleans did before they passed for white many years ago. It all boiled down to physical appearance: black or pregnant too young, stay away. I don't know how this traumatic episode still lives within me today. Perhaps it causes me to be a bit more timid when meeting new people, or maybe that is why my voice wants to shake when I am speaking in front of a group.

But my anger at the bookstore man has eased. When you know better, you do better; maybe today the man has learned compassion and understands the blows his words had on our spirits. I suppose he wanted to keep his store in good repute, or perhaps a former resident from the home had lifted something from the store, or maybe he had a young teenage child and wanted to guard her from our bad example. How could I have known?

But I couldn't consider his motivation back then: I was too full of anger. I can only assume he acted in ignorance. In his eyes, our appearance screamed whore, for he could not see past our shameful bellies to the sacred little spirits inside, waiting to be born. Our shame was our own. Our babies, I hoped, would be spared in their pure innocence.

CHAPTER 33
MY BODY GREETS D-DAY

The way my belly expanded on a daily basis frightened me. I didn't think there was any more "give" left. There was no place to put the chewed-up food so it sat there in my throat for hours after eating; the belly skin was tearing along the underside and itched; the baby's little feet got stuck under my ribs and some kicks brought tears to my eyes. Maybe the little thing was getting back at me for what I had done when I was 3 months along. My body was really too fresh, young, and small to accommodate this pregnancy, but yet it kept on.

Linda P. told me about Mother's Friend. It was this magic liquid that could prevent stretch marks from forming if you used it faithfully. Linda said that once you got stretch marks, they never went away. Then you would be haunted with the telltale signs of your pregnancy for the rest of your life. I kept a steady supply handy and spread it on faithfully every night after I marked off my calendar and before I crawled into bed. It was the consistency of olive oil and smelled like pine and lanolin.

When the baby dropped and settled into my pelvis, my belly became long and protruded straight out. I could have rested a dinner plate on top. I could breathe easier and swallow food better, but the stretching and burning got worse all of a sudden. Now, red marks like a rooster's tail showed up on the underside of my belly. This freaked me out—and then I noticed them on my butt and regretted my negligence for not smoothing the lotion on my derrierre. I was sick about it. But now it was too late. A red rash covered the underside of my belly. I scratched until my skin was bloody and raw.

My back ached. I felt heavy and out of balance. When I walked

I got a knife-like jab in my groin, every now and then, that stopped me flat in my tracks. I wondered if my body would ever recover from this.

I only had one pair of pants that still fit me. How I missed my little light and skinny body. At least my legs hadn't ballooned out. From the back, I looked like I did two years ago, but sideways or frontward, I was a freak. I was still the same person inside, but I looked totally different. I just couldn't wait to give birth and be light again. I thought that if this kept up, my body would burst. I took great pleasure in crossing off the days at bed-time. The horrid thing was that the calendar number was now minus three, which meant three days past my due date. With each passing day, I thought I might explode.

I don't think my body had matured enough to be having a baby. I perceived the changes as violent, and I watched as my skin, breasts, and belly suffered permanent changes. When you are married and have planned for a baby, these changes are taken with resolve because you know it is what you have bargained for and a small price for the glory of becoming a mother to a new baby. But when you are trying to ignore your changes and want no lasting effects because you have a secret to uphold, each passing day of increased growth is a horror. I knew there was no turning back, and I had no control as I stood by and watched the changes with each passing day. "If only the baby would be born," I thought, "I would be spared more stretch marks and it would be easier for my body to spring back to normal." I felt trapped and very frightened.

On June 27th, 1967, I went to the bathroom and a glob fell in the toilet. It was the plug they talked about, the bloody show. What a welcome color from down there. I had been praying for this since last October; it was a pretty sight, even if it was nine months late. Somebody had told me the bloody show meant that the baby was coming soon. I gave a shudder of anticipation, knowing my time at the home had an ending in sight. I went back to my room and lay down. Nothing happened that day. Nothing happened the next day.

Finally, on June 30th, I awoke from the night with a gripping pain in my groin. I thought this might be it. I lay there for another hour or so, until it hurt enough for me to get scared. I waddled down to the hospital floor.

The Martha Washington Home for Unwed Mothers was an all-inclusive facility. Our second floor was fully equipped with labor and delivery rooms and a nursery for the babies. There were no resident doctors because we weren't that busy, but a local doctor was on call when needed. The hospital floor was off-limits to us until our time came. So once you were in labor it was like you had a rare and coveted ticket. You finally got to see what it was like on the second floor, and best of all, it meant things were coming to an end. Girls who had access to the hospital floor were looked upon with envy and longing.

I was finally in labor and not sure what was to come, but I was more than ready for whatever it took to be done with my stay here and resume my normal life. I was a full ten days past the due-date indicator on the pregnancy wheel. I thought it was ironic that it was the day I had always expected, exactly nine months to the day from when that rubber broke and Mick shot the egg to life. I'd stopped scratching off the days on the calendar once I got to minus three—what was the point? For the ten days I was past due, I thought, "This is the day!" I was wrong ten days in a row, but now today was the day and I was finally doing it.

First they checked me to see if I was dilating. They said I was in the early stages of labor. They told me to take off my clothes and put on the white linen hospital gown. It tied behind my neck and let the cold air swirl around my backside. Next they took a razor to my tender parts. It pinched and pulled. Then I got an enema. I thought my innards would burst as I tried to hold the water in. Now that I was poked and prepped, I was ready for action. They walked me over to the labor room and told me to get in bed and lie down, that I should try to rest. The contractions were still coming, but not so hard that I couldn't doze off.

Soon enough the pain awakened me and I buzzed the nurse.

"It hurts," I said.

"How bad on a scale of one to ten?"

I didn't think I knew enough to give it a rating, but I said, "Seven."

"OK," she said, "we'll give you something." She came back about a half hour later with a hypodermic needle and told me to roll over. She shot it in my butt cheek. It was a narcotic to settle me down. It made me very sleepy.

There was nothing on the walls. No windows. A green-and-pink paisley curtain hung in the doorway to close off the room. The bed was hard and narrow. Sometimes, when I rolled on my side, I got too close to the edge and startled myself, afraid I'd land on the floor. Then, I would quickly roll onto my back so I wouldn't fall off. I was afraid to scoot over to the middle of the bed because any repositioning seemed to bring on the pains. They came in great waves, like whitecaps breaking on a rocky shore. As the pain crested, I involuntarily held my breath and clenched my fists. I wondered if I would make it through. Each one seemed worse than the one before, and I became engulfed in fright as the clock ticked on and the pains built to new heights.

I had to fight the impulse to push the call button. There wasn't anything that I needed, specifically, but mostly I didn't like being alone. The pain didn't seem right. It hurt more than I thought it should, and I was sure something was terribly wrong. I wanted some reassurance. A human—any human—would do.

The drugs put me in a state of delirium. I forgot where I was until I was jolted awake by another contraction, and then I'd look around and see the white walls, the gray steel cart by my bed cluttered with gauze pads and white puffy paper packages. Strings of reality coagulated into a vision of me in the home on the hospital floor and I would realize I was having a baby.

My skin felt numb to the touch. The narcotic kept me in a drowsy fog and I would be half asleep until the pain came back. Just like clockwork, the pain ground into me. It felt like a red-hot poker was being squeezed between the bones in my spine and their nerve endings. With some of the pains, I'd tighten into a ball and grip the sides of the bed and somehow make it through. Other times I would feel it coming on and I would panic and press the call button again. By the time the nurse got back in, it was over and she'd say something like, "What now?"

I would make something up, then, like "Can I have a blanket?" I wondered myself why I even called her. The pain was over and now things were tolerable. I was a pest and a baby. I didn't think I was handling this very well. I don't know what I thought anyone could do for me, but I wanted someone, anyone. I didn't think the pain should be this intense if everything was okay. I thought the baby must be stuck. I felt claustrophobic and unable to get enough air.

I guess I kept buzzing to be sure they hadn't forgotten about me in this lonely room. I worried that I might just lie there in my own fluids and die, and no one would notice until they wandered in and were shocked that they had lost a patient.

I reached for the call button again, but stopped myself. No, I couldn't bother the nurse again. Last time she seemed perturbed at my beckoning. I wanted to jump out of my body and run away from this place, but I hurt so terribly that I could never walk. And where would I go?

So I told myself that there was no way out of this but through it. I was strong. I could handle this. I reminded myself that labor meant that my time in limbo would soon be over. I comforted myself with these fleeting thoughts in between the catastrophic contractions. But most of the time I was in a puddle of panic.

The squeeze in my belly made me want to puke. My hair was matted into a nest of snarls from tossing it back and forth. Sweat had dampened my neckline and forehead, yet I was shaking like I was cold. My mouth felt like it was lined with cotton balls. I wanted water like a kid wanted Christmas. When I rang the buzzer and asked for a drink, the nurse told me that I couldn't have any liquids. She said it was because if there was an emergency and I had to have general anesthesia, they wanted my stomach to be empty so I didn't throw up and choke myself to death.

"Can I have something for this pain then?" I asked.

"It's not time yet for your next dose; just try to relax."

I thought she was nuts. Relax? I tried to think good thoughts. I thought about summertime at Bond Lake. I imagined myself lying lengthwise on the seats in the fishing boat with the cushion under my head, the waves gently rocking the boat side to side. I thought I could hear the rhythmic slapping of the water as the crests rolled under the boat. I thought about the sun shining on my face and warming my body. Then the next contraction came and I thought I would die.

OUR CABIN AT BOND LAKE

CHAPTER 34
THE BIRTH

I was dreaming that waves were breaking on shore and then I realized it was the sloshing sound of a mop going in and out of a bucket. It came from the hallway. I heard it slurp and then slide along the floor, up and down. A caustic smell of ammonia mixed with Pine-sol wafted into my room and triggered my stomach contents into a tight ball. The bolus in my gut rose and forced itself up my throat and out my mouth and nose. It splattered onto the linoleum. Then the smell of regurgitated pizza caused another upchuck. I said out loud to no one, "Oh God, please help me." The words gave me a hopeless feeling. I felt unheard. I wished Mom was here to tell me what was going on. I remembered her holding me when I was a little girl after I had fallen and scraped myself up. She wrapped her arms around me so my entire body was in her lap. I could hear her saying, "There, now, it's okay. Hush, little one." I could feel her smoothing my hair away from my face as I nuzzled up close. She made it okay.

I laid my sweaty head back on the pillow and closed my eyes. I swiped the back of my hand across my mouth. My stomach settled. Then I dozed off again. Sometime later, the nurse came in.

"My, what happened here?" she said as she looked at the slop on the floor. "Why didn't you call someone?"

"I don't know. It just happened too fast."

The nurse left and the janitor came in with the smelly pail to mop up my mess. I felt like I was going to lose it again. I laid my head back on the pillow, and the ceiling spun like a carousel. I put my hand over my nose to block the stench and breathed in slowly, in and out. I wanted to get up and run away from the smell, away from the pain, away from this place. My body had betrayed me. I couldn't get up or even move around; the hot poker in my lower back wouldn't let me. The drugs made my head woozy and light. I hated how my belly had just taken over my body and grown to enormous proportions. I hated the sick feeling in my stomach. I hated the stab in my back. I hated it all.

My eyes landed on a steel-rimmed clock fastened to the wall opposite the foot of my bed. I watched the second hand creep. It seemed frozen in a time warp. I closed my eyes and waited for the next inevitable rush of pain. The clock didn't tick ahead but the pains kept coming.

I buzzed again. "Please, I can't stand this anymore. How long does this take?" I asked the nurse.

"Labor can take a long time, especially for the first one."

It was midafternoon and the pains had started the night before. I must have been into it fourteen hours by now.

When the nurse told me we were waiting for Dr. Wigglesworth to arrive, I thought he sounded like he busted out of a Daffy Duck cartoon. I pictured a mad scientist type with Einstein hair and thick glasses. Soon afterward, two nurses came in with a wheelie cot.

"Where are we going?" I asked.

"Delivery room," she said, as she put the gurney alongside my bed.

Even though I had been laboring all night and most of the day, I thought, "I'm ready to deliver?" I was shocked because I didn't feel any baby coming. I just had this horrible hot and sharp pain in my back that cranked up a notch with each contraction. I was elated to be moving out of this hospital cell and that humans would be with me.

The nurses grabbed hold of the sheet under me and slid me onto the wheelie cot. Then they rolled me down the hall and turned the corner into the delivery room. Spotlights with metal shades hung from the ceiling. I squinted as my eyes tried to adjust from the dimly lit labor room.

They put the wheelie cot next to the delivery table and said,

"Judy, we have to get you on here. Scoot over and get your body close."

"I can't. It hurts too much."

"Sure you can. Just move your bottom over to the edge and we'll lift you."

I scooted over. It felt as if a boulder was grinding on my backbone; every movement pushed harder on the raw exposed nerve. Whether I was ready or not, the two nurses grabbed my arms and hoisted me onto the table. It was stiffly padded. I thought my back would break as it settled into the hardness.

I felt naked and exposed with the lights aimed at my body. I wanted to scramble around and find a dark hole to crawl into, but I lay there prostrate, under full view. I imagined myself as a bug under a microscope, being peered at and poked. The heat from the lights warmed my face and chest until I felt like I couldn't catch my breath. Beads of water collected on my temples. I felt light-headed and the room began to spin.

"Oh, I don't feel so good," I said.

The nurse was busy setting things on a steel table, but turned around and said, "Well, of course! You're in labor. That never feels good." I laid my head back, closed my eyes, and felt another contraction coming. I moaned with the pain. I wanted her to know how much it hurt; maybe she would do something.

Dr. Wigglesworth came into the room, but he was not like I pictured him. He was a big man and, unlike Einstein, bald except for a few tufts on the side just above his ears. His skin was smooth and cherry colored. When he walked in, he had an air of serious concern on his face. He stretched white gloves over his large hands and reached inside me.

"This baby is posterior," he said as he withdrew his gloved hand. We might have to use the forceps." I didn't know what posterior meant. I had been in labor now for half the night and most of the day. Stuck. It must be stuck.

"Now, Judy, I want you to roll over on your side. The doctor is going to give you a spinal."

"What's that?"

"It's a shot that will make you numb. You must lie perfectly still," the nurse said.

"Oh, I can't roll over," I said. "It hurts too much."

"Just try. You'll feel a lot better soon. We can't proceed unless you roll over."

I grabbed her arm and slowly rolled a quarter of the way. They grabbed my body and finished the rotation so I was on my side. It felt good to be off my back, but my upper leg started to cramp.

"Ahhh, oooh!" I screamed out in pain. A doctor came in and walked around to the back of the table. An icy wetness was smeared on my back. It seeped all over the middle and sides of my body, and then the cold liquid spilled down onto the delivery table; I was lying in a glob of wetness. I felt the needle prick into my back: at the same time a contraction started to build.

I wanted to move my body. It seemed like it was going to hurt more than ever with me in this position.

"Just lie still. You must not move."

"Oh, I have to move my leg. My leg, it hurts. It hurts." The cramp felt like a dagger in my thigh.

"Hold still, Judy."

One nurse had her hands on my shoulder and the other on my legs. Their grip was strong, like they were holding down a squirming dog. Within seconds I felt the needle go in, and then a rush of soothing numbness eased into my back and through my legs. The analgesic smoothed the jagged nerve endings and quieted the pain.

My eyes filled with tears. It was gone. The pain was gone, not a shred of discomfort. Within minutes I was numb from just below my chest to the tips of my toes. That stabbing, searing pain had left, whisked away as easily as dust bunnies under the bed. I imagined Bond Lake now, glassy and serene after a storm had passed. I felt like the sun came out and the birds started singing again. I became calm and receptive. I was so grateful. I loved everyone in this room with me. I wanted to do whatever they asked. The pain was gone, and I felt like a dancer who loves the music and knows the steps.

They rolled me onto my back again. The needle doctor packed up his spinal apparatus and left, along with Dr. Wigglesworth.

They took these long metal arms with foot holders on the end and screwed them into the end of the delivery table. They took my legs and set them inside the stirrups so my feet were higher than my head, way in the air, with my knees slightly bent. It was a strange position, like a bug stuck on its back, flailing to turn over with its legs straight up in the air. I didn't care, though. The pain was gone and I was golden.

The nurse said, "It's time to push. You hold your breath and push like you're having a bowel movement." Then she showed me. She took a big breath, then put her head down on her chest and acted like she was trying to blow the breath back out but couldn't because her mouth was closed.

The nurse put her hand on my belly, and when the contraction began she gave me the cue to start the push. I couldn't tell. I was too numb.

"OK, here it comes now."

I inhaled, but it didn't feel like my lungs could expand much. I held my breath and tried to imagine that I was pushing against the pain that I used to feel down there. Some air escaped through my lips as I pushed against nothing.

"No, no," the nurse said. "You have to keep the breath in; don't let it out."

On the next contraction I tried again, holding my breath for longer than my lungs wanted. I got light-headed and had to let the breath out. It seemed fruitless. It was all dead down there. I couldn't feel anything to push out or where the muscles were to tighten.

I did it anyway, on cue. I was happy to be a good patient. I felt good, pain free. I was a lousy actress, though, tensing my face and holding my breath as I went through the moves, trying to imitate the nurse's example.

"Do I still have contractions?" I asked.

"Oh, yes. They're there. I can feel them."

I liked that she had to tell me when I had a labor pain. All I felt was sweet numbness. I felt like I had a round-trip ticket to hell and returned home to heaven. I was just along for the ride now. I pushed on cue for two more hours. The nurse did an internal exam and walked out of the room. When she came back in, Dr. Wigglesworth was with her.

I felt an overwhelming desire to be cooperative and helpful. The doc was here: I was hopeful that the baby would be coming soon.

"Should I scoot down?" I asked.

"Just stay put. You can't scoot anywhere. You're numb."

"Well, I knew that, but I was just trying to help," I thought.

The doctor did another internal check of the baby's position and shook his head with disappointment. A second nurse walked in with a tray of shiny medical instruments and set them on the table. Wigglesworth put on a new set of gloves and took two silver slats off the tray. He put one side of the forceps deep inside me and then the next. It seemed like they clicked together like salad tongs.

Then he said, "Now on the next contraction, I want you to push like you have been doing."

Wigglesworth said to each nurse, one on each side of me, "I want both of you to apply fundal pressure at the next contraction."

The nurse had her hand on my tummy and gave me the cue to push. I inhaled, put my head down, and held my breath, pushing with mushy effort as both nurses placed their hands on the top of my belly, leaned in, and pushed the mass of baby toward the opening. At the same time, Wigglesworth pulled with the forceps. My body slipped along the table toward the doctor as he strained to extract the baby.

Now I got scared again. The force was so great, I wondered if the child would be okay. I also wondered what they were doing. I thought the baby must be wedged in there so tight that it wouldn't come out. What if it didn't come out? What would they do next? Each time the contraction waned, the nurses told the doctor it was subsiding—I stopped pushing and he stopped pulling with the forceps.

Nobody was reassuring me or giving me encouragement. No one said "We'll get this," or "We're making progress." Not a word. Just serious, intense looks on their faces. I wondered if my insides were ripping out with each pull of the forceps. I wondered what was wrong with my construction. Why wasn't the baby coming?

This procedure with Wigglesworth pulling on one end and
the nurses pushing from the other continued for about four more
contractions. Each time, my body slid closer to the edge of the table,
and each time they grabbed me under the arms and pulled me back.
Finally, all of a sudden, something broke loose and I felt the pressure
give. The nurses left my side, and there was a flurry of action. The
doctor was doing something below. I heard a suction noise. A
minute later, out it all came. I couldn't see anything, but I felt all
the thickness release. I heard a sputter and a gurgle and then quiet.
The silence was pronounced. "There should be a cry or something,"
I thought. The baby was out. Then at last, after what seemed like
minutes, a loud wail.

I could not have anticipated what happened next. I started
crying at the sound of its insistent voice. My body softened with a
spiritual connection and love for this little human. Although my
head knew a baby was in there, my heart didn't know it until I heard
it cry. I wanted this child.

I was ashamed to ask, like I had no right to know. It wouldn't be
my child, after all, but I asked, "Is it a boy or girl?"

"It's a girl," he said. I wanted her. Her cries were a call for me. I
wanted her close to my skin, to swallow her up to my chest and keep
her warm and safe. My heart ached for her. We had been through
this together. I wanted her so bad. But I was ashamed that I wanted
her. I had no claims.

I did not ask to see her: I thought I didn't deserve to see her.
She was in a baby bed on the other side of the room, but I couldn't
see inside. They didn't say anything about her, like, "Oh, what a
beautiful baby!" You know, the normal delivery-room banter. Just
silence. I suppose they thought they were protecting me. I suppose
they thought I didn't care, since I was giving her away. But I cared. I
cared way too much.

"Is she okay?" I asked.

"Yes, she's a little bruised up, but she's okay."

I was thankful. I wondered why I was thankful when I had been telling myself for nine months that I didn't care.

They took her away. They sewed me up. "You might be a little sore down there," the doctor said, "but we will give you some icepacks and medication to help with the pain." He also told me that if I have another baby, I might tell the doctor that this one presented posterior.

"What does that mean?" I asked.

"Well, she was face-up instead of the usual face-down." This must have been why I felt like I had the hot poker in my back. The back of the baby's head, not the softer face tissue, had been pressing against my spine.

CHAPTER 35
RECOVERY

They wheeled me back to the recovery room and I slept for several hours. I woke up with a stabbing headache, but the nightmare was over. I had the baby. I did it. I wasn't pregnant anymore. I wondered about the baby. Where was she and who was taking care of her? I hoped they gave her more attention than I got when I was in labor.

They brought me some water to drink, and a tray of pork chops and mashed potatoes. I ate every shred, then fell asleep.

Around 7:00 pm I woke and thought about calling Mom. I wanted to tell her it was all over. I asked the nurse if I could use the phone that was down the hall. The numbness was gone now. I could feel a very sore and tender bottom. My ribs ached, and my head felt like a saw was moving across my temples. I swung my legs over the side of the bed and sat up.

"I feel like I'm going to pass out," I said.

"Just sit for a minute," the nurse said. "If you need to make a call, I can wheel you down there if you feel up to it."

The phone hung too high for me to reach the rotary dial from the wheelchair, so the nurse dialed the number. Since Mom was up at the lake, I had to be careful about my choice of words. We were on a party line, which meant that anyone in Wascott could pick up the phone and listen to our conversation. I had to talk in code.

"Hello." It sounded like Hugren.

"Can I talk to Ethel?" I asked. I didn't know if Hugren recognized my voice, but I didn't want her asking me any questions.

I waited and imagined Mom wheeling over to the phone to talk.

"Hi, Mom, it's Judy. I just called to tell you that Sally had her baby."

"Sally?" Mom sounded confused for a second. "Oh, my, that's good," she said. "Is everything okay?"

"Yes. It was a hard birth: a baby girl, eight pounds, four ounces. Delivered by forceps. Everything's fine, though, and it's all over."

"Oh, my," Mom said. "When does she come home from the hospital?"

"I think in about a week."

"OK, then. Thanks for letting me know. So everything is okay then?" Mom said.

"Yep, everything's fine. I just wanted to let you know."

Mom sounded tentative on the phone. Maybe I wasn't supposed to be calling her. Maybe that was up to the facility, to notify the parents. I suppose Mom was afraid of what I might say and who might be listening in. Maybe she had company over at the cabin and couldn't ask any more questions. We hadn't talked for several months.

I hung up with a lonely feeling: Mom was three hundred miles away. I knew she was disappointed in me, and I was saddened by her cool tone of voice. Maybe she acted like that just because she was on a party line. Still, I had lingering doubts about her love for me. I was glad she hadn't seen me during those later months: me, so young and full with child. I was glad I didn't have to see anyone while I was in that state. It was good I went away.

People have asked when they hear my story, "Well, where was your mom? Why wasn't she there with you?" Since the story was that I had a contagious disease, it wouldn't do for Mom to be coming up to visit me, and most of the time she wasn't up to it. If the secret plan was to work, they couldn't be taking trips up to Wauwatosa, Wisconsin. I didn't blame Mom. I couldn't admit she had anything I needed. I was serving out my sentence for the wrongs I had committed. But today, I think, "How could she not know I needed her desperately?" She must have ached as much as I did to know that she had to stay away. I believe she did know I needed her, but she was adhering to the plan. Even if she was healthy and up to it and wanted to come, visitors were not allowed on the hospital floor or inside the home. It must have broken her heart to know that I was laboring alone and handing over my newborn child to strangers. We were both victims of the plan.

They told me that I could go to the nursery for visiting hours between 3:00 and 5:00 pm each day. The nursery was down the hall and around the corner from my hospital room. By the second day I was able to get up and walk around a little bit. This is when I decided to go see the baby. I stood outside the glass window, looking in. There were two cribs with babies. An attendant walked out and I asked, "Do you know if the one over there is mine?" as I pointed across the nursery room.

"Does the baby have a name?" she asked.

"Helen," I said.

"Yes, that's Baby Helen. You can come in and hold her if you want."

"No, that's okay."

The baskets had clear sides, so I could see her even though I was peering through the glass across the room. Her beauty amazed me. I know all mothers think their child is exceptional, but compared to the wrinkled scrawny one next to her, she stood out like a rosebud in a field of weeds. There she was, a little cherub with a mop of hair and chubby cheeks. She had a big red mark on the side of her head and cheek. It must have been from the forceps. Poor thing. She was lying on her tummy, asleep in the bassinet. She looked healthy though. Her little square jaw reminded me of Mick; she looked so much like him with her dark hair. She had a perfect miniature nose. As my eyes moved over her, I swelled with pride, as if I had something to do with her beauty. I had seen newborns before, all wrinkled and squinty-eyed. But her skin was soft and plush, a perfect rosy cameo color. If it wasn't for the bruises on the side of her head, she could have been a Gerber baby star.

My body yearned to walk inside the nursery and pick her up. I took a deep breath and remembered how Jackie's babies smelled when they came home from the hospital and how I loved their aroma. It was that baby powder mix with their sweet milky breath. I remembered how they would arch their backs and put their fists up by their ears as they stretched and yawned. I could imagine what it would be like to hold my baby and nestle her peach-soft skin next to mine. After I got her in my arms, I would take everything in. I would smell her babyness and run my fingers over her tiny hands and touch her toes. I would feel the light weight of her against my body and hold her close to my heart so she could feel it beating, so she could feel the love I had for her.

I put my hands on the cold glass of the nursery window. I looked down the hall. No one was around, so I let myself cry. I wanted her so bad. I wondered if, maybe, I should go in there and hold her. They said I could. She was mine for now. No, I couldn't do it. If I held her once, I just might not ever be able to let her go. That seemed like dabbling in fire. I could just see the frightful scene I might make, them telling me, "No, you can't have her. You signed the papers. She belongs to her real parents," and me clutching her next my body, crying, "No, no, no," unable to let her go.

No, holding her would not do. It wouldn't be good for either of us; there was no future in it. It would rip my heart out to have to hand her over. I had to protect myself from that hurt. It was better to cut the ties right now. It was better to forget, to never feel the sweetness of her body close to mine. That way I wouldn't know what I was missing. Yes, it was better for both of us to leave her be.

So I continued to watch, with tears in my eyes. I saw her yawn and turn her head. I watched her fall back asleep, then open her eyes and look around. She seemed content. She seemed to be doing fine. I didn't want to disturb her serenity. After standing in front of the glass watching her for about a half hour, I went back to my room, lay down, and slept again.

At the end of the day I moved back up to my room on the third floor, but I still had the privilege to go to the hospital floor during the nursery visiting hours. On the third day after the delivery, I passed a new girl on the stairs. I hadn't seen her before and her belly was small.

"Hi," I said. "Did you just get here?"

"About three days ago. When are you due?" she asked.

"Oh, I already delivered."

I was so proud to say it. I was hoping she would ask, smug in my knowing that she had no idea what was in store for her. Poor girl. She was just starting at the home. I felt aloof and cocky inside. I hoped she noticed I came out of the door on the second floor. I had access.

The next afternoon I went back to the nursery, but still I stayed on this side of the glass. One of the girls was inside holding her baby, but I just stood there and looked through the diamond-shaped, wire-mesh window. Baby Helen glowed with beauty, like stars on a moonless night. Her red marks were fading just a tiny bit.

On one of my visits, I watched the nurse hold her and feed her a bottle. I was relieved that they seemed to be taking good care of her. But one time when I got there she was crying and no one was around. I went to the nurses' station and told them.

"Baby Helen is crying. Do you think she's hungry?"

"We'll be in there as soon as we can," the nurse said.

I walked back and watched through the window as she cried for another ten minutes. It made me so nervous. "What does she want?" I wondered. "How can they let her lie there so hungry and needy?"

Finally, I watched the nurse walk in with a bottle. She picked her up and fed it to her. It was wrong that it wasn't me feeding her. The sight of it sent a shock of longing through my heart. The nurse didn't hold her close, just laid the baby on her lap and held the bottle so she could suck. She didn't seem to care that much. I would have cared. I would have held her close when I fed her.

On the fourth visit, I wanted to hold her so badly and talk to her and tell her that I loved her. The ache was deepening, so I decided I wasn't doing myself any good to be standing out there longing for her. I made the decision to make this my last visit. I went back to my room, lay on the bed, and put my face in the pillow. It was over. It was time to move on. But if it was over, why did I feel this hole in my heart? I felt worse than before I had the baby. I was supposed to be happy now. A new chapter of my life was starting, but I was having a hard time turning the page.

CHAPTER 36
THE BABY IS TAKEN

I would be leaving the home in two days. It was early July, but the weather didn't know it. A north wind brought sheets of rain. I had just gotten up from my bed to peer out the window. My baby was now five days old. A bolus of grief sat in my throat and gripped me with a sorrow that only a mother can know. My baby was not in my belly. My baby was not in my arms. Something was very wrong.

I thought back to my early pregnant days when no one knew about my predicament, and I remembered how I wanted it out of me. How I prayed rosary after rosary that it would disengage and slip out, freeing me of the nightmare. I flashed back to the times I punched myself, just below the belly button. How could I have done that? How could I have been so naive to think it might work and to not consider that I might be harming a growing child within me? All I felt was a lump, a growing lump just above the pelvis. It was the bane of my existence. I hated myself for what I did. Thank God it never worked. Thank you. Thank you. Now that unwanted lump had turned into a perfectly gorgeous child. I hadn't held her, yet my love for her ran deep.

The window was full of rain spatters, muting my view. I glanced out over the parking lot and saw a red Buick pull in and park just below my window. As I looked through the sheeting rain, I could tell by the red hair and the way she moved that it was Catherine Cavanaugh, my social worker. She was dressed in a full-length black trench coat, her arms wrapped around her body to keep the wind out. Her eyes were on the ground as she walked briskly to get out of the rain. She reached the building and went in the back door.

I stared out at the parking lot. It was empty except for the red

Buick. The asphalt along the edge was broken into black chunks, maybe from the heat of the summer. Brown and green weeds sprouted through. The once-purple lilac bushes had lost their blossoms to summer.

Linda P. walked in the room.

"Judy, what are you doing?"

"It sure is gloomy out there, just like I feel."

"Why should you be sad?" she said. "You had the baby and you're going home. You're so lucky. I'm stuck here for another month."

"Yeah, I'm glad to be done with it," I said. "But I thought I would be happy to be done with the birth and it'd be so easy to say good-bye. I don't know what's wrong with me. I'm so sad." I turned away from the window to look at Linda.

"Well, I'd sure be happy if I was done with this whole thing," she said.

"I feel bad about giving her away. She's so beautiful. I signed the papers, but I still don't know why I did it."

Linda sat down on her bed. "Oh, she will have such a better life. Most of the girls here give their baby up. It's just what you do when you get yourself into trouble. You're doing her a favor. How would you take care of her, anyway, if you kept her?" I walked over and sat down on my bed, facing Linda.

"I don't know. I don't know if I could. I suppose her life will be better with a family that can care for her." I was engaged in the plan, but I felt like a fraud. When I signed those papers a month ago, I didn't do it because I loved her and wanted the best for her. I did it because I didn't want anyone to know I was pregnant. I didn't want anyone to see the shame I held deep within, hiding the secret of my immoral behavior. It was a lousy reason, shallow and uncaring.

I got up again and stared out the window. My heart ached to hold the baby and kiss the baby and love her and change her diapers and feed her and care for her. But it was too late. It was a done deal. She was all set to go to a new family.

"Did you hold her?" Linda P. asked.

I turned away from the window to look at Linda.

"Oh, no, I couldn't. They said I could, but I thought that if I did I'd never be able to let go."

I heard a shuffling below the window and turned my head to look out again. The rain was still falling and the sky was full of dark, low-lying clouds. Catherine Cavanaugh was walking to the car with a pink bundle in her arms. She walked fast and put the bundle in a bassinet in the backseat.

"I have a feeling that's my baby," I said. "She's leaving now."

Catherine closed the door to the car and got in the front seat. The car started, and she backed out. I watched her pull away.

"I have to go check something out," I said, and ran down to the second floor. I took the long hallway to the nursery. I peered through the triangular wire cross-hairs of the window. Sure enough, her little bed was empty. She was speeding away in Cavanaugh's car. She was gone. I wouldn't ever see her again.

I pressed my hands against the nursery window and pushed my cheek against the cold slick surface. My knees felt like noodles, and long hard sobs erupted from deep within my gut. My baby was gone. I let her go. I never held her. I signed the papers that gave her to some strange woman. They didn't even tell me she was going today. Maybe I could have said good-bye.

I wondered who would be feeding my baby tonight. I took big chunks of my hair and pulled it slowly through my hands. Icy fingers of grief stabbed at my heart and gut. I feared I would never be okay again. I was drowning in hopeless sorrow.

CHAPTER 37
HOME TO GLENVIEW

It was now July 7th, 1967: one week after the baby was born. So much had changed with the birth. I was no longer pregnant. I had nothing physical to keep me in the slot of shame, yet the effects lingered. My belly was a sagging pouch of skin, fat, and fluid. And I felt empty. So empty. I couldn't walk very far, because the stitches down below started to ache and throb. And sitting caused a burning sensation down there. I preferred to stay lying down. I slept a lot during those days after giving birth. I suppose my body needed to recuperate and so did my brain. Sleep was still my friendly escape.

I looked out the window again and noticed the empty space where the Buick had been. I remembered the scene from a few days ago when the car sped away with my baby inside. I, too, would be leaving soon. Our job was accomplished. Now that it was time to go, I was afraid to face my family. I was scared to have them see me like this. I had always been so skinny, but now I had some meat on my bones. My belly wasn't tight and slim. Now it shook when I moved like ripples on the lake. My breasts were huge. I hated what the pregnancy did to my body. My bottom was still sore, like it had a hundred paper cuts. I sat down gingerly. They gave me a doughnut, inflated like a small inner tube, to perch myself upon, but how could I bring that thing home? I would be too embarrassed to use it.

I worried about my reentry. After I got home and saw people who knew I had been ill, they would wonder just how sick I was. They would wonder how I plumped up so nicely when I was supposed to be bedridden. I was supposed to have had a deadly disease. I was supposed to have been so sickly that I had to be shipped away to be cared for by an estranged aunt. I thought I should have been elated, but I dreaded going home.

I ran my hand over my stomach. This belly of mine was impossible. It should be flat by now. Maybe in time it would be, but I didn't have time. I was going home today! I remembered the girdle I had at home, sitting in my drawer. I could wear that for a while. This time it might work, because the skin and my belly underneath were loose and soft. It just might compress things. I felt a slight wave of relief. I thought I was done with the girdle thing. Funny how things go—I just couldn't seem to shake this nightmare.

I was almost done packing. I left the bottle of Mother's Friend on the nightstand for the next resident, along with some pregnant clothes. Then I grabbed the last thing in my locker, the calendar. It had been forty-one days since I arrived. Now my life would start anew. Yet shades of the nightmare lingered like bad breath.

The good thing about leaving was that I wouldn't have to wash any more giant pots and pans. I wouldn't miss the gloom that haunted this place, and I didn't have a bunch of friends here that I would miss. I wondered what would become of Linda P. She was still in waiting. "Good riddance to the watermelon seed eaters," I thought. All of us with extended tummies, like we had sprouted a watermelon right inside our guts. Good riddance to Judy L. Soon I would resume life as a normal person with a full last name.

I had my bags packed. Jeff would arrive soon. I noticed the curtains were blowing from the open window. I walked over to take one last look at the empty parking lot. From somewhere deep inside, tears came again. I told myself to get on with it. It was all over. It was time for a new life now. I told myself to be strong and keep back the tears. Don't dwell on the negative. I blew a kiss out the window and wished for it to land on my little child, wherever she was. I wished her a good life. I prayed to God that she had a good mother. I clip-clopped down the stairs for the last time, dragging my brown leather suitcase, my green book bag slung over my arm, and my purple velvet case.

Jeff drove me back to Glenview in his red Mustang convertible. It was a warm, balmy day and the wind blew my hair about. I was finally free. I looked up at the crisp clouds that dotted the sky and

felt thankful that I was on my way home and it was all over. The
sense of movement and speed was exhilarating. I had been so stuck
and hampered, so full of boredom, gloomy fear, and regret; now I
was free. The force of the summer wind as we sped along refreshed
my body and seemed to blow the grief away. I felt like an escaped
prisoner; no longer a member of the down-and-out. I had paid my
dues. I was free.

Jeff and I talked a little at first. I told him the birth was horrible,
and that I was glad my time was over. I said I couldn't wait to see
my friends. I remember thinking as we sped along the highway that
I had come through it and I was on the other side now. I was still
intact, a normal teen, yet scarred by the shame that I would continue
to keep well hidden.

I wondered if the secret had been preserved. I thought it would
be ironic if I came this far, performing all these manipulations to
keep up appearances, and someone told someone and they all knew
about me. I dreaded facing my classmates. I would never know until
I saw them in the fall, and then I would know by how they looked
at me and how they acted. I hadn't talked to any of my friends since
last March. That was three months ago. I suspected Annie and Jane
would be curious. I hoped no one started asking me questions about
my disease.

I thought about my inward journey for the past nine months:
looking for my period, realizing I was pregnant, telling Mom and
Dad, staying in the country at Helen and Ed's, the lonely Home
for Unweds, the hard birth, watching my baby from the nursery
window. It was all over now, and I was starting afresh. I felt a spring
deep inside of me start to bubble up, a feeling of newfound strength.
I thought to myself, "If I could go through this and come out on
the other side without going crazy or killing myself, I could handle
anything that would come my way in this life." I was proud of the
way I handled this. I was strong. Nothing could ever shake my
strength of character. I was overwhelmed with a feeling of empathy
and love for those who had suffered hardships of all kinds. I had a
desire to offer help in my days ahead. An outflow of compassion
swelled inside of me. I didn't think I could ever judge someone for

doing wrong. I wouldn't know what wrong was unless I had walked in their shoes. The bookstore owner could not know how he caused us to suffer by passing judgment on us. I forgave him. He did not know. He never walked in my shoes. I didn't know how or what I would do in my future, but I felt like I'd had an experience that would aid me in service to others.

I had a welcome, long-overdue burst of joy on that ride home to Glenview. I found strength in reminiscing about what I had been through and how I had handled it. I thought that I would just go back to being the same kid I was before I got pregnant. But I couldn't know then that I would be changed forever. Not only would I never return to the innocent, confident teen that I had been, I would hold the sorrow of my lost child for the rest of my days. It would lessen with time, but it would never be easy to forget and I would not heed my father's words to keep it all in my past.

JUDY 1968 SENIOR YEAR

CHAPTER 38
THE ROTTEN AROMA OF A LIE

After being gone for three months, I was finally back in Glenview, snuggled into my own bedroom with the pink lacy bedspread and matching skirt on my French provincial dresser. My rosary with the clear blue beads was still on my dresser. It had been a long time since I picked it up and prayed the chains of desperate Hail Marys. I took the circle of beads, held them close to my chest, and put them in my top drawer. I didn't have anything to pray for.

I loved having a window I could open without worrying if it bothered my roommates. I could leave the curtains open. I would let the summer wind send its softness over my skin as I slept. It was strange to be home at this time of year. From the time I was a baby, I had spent every summer up at the Wisconsin cabin. Mom was still up there, but Dad was home because he was working. He usually came up to the cabin for long weekends. Dad would soon be driving me up north so I could finish my summer at Bond Lake. When Sunday came along, I wouldn't go to Mass. Dad never went on his own, but I didn't really want to risk running into people I knew just yet, so I stayed home and slept in.

The day after I got home, my breasts started swelling. I thought this could be a good side effect of the pregnancy. But by the second day, they were freaky big and they hurt and were hot. I didn't know what was happening. I was embarrassed to tell Dad, but I just had to. It hurt too much. I heard Dad in the kitchen and went downstairs. He was putting coffee grounds into the percolator.

"Dad, I think I should go to the doctor. My chest is really sore." I hated saying the word "breasts"; I didn't think I was supposed to have those.

"I'll call Keller," Dad said, as he put the pot on the stove. He walked over to the wall phone in the kitchen.

After a few minutes on the phone, Dad relayed the doctor's advice. Dr. Keller said it was a crime that they hadn't given me some dry-up pills, but at this point I just had to ride it out and could suppress the swelling with cold compresses.

I walked back upstairs like I was balancing a plate on my head, smooth and slow, up to the bathroom. I let the water run until it was icy cold, soaked a couple of washcloths, and wrung them out. I took them to my room. I lay down on the bed and put the cloths on my swollen breasts. The coolness felt good on my hot skin. I thought that this milk just showed how much my body was aching for the baby that should be next to me, hungry and nourished by my milk. It was only right. It felt like she was ripped from me, a hundred miles away, drinking a bottle full of fake formula, given to her by some stranger. I felt cold and freaky. This was only what I deserved, though. She wasn't to be mine. I found it loathsome that I didn't deserve my own child. I thought, "I am too bad and dark to deserve my own child."

Soon, the washcloths warmed to body temperature. I took them off and threw them on the floor. I lay there and gingerly rubbed my hands over my breasts. They were full of knots, throbbed, and kept expanding. It was like my belly; how big could they get? The bulge spread under my arms. When I put my arms down to the sides, I could feel the swelling and it hurt to rub against the swollen knots. "I hate this," I thought, and rolled over on my side and drew up my legs. Then I cried from the hurt of the fullness in my breasts and the emptiness in my heart. I fell asleep. I dreamed I was babysitting for my niece: she was crying and I didn't know how to make her stop. When I woke up, I was in a puddle of milk. I changed my clothes and sheets.

The next day I woke up in a funk. Being home wasn't like I expected it would be. I remembered the days of summer: I rose, full of anticipation for doing fun things with my friends. I was hardly able to wait for the day to start and vibrated with the excitement of a whole free day ahead of me. But I didn't feel like that now. Normally

I would have a million phone calls to do this or do that, but no one was calling. Of course not. No one knew I was home. Besides, I was scared to face anyone and I didn't know what I would say to them. I thought my friends were probably all involved in their summer activities and might not have time for me. I hoped when I finally saw people I could act joyful and lighthearted, even though I felt dark and worn-out.

After the sixth day at home, my loneliness prompted me to call Annie and tell her I was back. I thought it would substantiate my story if I made an appearance before we left for upnorth. I had only been gone three months, certainly not time enough to carry and have a baby. Right? I hoped no one would be asking details about my kidney disease.

Annie was sweet to arrange a get-together with Jane and some of our other friends over at her house. It would be great fun to see them. Jane, my sweet Jane, always listened to me and was interested in what was up. She had a resident quip on the tip of her tongue waiting to be spilled out at the first opportunity; funny words that made laughter bubble as easily as water from a mountain spring.

I picked out a madras plaid blouse, but while buttoned, it pulled too tightly across my chest. I shuffled through my clothes and tried on three different shirts until I found one that was tight but tolerable. I pulled out the girdle that was still in my bottom drawer and put that on too. It helped. I found a pair of shorts that fit.

I thought I looked a lot different from when I left. Those two raisins on a breadboard had morphed into mammoth muffins. I wondered if I should stuff some Kleenex in my bra in case I started to leak, but that would just make me look bigger yet. I carefully folded two tissues so they would lie smooth and flat and I put one in each cup of my bra. It seemed that milk seeped out when I least wanted it to, but of course I never wanted it to. I thought it would be better to suffer the extra bulk than to risk a wet bull's-eye in a conspicuous area.

When I got to Annie's, I tried to round my shoulders and make my blouse sag. I gave Annie a hug hello and could feel the rocks smash with our embrace. Annie's mom had a look of disapproval on

her face. Was it for my benefit? We were sitting on the couch when
one of my friends, who was not privy to my secret, said, "Wow, you
got big while you were gone," obviously referring to my full chest.
I didn't expect anyone to comment on the obvious. I flushed neon
with embarrassment, and then fright shot through me—fear that my
secret was exposed. Annie's mom was in another room, yet I feared
she could hear the reference to my large chest. Then I was afraid
that someone who knew would say something that gave me away.
Embarrassment prickled my skin. I just said, "Yeah. I'm older, you
know. I guess I grew," or something dumb like that. What to say?

Even though I could hear Annie's mom shuffling around in the
other room, she didn't come in and talk to us. I had a weird feeling
about her, kind of like she could smell the rotten aroma of a lie.

Many years later, Annie told me that when I left that day, Mrs.
F. quizzed Annie.

"Ann, what was wrong with Judy?" she asked.

"She had some kind of kidney disease," Ann said.

"But why did she have to leave home for so long?"

"I guess because her mom is sick and couldn't take care of her."

"I never heard of such a thing," she said. "Tell me what really
happened to Judy."

"She was sick, Mom, I told you. Quit asking about it. She was
sick, that's all I know."

Years later, Annie confessed to her mom, and told her the truth
about me. She was a good friend to stand by my story, and I feel
rotten that I asked her to lie for me. I shouldn't have gone out in
public until my chest shrank, but I didn't know if it ever would. I
guess I had hoped no one would notice that my breasts were large,
but Mrs. F. was no dummy.

When I first got home, I hid behind an invisible wall that gave
the message: off-limits. I think Dad had instructed everyone, too, to
keep a tight lip and just act like I had never been gone and nothing
had ever happened. This was the best way to ensure the secret was
preserved, like it was stuck in formaldehyde: dead and isolated. Each
time I saw someone for the first time after being gone, I dreaded

it; as minutes and then hours went by without any reference to my absence, I'd relax with silent relief. Everyone seemed to be playing the hush-hush game, and I was thankful.

Anytime my mind lit on the vision of Catherine Cavanaugh leaving the parking lot with the baby, or the pull of the forceps, or the hot dogs and ketchup at Helen and Ed's, I just stuffed it down and didn't dwell on it. Like a burning rise of fluid in my throat, I continued to swallow until it formed into a dark feeling, like something was wrong, but I couldn't name it. I wrapped my emotions with a protective coating and buried them deep within me.

The silence let me grieve in some dark unknown place within my own heart, alone and secret. I don't even think I knew I was grieving. Perhaps I felt nothing. I was numbed by stuffing the grief of losing my baby, and my shame. I tried to put it all behind me like I was told to do.

My brother-in-law, Jackie's husband, Dave, was an exception to the silence. Although he didn't say much, I could tell by the tone of his voice that he understood. The first time he saw me, he walked up with arms outstretched and gave me a substantial hug. Then he said, "Awww ... God bless ya, Jude." He had tears in his eyes. I knew he understood. I felt like he accepted me and didn't judge me either. I never forgot that precious moment when I needed the understanding and love the most.

After a week at home with Dad and Jeff, I went back up north to spend the rest of the summer with Mom. When I walked in the cabin, Mom said she missed me. She gave me a big hug and said something like, "It's all over now, honey. No need to look back. Now you can get back to your normal life."

"Yeah," I said, and felt relieved because of the way she hugged me. It meant that she still loved me. No further references were made to my time away. Not that day and not ever.

After I arrived at the cabin, it was sunny and pristine but my heart was heavy with a mustiness that thickened the air with an unfamiliar gloom. I didn't understand my sadness and internally lashed out at myself for feeling that way. I thought I should be happy it was all over. This was what I had been yearning for the past nine months. After all, I was getting back to normal. My breasts had dried up and now they were back to their tiny selves. My stomach was almost as flat as it was a year ago. I should be happy for my child. I should be happy she had parents who were taking care of her. Most of those summer days were gray and colorless. No ups and downs, just steadily flat. I had no friends to hang out with at the cabin. My days were filled with reading books, swimming, and some waterskiing whenever I could get Jeff to tow me behind the boat. Mom always went to Mass in Minong or Gordon and I felt obligated to accompany her. So I went each Sunday, but I wasn't getting any spiritual uplift from my visits. I just sat there, going through the motions and waiting for the Mass to be over. I didn't go to communion because I hadn't been to confession—and I knew you had to have your soul clean to accept the sacred host. Perhaps it was because my sins were too weighty to confess, but I never did return to confession.

In the past, I had always been excited about school in the fall. Childhood summers at the cabin were isolating and lonely for the most part. I loved getting back to my friends and the days of having too much to do. This fall was the same, but I had some serious apprehension as I worried about someone asking me about my sickness and details of where I was and what I did. I was thankful to have had the summer vacation as a buffer between the two months of school I had missed. Regina was situated in a quiet neighborhood in Wilmette, Illinois. It was a sprawling building with a bridge that connected the auditorium with the classrooms. Large, grassy areas with stately maple trees surrounded the school. The freshly waxed linoleum made the halls shine. We had lockers that were assigned alphabetically. I had the same kids next to me and also in some of my classes, the ones whose last names started with "K, L, or M." So the first person I saw when I came back was my friend Katie K. She wasn't in on the secret but knew I had been gone. She said she was glad I was better and back to school. Then she wanted to know what was wrong with me. "I had nephritis," I told her. But I said I was better and asked if she remembered the assignment for French class.

I watched my classmates, but didn't see any expressions of suspicion. I came to believe that I had pulled it off. I was sick and now I was back. I resumed my spot at the lunch table with Annie, Jane, and Carol, but was serious and heavy hearted. I didn't seem to come up with any clever words or jokes until I had been back for several months. Still it was good to see them again and all be together. Each said, they had kept the secret but none asked what I did, where I went, or what happened to my baby. It was better to keep it all unsaid. I was glad at the time but oh how I needed to talk. I eased back into my senior year, clunky and unsure of myself, but present and having a period every month.

Forty years later at my high school reunion, I asked some distant friends if they knew what happened to me back in 1967. Not a one of them had any idea I went off and had a baby, which is just a testament to the great friends I had in Annie, Jane, and Carol. I loved them for "crossing their heart, hope to die, swearing to God, no peein' in the pot, and no pickin' your snot." They were the best a wayward girl could ever hope for.

CHAPTER 39
MICK AGAIN

For the first year after I got back, I didn't contact Mick nor did I hear anything about him, but I often wondered what he was up to. I had a date or two with friends of friends and patted myself on the back for not being interested in sex, having learned my lesson. I'd wait for marriage. Of course, I wasn't tempted because I wasn't in love and my resolution was easy to keep. I was finally pure and good, but for me, it felt a little too late. I was still grieving over my loss of virginity and didn't quite know how to purify myself.

It was time to apply to colleges. I had taken the ACTs in my junior year but my scores were mediocre, probably because I was preoccupied with my horrible secret. The rejection letters were a blow to my already fragile ego, and I took the news as evidence of my lacking. I had applied to Michigan State and the University of Illinois but had to read those nasty letters, "We regret to inform you … do not have the qualifications we are looking for…." I decided Southern Illinois was the best of my options, so I planned to attend school in Carbondale in the fall. It was a shame because I had mostly As and Bs before I took the plunge into the darkness.

I graduated with my class of '68 in June: it had been a year since the birth. It was a strange summer because I had decided to forgo Bond Lake for the opportunity to work in downtown Chicago in a high-rise office. It was my first job and Dad thought it might be a good experience for me. I would be leaving for college in the fall.

One summer evening my girlfriends and I went over to the old Glenbrook kids' hangout, Roosevelt Park. Wouldn't you know, I ran into Mick. When I saw his brown eyes and his tight body with its air of confidence, the sparks flew. I still loved the way he squinted his eyes when he laughed and his lips parted, exposing his straight white teeth. He said I should come by his apartment sometime. He was living in Chicago near the "L," so I could hop on the train and only walk a few blocks to get to his place.

The excitement of reconnecting at his city apartment was dampened by a sick feeling in my gut. Of course, I couldn't tell my parents that I was seeing Mick again. I had been directed to be done with all that. So the dread of hiding and worrying about getting caught came back in full force. Again, like before, I did it anyway.

The view of the city from the train was a culture shock for me, being that I was raised in the clean, shining, and affluent suburbs. The litter between the buildings, clothing pinned to lines on the porches, and the shabby curtains hung to block out the passersby gave me a gritty-city feeling that nicely framed the guilt and dirtiness I felt as I walked over to Mick's apartment. I walked fast, looking at the ground, then consoled myself by thinking that nobody I knew would be running into me here—in the heart of the windy city.

Mick was like a mangy dog that kept following me: I loved the thing even though I knew I would get cooties if I petted it. I loved him enough that I couldn't help myself. I don't remember us talking much about what happened to me. I told him that yes, I had the baby, and it was a girl. I thought about telling Mick that she looked just like him, but I was afraid it would make him feel bad that he should have been the daddy and he couldn't remedy that. So I kept most of the details quiet. He didn't ask me what those three months were like when I went away. I was relieved. I was happy to get off the subject and leave my sacred secret in the silence. I was afraid that if we talked about it, the sound waves would creep over the planet and people would know. I kept quiet.

Mick was off to new adventures. He was smoking pot now. The last I heard about marijuana was from the grade-school movies that featured pushers lurking around in alleys near school yards, ready to grab our souls and take away our free will. The movies told us to stay away from marijuana or we would soon be addicted to heroin.

"Pot? Really?" I asked.

"Yep, it's cool. It doesn't hurt you. Teaches you to be in the moment. Everything looks good on pot. You should try it," he said.

"But aren't you afraid you'll get addicted?"

He chuckled in a way that seemed to say, How could you not know? Then he said, "You don't get addicted to pot. That's just propaganda. It's like smoking a cigarette. You can quit when you want. It's no big deal. My friends really dig it."

"Like who?" I asked.

"Oh, Lennie and Kurt. We get together and smoke and laugh a lot. It's a kick."

"Aren't you afraid it'll make you want to try hard drugs, like heroin or something?"

"Oh, no, that's dumb. I'd never do that."

"Really?" I said.

For several days I thought about Mick's presentation and my fear started to soften. It sounded like fun if it made you laugh. I wanted to share the weed with Mick. I wanted to be part of the group.

As an office clerk in my summer job, I sorted stacks of delivery tickets for a trucking company. I felt unimportant and bored much of the time. I watched the clock and eagerly cleaned off my desk at 5:00 when I could punch out and then take the L over to Mick's. It was easy to do this without Dad knowing. I was just home from work a little late. I could have been shopping or whatever.

The next time the boys passed the joint, I took a puff. It felt like barbs of hot steam poked my lungs and ended in a coughing fit. They looked at me like I had committed a mortal sin. I was wasting the expensive and coveted weed. The next time I took a tinier puff and was able to hold the smoke in my lungs for several seconds. Then, with practice, I could hold it longer to get the full effects.

At first I couldn't feel anything and thought it must have been wishful thinking that made them high. But then, around the third time, I said something like, "This stuff blows your mind." And the friends laughed because they knew I was finally high. My eyes landed on some object in the apartment and I found myself staring, entranced by the intricacies. It seemed like I could actually feel the beauty my eyes took in, somewhere deep in my body. It was astoundingly sensual. And I loved the friends in the room. I felt close, like we were in a special club: The Enlightened Society of Weed Worshipers. We knew things others didn't. We were hip. Then someone said something that made us all laugh hilariously. What? It didn't matter. Sweet or salty food tasted like the first bite after a forty-day fast, the first bite, over and over again as I devoured a whole bag of salty crunchy things.

The mornings after, when I got ready for work, I felt dark and criminal for smoking pot. I was tossed into that gloomy feeling of guilt and remorse when I got back with Mick. Now I had an added arrow in my quiver of shame: I was doing drugs. But I liked the stuff. It took away the angst when I was high and I felt loving and light. Until, of course, the effects wore off, and then I was depressed and looked forward to the next joint that evening.

After Mick and I got back together, I made a visit to Dr. Keller and got the birth control pills he promised he would prescribe if I ever needed them; so much for my pats on the back.

A few weeks before it was time to leave for college, I got a call from Mick. He had been on a road trip with Kurt and had some bad news. He met a girl in Colorado, he said, and fell for her. He was surprised at how it hit him off guard. Did I really need to know these details? I couldn't believe he was telling me this. I remember his words: they crushed me. He said, "I never knew love like this before. Love is like a rock." All I could think was, "He found something better than me."

That fall, I was supposed to be excited and happy to be leaving home and on my way to college. But I felt like I had to settle on third or fourth best because of my rejection letters. I was also mentally sick with the loss of Mick. I couldn't help thinking about him and the girl from Colorado and imagining them together: holding hands as they hiked through meadows, stopping to look at wildflowers, laughing with their rocky mountain high. Daggers of anger and jealousy pulverized my tender heart. When I think back on it now, I should have seen it coming. Mick was not committed— and where was our love going to go, anyway? We couldn't get back together in a public way because of my father's prohibition. It was a doomed love affair.

I stared out the window as we drove through the cornfields on our way to a school that I didn't even pick for my first choice. I thought it was a school for dummies. I thought the good schools were the ones that didn't want me, along with a bunch of schools in California and other exotic states to which I'd applied. I thought it was just so not cool to be going to SIU.

My year at Southern turned out to be a year of changes. I must have been placed in easy classes because of my ACT scores. I whizzed through the courses and got all As. Compared to the nuns at Regina, the professors didn't demand much. I lived in a dorm and had a sweet roommate named Lucy, and just before Christmas I hooked up with Johnny.

Johnny was an old acquaintance from back home in Glenview and too cool for me back then. He had wavy blonde hair and blue eyes, and resembled John Lennon. His body was tall and well defined. I was flattered that he took a liking to me, this outrageously cute guy who loved to draw and take movies. Johnny attended SIU for the fall quarter, but dropped out and moved to California. He asked me to come visit him during spring break.

Mom and Dad were appalled. I suppose they were scared I would get in trouble again and didn't like me going off to the other side of the country to see a strange boy. In spite of their disapproval, I hopped a jet plane headed for LA. I was 18, after all.

During my visit, I took my first slice of orange wedge, LSD. Johnny and I camped at Big Sur next to a large river that flowed into the ocean. We took the acid when we got up in the morning and then walked to the sea. The path to the beach wound through towering pines and thick ferns. The forest was thick with the sappy pine smell and the humidity from the sea. By the time we got to the ocean, we were flying high. It wasn't anything like pot because it physically changed how things looked. Stars and sparkly traces flew off Johnny's arm as he moved, like a falling star or a comet. The visions delighted my senses. I wanted to cry in awe and my body vibrated like it was in a state of orgasmic wonder.

Johnny took my hand and led me to a large rock that was just off the shore. We climbed on top. The sun was bright and warmed my skin. We sat perched up there, several feet from land, out in the blue sea. The waves came in and crashed, spilling over our bodies and releasing their salty spray as we held on tight, afraid we'd be washed away from our stronghold. We held on to each other and laughed after each wave passed: laughed that we stayed put, and laughed for the refreshing feeling of the waves washing over our faces, arms, and legs.

"Don't look at the sun," Johnny said. "It'll hurt your eyes." We had to remind ourselves of the most basic safety tips because our minds were off into outer space. Of course our pupils were dilated to saucers, so this was good advice.

Over and over the ocean waves immersed us in their rhythm. Soon my skin was the same temperature as the water, and I couldn't decipher the barrier between my body and the ocean. The pulse of the sea was my heartbeat, the rise and fall of the waves, my breath. I became the sea, the sun, and the heavy humid air. I felt like I could fly. I felt one with God.

We only took LSD a few times, but something changed within me. I don't know if it was the orange wedge that did it or if I was just ready, but I began to revere all things natural and of the earth. When I got back to school, I stopped wearing make-up: I thought that was disingenuous. I stopped cutting my hair and let it fly in the breeze. I stopped wearing frilly, fancy, or binding clothes in lieu of loose cotton and natural fibers. I strove for a pure version of me; I was one with the earth, like a Native American who had found sacred ground. I felt one with God while I watched the waves come in and crash on the rocky shore. I was spiritually uplifted watching pelicans dip for fish on the seashore or the clouds form into puff balls against the indigo sky.

It had been several months now since I had attended Mass; my white leather missal was left at home, tucked away in my skirted dresser drawer. The ritual of the Catholic Mass—stand up, sit down, now kneel, now stand up—began to feel ridiculous. We were sheep following man-made directives with no other purpose than to prove we were followers. I didn't think God heard me when I prayed those million rosaries to my savior. I wasn't saved from my trouble. And besides, if my Catholic God did hear me, I knew he didn't like me much. I had fallen away and violated his sacred law of purity.

And the guilt, that raw dark wound I felt from failing to abide by the moral code, was all that necessary? Was it perhaps even harmful to my fragile young psyche? Maybe all that I had suffered could be eased. I started to realize that I had to buy-in to the guilt to let it eat away at my self-esteem. Perhaps I could forgive myself and love myself for who I was and what I had been through, and the guilt could melt away.

I started looking at organized religion as a collection of dogma that mostly served to produce guilt and shame, yet I grieved for my loss of faith. I reminisced about my childhood days, when I felt protected and guided by God. I wanted to pray, but when I tried, the words seemed hollow and meaningless. I wanted that feeling of rejuvenation as I attended early Mass before my school day started. But now, nature became my new god; walks in the woods grew to be more satisfying than Latin words and mindless ritual.

I believed in giving love and sweet caring because of how it made me feel, not to please God. I did it for goodness' sake alone, not because I was afraid of burning in hell. I wasn't sure what happened to us when we died, but I suspected that we just turned to dust. That was a frightening thought, but if the God I believed in might not exist, then heaven probably didn't exist either. It was easier to believe there was no hell. I couldn't believe a loving God would ban people to hell and let them burn forever. Maybe man invented this stuff to manage the congregation. To make them follow the desired path, and to invent answers to the meaning of life.

For many years, I longed to return to that place of oneness that I felt from the effects of LSD at Big Sur. I took acid a few more times, but I never had the same spiritual awakening as the trip to Big Sur. It began to feel like it was too risky to increase the dose to repeat the experience. Rumors went around saying some of the acid was cut with nasty stuff that turned your mind to mush. How could you know? Then I had friends of friends who reported flashbacks that permanently screwed up their minds. Then there was the news report of some dude who took LSD and jumped from the fortieth floor because he thought he could fly. As the risks piled up, the drug lost its appeal. But I continued during my adult life to yearn for that place of peaceful oneness, to seek a path of spirituality that was introduced to me by the LSD.

DAVE AND JUDY'S WEDDING IN THE MEADOW 1970

OUR CABIN IN FRASER COLORADO

Part III - Coming to Terms with My Past

 ## Chapter 40
Rocky Mountain High

Johnny stayed in California and I returned to Southern Illinois for the rest of the semester. At the end of the year, I decided to transfer to my dream school, University of Colorado in Boulder. Now that I was a sophomore with good grades from my freshman year at SIU, I could gain admission. Boulder was full of hippie-type free thinkers, nestled in the Rocky Mountain foothills, and in my opinion, way cooler than SIU.

By the end of my first semester, I met the man I would marry. I remembered Dad's words about not revealing the secret to my husband, but I didn't want to start off a relationship with that burden. Dave would load up his guitar and we'd hike above the Flat Irons to Dream Canyon. We called it our church. Nestled below the Continental Divide, perched on the side of a rocky outpoint, we gazed at the pine-studded canyon cut by the river far below while Dave sang, "In My Life" by the Beatles. "There are places I remember all my life … but of all these friends and lovers, there is no one that compares with you." The stunning panorama sent our spirits soaring, or maybe it was the killer weed, but it was up there that I told Dave my secret. He didn't react with shock or judgment but took it in stride as he strummed and sang. I was grateful and falling in love.

We started out living together, which, for Mom and Dad, was salt in my wound of shame. "Oh, Judy, how could you do this?" Mom lamented. She cried over the phone and that made me cry. I thought, "She just doesn't get it. Here I've met this cool guy who can sing and play the guitar and I'm in love and she's crying about it." The wedge that kept us from understanding each other after my teen pregnancy widened.

Mom hadn't met Dave yet and apparently got worried about his appearance when she heard his name was Rodriguez. She phoned me to ask her burning question: "Judy, is he dark?"

I knew this meant dark-skinned, but I whined, "What do you mean, dark?"

"Well, you know, dark-skinned."

"No, Mom, he's not darrrrk. His grandpa is from Spain; they're fair-skinned."

That still didn't make Mom like him.

In an effort to shed the lingering shame of my teen pregnancy, I told myself that I didn't care what my parents thought anymore. I was losing at the game of pleasing them, anyway. Ricky Nelson sang, "You can't please everyone, so you got to please yourself." These words rang true. I tried to be strong and independent, devoid of caring what others thought, but why did Mom's reference to me "living in sin" cut so deep to my core? And why did I cringe with embarrassment when we checked into a hotel without being Mr. and Mrs. if I really didn't care what people thought?

Dave and I didn't call ourselves hippies, because we weren't living in Haight-Ashbury or giving free love, but we believed much of the hippie creed: free thinking. We questioned the cultural standards, including marriage by law, my Catholic religion, and the pursuit of financial success.

Growing up, I had everything I needed in a material sense. Yet Dad came from nothing and started working at the age of seven, sweeping floors in a newsroom to help feed his family that had just arrived in Chicago. Survival was Dad's daily concern. Because of his hard work and entrepreneurial spirit, I was never hungry or cold, and I never had to get a job. At home, Dad just took out his money clip and peeled off a few bills whenever I told him I needed something. By the time I was in my twenties, it was easy to throw out Dad's measuring stick for success and abandon pursuit of the almighty dollar. Today I have conveniently softened my views and no longer believe that pursuing your inner values and making money are mutually exclusive.

Cop out or not, Dave and I had to eat, so he worked for $4.25 an hour at a ski shop, and I worked as a maid for $3 an hour at the Idlewild Ski Lodge. We rented a one-room cabin in the Fraser Valley from Dave's Grandma Miller for $40 a month. Fraser was called the icebox of the nation. Our cabin was the real icebox—no insulation, no water, and no electricity. We kept warm with our potbelly stove; Dave woke up several times a night to stoke and feed the fire as subzero drafts swirled through the cracks in our barn-board walls. My dad used to say, "Ferchrissakes, Judy, you can't live on love alone." I can imagine how heartbroken he was to see how far astray his daughter had been led by this cowboy from Colorado.

Dave and I acquiesced to a legal marriage, but for us, it was just a piece of paper we signed for the sake of the old folks. In a mountain meadow outside our cabin, Dave's Grandma Miller, a freelance preacher, helped us with the "I do's," which we never said—too conventional. Instead of exchanging rings, we shared water, like the aliens from the book Dave was reading, *Stranger in a Strange Land*. I wore a handmade, yellow-Swiss-dotted pioneer dress; Dave wore a red-plaid flannel shirt, blue jeans, and mountain-man hiking boots. Mom, Dad, and my brothers attended, worrying about the lasting nature of our vows and shaking their heads at the bizarre ceremony, yet also a little relieved that we would no longer be living in sin.

When I met Dave, he was working as a welder at the Coors Beer factory in Golden, Colorado, saving money for an extended trip. He said he'd marry me as long as I was willing to join him in his dream to travel the world. It sounded like an appealing adventure: blinded by love, I followed his lead. We used our wedding money and an inheritance from my godmother, Deds, to travel through Mexico, Central America, and South America. We took a boat to the Galapagos Islands and rented a cabin in the highlands of the main island. We foraged for fallen avocados as soon as they fell from the trees, harvesting them before the birds could convert them into seed carcasses. We rented a hut on the shores of the Bonda River in

Colombia and picked wild mangos. We hiked along the Inca trail in Peru to visit the ruins of Machu Picchu. We were roughing it but were seasoned for hardship after living in the cabin in Fraser. We stretched our $5,000 for a year and a half by shopping at farmers markets and staying in hotels for $1.50 a night.

At the end of our travels, we realized it didn't matter much where we landed, but a place was what you made it. Each city began to look like the one before. Having spent time with the poverty and filth, we longed to be back in the United States, where the toilets flushed and the tissue paper was handy. We moved back to Fraser, Colorado, and I soon became pregnant with our first child.

Determined not to repeat the horrific birth experience I had at the home, I devoured books on home birth, and on January 28th, 1974, gave birth to Kiona in our cabin in Fraser. She was the baby who would be mine to keep. I didn't hold her right away. There were complications with the placenta, and she lay quietly in her bassinet until long after the doctor had gone. I picked her up and marveled at her rosebud mouth and full head of hair. This time I was proud of my body and how it could grow and birth a child. And how did she know how to suck with such fervor on the first try? It must have been her exceptional intelligence, I mused with motherly pride.

As I nursed and rocked her in our mountain cabin, my love for her blossomed. She went everywhere with me in a papoose carrier. We cross-country skied to the laundromat to wash diapers. I brought her from room to room with me as I cleaned the ski lodge. During her first year, I didn't trust a babysitter to care for her properly, so I never left her. My Kiona was precious and my world revolved around her needs. This was sweet and at the same time overwhelming.

The love I felt for Kiona caused me to second-guess my decision to give away my own child in 1967. I hadn't made an informed decision. I wondered how I could have let it happen like that. Now it seemed inhuman and heartless. I wasn't much better than the mother gerbil I saw gnawing on her newborn like an apple in her paws. The whole birth and relinquishment was contrived, unnatural—unconscionable. What if I gave her away to incompetent people, thieves, or thugs? I didn't know anything about them. Did they have enough money to give her a good life? Did they laugh together? Did they love every little thing about her? I didn't linger on these doubts or let them take over, but they sat there, silent, churning in some uneasy place in my heart. I yearned to know what became of this child I gave away.

After our trip to South America, Dave heard about people strapping kites on their backs and jumping off mountains. Adventurous at heart, he learned the hard way, spraining ankles and getting caught in turbulence on the Continental Divide that bounced him around like a rag doll under his hang glider. I was sure I would be widowed at a young age, but his skills and wisdom improved until he became the Masters of Hang Gliding Champion in 1978.

We moved from Colorado to Utah to start our own business, Wasatch Wings, because of the ideal terrain and weather for teaching and flying hang gliders. My dad financed our start-up business, although he was skeptical about its money-making prospects. We struggled. It was a seasonal business. We laid ourselves off each winter so we could draw unemployment. We were milking and benefiting from the system we criticized, yet living our dream of making money at something we loved. We barely made enough to feed the family and pay the rent. My main jobs at Wasatch Wings were bookkeeping and designing and sewing hang-gliding harnesses.

I never was as passionate about flying as Dave, but I did manage to learn to soar, staying aloft for hours above the Widowmaker in the Salt Lake Valley. The ridge got its name from the motorcycle races that were held on the steep incline. I spent my hang-gliding career teetering between the love of feeling the wind beneath my wings and fright at being suspended thousands of feet from Earth by aluminum tubing and Dacron. I was careful to fly when conditions were smooth and the weather stable. During the years, we lost friends and professionals to the sport, but kept at it, always trying to make the sport safer.

By 1979, I was pregnant with our second child. Eventually we upgraded our living situation to a single-wide trailer complete with running water and an avocado-green washer and dryer set that my dad bought for us. This is where my not-so-little Tessie, nine pounds, thirteen ounces, was born at home with the help of a midwife. Kiona was now five and was by my side as Tessie slipped into Dave's hands and took her first breath. I hadn't been planning on a second child right then, but was grateful that she found her way when she did. She was my blessing in disguise.

My yearning to make the birth experience better for women, and perhaps a desire to heal from my teen birth, propelled me to study and become a lay midwife. The home-birth movement was well established in the Salt Lake Valley, perhaps because of the underground polygamist fundamentalists who all had their babies at home. I studied for seven years as an apprentice under another lay midwife and eventually delivered babies on my own. I felt a deep spiritual connection as I gave support to laboring women and was privileged to be present when their babies took their first breaths. But, as a lay midwife, again, I found myself on the fringe of society, going against the establishment and subjecting myself to scorn by the medical profession and some of the public who shook their fingers at our activities. Doctors did not believe lay midwives had the education, skills, or technology to be delivering babies at home.

But we believed in it like a religion. We attempted to weed out the high-risk cases by doing prenatal checks: if there were any warning signs, like high blood pressure, protein in the urine, breech presentation, or a stalled labor, we would refer the woman to the hospital. We heard stories of botched hospital births and blamed it on trying to fool nature with the flow of drugs to speed up labor, slow it down, take away pain. We believed that nature had it perfectly designed and we didn't want to intervene unless safety was being jeopardized. We were diligent in our pursuit of safety. It worked, most of the time. But if you are in the profession long enough, there creeps up the unforeseen complication. Seven years into it, I helped deliver a baby with shoulder dystocia, which means the shoulders were stuck in the birth canal after the head had delivered. We took the baby to the hospital shortly after birth. The resilience of the newborn amazed me, again, and the baby was okay, but this incident scared me enough that I quit lay midwifery to go back to school to become a doctor.

After three years, I got my undergraduate degree and finished the requirements for medical school with a high GPA. Maybe it was my age—I was now forty—or my mediocre scores on the entrance exam, but I wasn't accepted to the University of Utah Medical School. It was a bitter disappointment. I had secretly questioned whether I had the right stuff. I thought I was probably smart enough, but didn't know if I had all it took, emotionally. Displays of anger still put me in a frozen state, and I wondered how I would react when I was in training and got scolded by one of the doctors. I could just see the unwelcome tears start to flow. Was I tough enough? I also worried about births with a negative turnout. I was sure I would second-guess whatever I had done. Birth can be a risky business regardless of whether it is at home or in the hospital.

Yet, I loved the work. I was honored to stand by the laboring moms, offering encouragement and back rubs, and finally, sharing in the baby's miraculous first breaths. I felt spiritually connected to the dear women whose births I attended. Perhaps these home births served as a way to redo my own teen birth and make it better, vicariously.

Even though I told Dave about my teen pregnancy, I was still obeying the vow of secrecy, not necessarily because of my dad's instructions, but because it had saved my reputation and I was ashamed. My intention was to just slice those nine months out of my life: simply put a patch over the time that was ripped from my life.

But now, with the birth of Tessie and my work as a midwife, the patch was wearing thin. I came to understand that the only way to heal from the trauma was to take off the cover-up and attend to the wound. Take a good look. Let it air out. Share the secret.

So I plowed ahead, wanting to be done with the shame even though it stuck like a scarred adhesion. With forced determination, I gradually broke the silence, offering a sentence or two when the subject of teen pregnancies came up in a friendly conversation, saying something like, "Oh, that happened to me." My throat would squeeze and my voice would shake. Then I expected someone to say, "Really? What happened?" I wanted desperately to talk about it; they just pretended not to hear me. I am sure they could sense how uncomfortable I was exposing my festering wound.

Intellectually, I now understood that guilt and shame were taught to me by society, my parents, the nuns, and the Catholic Church—and that I didn't have to keep reliving it. But these things are deep seeded. It wasn't just a question of intellectualizing what I had been taught and how it played into my regrets. I still had some work to do.

By the time my daughters were five and ten, we had moved from our trailer in the mobile home park to a sprawling rented home in Cedar Fort, Utah. I had watched the movie about dealing with the grief of losing a baby, which prompted the healing episode of tears with the Cabbage Patch doll. I was realizing that even though I gave away my baby, at least I gave her the gift of life. A bit of sunlight crept in and set me forward on the path to easing regrets.

MY DAUGHTERS TESSIE AND KIONA 2010

OUR HOUSE IN PEPPERWOOD

CHAPTER 41
A STROKE OF GRACE

My children were growing; we now lived in Pepperwood, an
upscale neighborhood in Sandy, Utah, nestled in the foothills of
the Wasatch Mountain Range. It wasn't that we could afford this
lifestyle from our hang-gliding business, but due to the sale of stock
in my father's company, we were able to upgrade considerably. Our
house was filled with mountain views on an acre of land, financial
worries were eased, and my loved ones were healthy—yet my sense
of well-being was rocky. Something vague was awry. Perhaps it was
a lingering memory from the hundred days when I held the secret
of the pregnancy to myself, constantly worrying about what would
become of me. Perhaps it was just the lingering shame, or perhaps it
was the worry of what became of the child I gave up for adoption.

The physical ache for closeness that I felt at Baby Helen's birth
morphed into a more subtle concern for her well-being. When I
gave her away, I never allowed myself to question my decision. I
couldn't get married at such a young age; no one did that. I couldn't
keep the baby: how could I raise it? I couldn't get an abortion
because the window for that option had passed before I told any
adults. Adoption seemed like it was my best choice. Yet I questioned
whether I did the right thing. I still missed her and I had never even
held her, so where was my longing coming from?

The memories sat like wet leaves on a fall fire, too heavy and
moldy to burn: the toxic smoke clouded my days. I walked around
in life doing this and that and learning to live with this smoldering
smelly feeling in my gut of sorrow, pain, and shame. I couldn't be
completely clear with anything because of the smoke, yet I was afraid

to poke the fire and dig down to get to it.

The ache of longing, that shadowy lump in the left side of my body, was still tangible. It may have been the trigger for recurring nightmares of botched babysitting episodes that went something like this:

I am walking out of the ladies lounge at Marshall Field's. I am hurrying from ladies dresses to the shoe department, looking for something, when I gasp as I remember I left the baby in the bathroom. A shroud of horror puts me in a panic. I retrace my steps, scramble to the escalator, run up the moving steps, and try to pull open the door to the ladies lounge, but it is too heavy. I run to look for the maintenance man to help me. None of the clerks know where he is.

I know the baby is in there. I have to get her. No one seems to be able to help me. I am frantic and worry about telling my sister I lost the baby I was supposed to be watching. I feel irresponsible and careless, and a sinking remorse at my selfish insensitivity for letting the baby's sense of well-being slip my mind.

Or, another dream:

Again I am in charge of someone's baby, but I drop it and her head falls off. "You can't just stick a human head back on," I think. "It can't work." But I have heard of how a lizard can grow another tail, and I think I will give it a try. I have to do something before someone sees how careless I have been. So I reach down to the floor and pick up the head. I turn it so it faces forward and set it on the baby's neck. It seems to miraculously stick. I think I see the baby blink. I am relieved: it worked. But when I start walking with the baby in my arms, the head gives a little wobble and gets too far sideways and falls off the skinny neck again. I never find the baby dead, but suspended in this space between life and death. I grieve and blame myself. I want to think the baby will be okay, but I have sinking doubts. I am ashamed of my carelessness. My heart, head, and hands quiver with regret and worry.

After a dream like this I am relieved to wake up to the morning, but the dreadful feelings often lingered throughout the day.

I noticed a lessening of these unsettling dreams after my session with Lana. By some stroke of grace, I met Lana at a conference for midwives. I didn't plan it, but she ended up being the stoker of the smoldering fire, helping me uncover the leaves so I could let the fire burn. She was one of those grown-up hippie types, decorated with a pink-and-purple tie-die gracefully swooped around her plump yet agile body. Her voice was smooth and soft, like whipped cream, and her hair was whisked up into a loose knot fastened with a teakwood stick. She moved deliberately in her space and seemed to be aware of everything around her. Her eyes sparkled with inner knowing. She was a trained psychologist, and the gist of her message was that getting in touch with your own birth can help you become a better midwife. "It could help you understand the perspective of the newly born," she said.

I had heard about the benefits of rebirthing. One story told of a person who was no longer claustrophobic after a session that traced this fear back to an oxygen-deprived birth. I didn't know what fears I might uncover, but I hoped the lesson would be profound. I liked Lana instantly, so I signed up for a private rebirthing session later that afternoon.

We were in the basement of an old church. The walls of the room were gray-painted concrete block. Brown particle-board folding tables lined the walls. When I walked in, Lana was sitting in the middle of the room opposite a straight-backed chair with a black-vinyl padded seat. A few metal fluorescent lights hung from the ceiling, giving the feeling of an overcast day.

"Hi, Judy," Lana said. "Have a seat."

I sat down and faced her.

"Thanks for coming. Are you ready for an inward journey?" she asked.

"Hope so," I said as I shuffled in my chair. "Will it be like I'm hypnotized?"

"Not really," she said. "Some say it's similar, but you'll be fully aware."

I took off my sweater and put it on the back of my chair, then immediately felt chilly.

"This is kind of scary," I said.

"Judy, I understand. Of course you would be a little afraid because it's a journey into the unknown."

"What exactly will we be doing?" I asked.

"I'll take you on a guided inner journey to help you remember your very own birth. Our first early experiences shape who we are and influence our lives. When we bring them to light, we get in touch with our true selves. Sometimes it leads you to a better understanding of why you act the way you do."

On her direction I took three deep breaths. I noticed that my hands were clenched in my lap. I reached behind me to get my sweater and draped it over my shoulders.

"Now as you breathe, I'd like you to let your thoughts flow freely until you find a sweet place in your mind's eye. Do you have a place you love? It might be a mountain valley or an ocean beach. Can you imagine it?"

"I'm up north on the lake," I said.

"Good. Can you describe it?"

"I'm lying lengthwise with the boat's seat cushion for a pillow. I'm gazing up at white clouds, cauliflower plumes. The boat is rocking gently; the waves are lapping at the sides in a soft click. The sun is warming my body."

Lana said, "Good, now just stay there for a few moments and feel the sun getting warmer. What do you smell? What sounds are around? Relax into the moment."

I could hear a loon in the distance. The thought made me chuckle, because I wondered if it really was a loon or my brother Jeff mimicking their call. He had a talent for such things. I imagined the loon diving underwater. Then, I relished the soft silence that soothed my jagged mind. I recalled the pungent smell of jackpine sap.

"Let's stay here and silent for a minute or two."

I noticed my hands were unclenched. I rubbed my knees in small circles. My breathing slowed.

"Good. Now, Judy, I want you to switch gears for a moment and go back to the earliest time you can remember," Lana said. She moved in her chair so it squeaked.

"Can you now go back in years?"

"I'll try."

"What do you see? Can you describe the scene to me?"

I scooted back in the chair and clasped my hands again. My mind gave way to a snowy screen of nothingness. The blank made me nervous. I surfed through a stack of memories, but it was like reaching in a grab bag and clutching the bottom of the sack: nothing specific.

"Take your time," Lana said.

This eased the pressure, and a scene appeared.

"I'm two. I'm playing on the pier," I said.

"Good, now what else do you see?"

"I have a bailing pump in my hands. Leaning over to suck up water. It's aluminum with a red barrel and a long rod. I pull the rod part up; push it back down but it goes down easy. I lose my balance. I fall. My feet can't find bottom."

Now I became quiet. I could hear my own heart thumping.

"What are you feeling?" Lana asked.

"My nose burns. I want to cry out but I can't. I can't get air. Help me. I'm suffocating. I see light above the water. I fight toward it, whipping my arms and legs. I can't get air. I gulp water. It's dark."

Again I am still and Lana asked, "What happened then?"

"Uncle Phil. He pulls me out."

"So he saved you?"

"Yes. Mom is holding me now. She wraps the towel around me. I'm crying, coughing, screaming."

"Tell me more."

"Mom says, 'Hush, hush, now you're okay. You'll be fine. You just slipped off the pier. You're okay now.' She squeezes me tight and rocks me in the lawn chair. She says, 'There, there, little one. You're going to be fine.' Then she tells me this is exactly why I should never go out on the pier unless adults are around."

"OK, Judy, good work. So you were okay and your mom was there to comfort you?"

"Yes."

"Now gently bring yourself back further in time and try to recall the day you were born. You can take your time. We're in no hurry here."

I liked that she said there was no hurry. I closed my eyes and tried to flash back. Nothing.

Lana waited a good long minute and said, "What are you feeling? What do you see?"

I figured some image would come up if I just started talking.

"I'm all warm and comfortable inside and then the pressure starts pulling at my head," I said.

I felt insincere. I couldn't seem to get into it.

"OK, Judy, what else are you feeling?"

"I feel kind of stuck, like I can't get in touch with my birth," I said. "There's like a curtain around it. I think there's something different that I need to experience right now."

"OK, do you know what that might be?" Lana asked.

Now my palms began to sweat and my pulse thumped in my ear drums. What was it?

"I had a baby when I was seventeen," I said. "I keep thinking about that."

"Good, Judy. Tell me more."

"I could feel my baby's birth, if I try. Not my birth, but hers. I feel in tune with her."

"That's good. What do you see?"

"It's dark. I feel a tightening. My head. My head is getting tighter … like a vice."

"Now," I thought, "this feels true." Then the story gushed forth as I felt the birth of my baby from her perspective.

"Now there's something cold and hard … along the side of my face. My ear is pinched. It hurts … stings. I feel a pull on my head. It hurts … ripped apart. Pressure … on my chest. There is pulling. Loud voices. Clear and too sharp, not muffled anymore. My head … squeezed. I suck in fluid."

"Tell me more, Judy. What do you feel?"

"It stings. I get free from the tunnel. I open my eyes … shapes around me. I breathe. It burns. The light burns. I feel cold air on my wet skin."

"Good, Judy. Go on."

"I'm suspended in space, but a hard surface is under me. My arms flail to feel something … to hear the beat of the heart… Cold… Quiet… Empty."

"You were alone then in a crib or something?"

"Yes. I cry out … the screech startles me. My lungs hurt… I long for warmth… I punch with my arms and legs … stiff. I miss the warm softness from inside…"

"So you were cold?"

"Yes … frantic. My head hurts. My eyes and lungs burn. I cry and cry…"

I paused again and sat, catatonic.

"Go on, Judy. Now what happened?"

At this point, it occurs to me that maybe I am remembering my own birth; but no, it seems like the birth of my Baby Helen and I can't bear to feel any more of her pain. I am overcome with her sadness at being born. I start to remember my own feelings at her birth, like a new movie scene. I continued the story, but now it was from my perspective. I continued….

"I go and pick her up. I wished I had picked her up. I didn't really do it, but I wanted to…," I said.

"That's good, Judy. Tell me the story like you wished it would have happened. Good work. Tell me more."

Lana's words opened the gate. I felt like wherever I was going was good with her and good for me. I continued.

"I pick her up and hold her close. I walk over to a rocker by the window. I sit down. Immediately she settles down. She is exquisite, beautiful beyond belief. I take her tiny feet and set them in my hands. They fit perfectly. She smells like a heaven rose. I wind the soft, snuggle blanket around her tightly. I hold her face close to my heart, her belly next to mine. I feel her little body warm as I give her my heat. I am holding her close. The love is intense, like the love of God or Buddha, and greater than anything I have ever felt."

In the straight-back chair I bent over and began to cry as the wash of love rose from my soul into great sobs of love, sorrow, and joy.

Then I told her, "Little Baby Helen, it's going to be all right.

Everything is fine. You are going to be okay. I'm your mama and I love you and I have always loved you."

Then I became aware of myself. I found myself crying out loud in a hysterical fit. My behavior scared me as I rocked my imaginary baby.

Lana must have sensed my fear because she said, "It's good to cry. Go ahead. Keep going. You're doing just fine, Judy."

"I'm singing, but it isn't my voice. My mouth is moving and I can feel the air coming from my lungs. The sound is angelic. Silent night, Holy night, all is calm, all is bright.

"Good, good, go on."

"I'm rocking slowly with her in my lap; the rails are creaking as the chair sways back and forth. I look in her eyes and see that she has returned to a place of content and safety. My body melts right into hers. I want to stay here forever holding her and rocking her and looking into her sweet little face. She is perfect."

While I sobbed I realized that I was just letting myself go to that crazy place of imagination. I could feel my rationality slipping away. I was afraid that I was losing it altogether. A voice inside said, "Let it go; let it be. Just go with it. You need this. It is good." But what if I never came back to reality? Wasn't this what it was like to be schizophrenic? Living in a world that only exists in your mind?

Lana said, "Go ahead, my child, it's okay. Tell me what you see now. Tell me how you feel. It's okay to cry. It's good to go here. Feel it all. What are you feeling now?"

"I'm stewing with love for this child in my arms, rocking gently."

As I lived this scene, I became inspired. This was the grace. I was inspired with the feeling that my Baby Helen was all perfect and all beautiful and her intent for birth was strong. Her existence was right and true. I was the vehicle that gave her the gift of life. It was something way beyond a simple accident with the prophylactic. Her life was sacred and I was simply her way to this world. Circumstances were inconsequential. This thought shed a light on me that sparkled away the shame and regret that had held me in its grip since 1967. I could feel the pain slowly spilling out of me, like water through a bucket hole. It was released, unplugged. I let it go. I let it flow where it may. It seeped into the earth. Gone. I felt free.

After Lana's session in the basement of the old church in Salt Lake City, I walked outside. A thin coat of melting snow slushed under my feet; the full moon hung above Lone Peak and the air was warm with the hints of spring. It smelled like wet leaves on their way back to mother earth. I did it. I let myself go there. I relived the birth. I felt the pain like it was yesterday and I lived through it. I walked out feeling like I could flit on the tops of the cedar trees and hold the moon in my arms.

CHAPTER 42
SEARCHING FOR BABY HELEN

The session with Lana brought air to the smoldering leaves so they could burn away. The fire roared as I sobbed and felt every shred of loss and sorrow. Just-cooled cinders evidenced the passing pain, leaving me with peace and acceptance for what is and what was. In the end, it left me free. I found forgiveness for what I had done. Regret slipped away like dew on a summer morn.

I know the mind knows the difference between reality and fantasy, but I wonder if the body knows the difference. I experienced Helen's birth in reality in 1967. Then, eighteen years later, I was able to go to a fantasy place that was fabricated in my mind. I relived the experience, changing it to be the way I always wished it had been. It was kind of like I was dreaming while awake. On some gut level, the rebirthing experience was as real as if I had travelled in a time machine and changed history.

With the aid of Lana, I felt safe enough to allow myself to revisit the painful memories. I gained new insight that eased my shame, guilt, and sorrow. It felt like real life, this rebirthing experience. How was it different from dreams? And how are dreams different from the real world? Does the psyche and body really know the difference?

In the middle of the night I have awakened crying, falling through space, laughing, or flying through the air: then I awake in a daze, like I have been on a trip somewhere. You know that stuff, the emotions, that carry from deep slumber and color the day? After many years of marriage, Dave and I were finding our goals and aspirations at odds. When we were in the thick of disagreements, I used to rise up, tied in a knot of anger. Although my rational mind understood that my emotional state was the repercussion of the dream, my gut didn't know the difference, and I would spend the morning stewing in angst. My dreams often reflected the trials of my waking day.

Perhaps dreams help us iron it out, rework the problems. What if we can control these dreams and direct our images and thoughts to orchestrate healing, or to create the life we want: lucid dreaming at will? Do we create our own reality by our mindful images? And since we can control our own thoughts, can we control our own dreams and then our own reality? Sometimes we need a fresh outlook to realize we have this control. It can come in the form of a healer, like Lana; the form of an enlightening book; or the form of a compelling movie. The mind's experiences are powerful enough to shape our future.

After the rebirthing, the shameful babysitting dreams lessened and I was able to talk more openly about my traumatic teenage pregnancy. I realized the silence of secrecy was harmful, because in speaking up, I was showing love, forgiveness, and acceptance of myself. It was only a few sparse words at first, and my palms would get sweaty and my heart would race. But I kept at it, knowing that speaking up was good for my soul.

I was taking baby steps. The first step was the Cabbage Patch doll, when I pretended she was Baby Helen and I could tell her everything I wanted to say back then. Then it was the rebirthing session with Lana, when I appreciated Baby Helen as a gift and found forgiveness for myself. The third step would be reconnecting with my adopted child. Perhaps the first two steps were getting me psychologically prepared to begin the search. My desire to know what happened to Baby Helen kept bubbling up like the springs at Yellowstone: quiet for a while, then a gurgle, then a bubbling spout, and then quiet again. Then the cycle renewed. What happened to my baby?

I hoped to find out that her life was good. This would ease my worry about whether I did the right thing. I wanted to know where she was and what she was doing. I dared to hope that I could bring her back into my life. Whatever that meant would be entirely up to her. I was afraid, though, that she didn't want to know me, or that she had no interest in finding her birth mother. But unless I searched and found out, I would never know. It wasn't like she was seeking me out. It had been twenty-three years now.

Then I read about an organization in Mothering Magazine called ALMA, which is the Spanish word for soul and stands for Adoptees' Liberty Movement Association. The organization believes that, "The denial of an adult human being's right to the truth of his origin creates a scar which is imbedded in his soul forever." ALMA provides support to adoptees who are seeking their birth parents so they can solve their biological puzzle. I found out I could register as a searching birth parent, and if my child contacted ALMA, she could find me based on her birth date. I was excited to have a path that might solve my greatest mystery. I sent for the registration papers.

Since I hadn't practiced revisiting my memories from 1967, they lay dormant in some tucked-away place. Trying to remember in 1990 was like walking through sticky, heavy mud. Perhaps I was suffering from post-traumatic stress syndrome, but at first I couldn't muster up the answers to basic, important questions, like the date of birth or even the year. Slowly, I navigated through my past, bumping into clues as I reactivated the memory links to past events. It was like stumbling on rocks in a meandering stream. Soon I had enough details to fill out the forms for ALMA.

Birthdate: June 30, 1967. I remembered this because I recalled that the baby was born exactly nine months from the date I conceived, and I knew the fateful party was the last day of September. Time of birth? That was impossible. I thought it was in the afternoon, but I wasn't sure of the time. So I left that one blank. I filled out the rest and carefully folded the forms into an envelope. I hoped this would be my ticket to finding my lost child. I licked the envelope, stamped it, and walked out to the end of our sidewalk. I slid it into the mailbox and flipped the red flag up for the postman to take it. I had taken my first step toward finding Helen.

Now there was a whirling in my belly, a vortex of hope. Any shred of information about her would satisfy my yearning to know of her whereabouts and her life. I hoped this whirl of hope would suck her back into my life someday soon.

It was now June of 1990. When I opened the front door on my daily trek out to the mailbox for news from ALMA, I was often taken aback by the surrounding beauty. I looked up and pulled the mountain air into my lungs, giddy with anticipation of news. The mountains looked different every day. Their massive panorama changed with the seasons, like a slow slideshow. In the fall, as the tree leaves changed from yellow and orange to red and brown, they looked like colored popcorn running along the ridges. By wintertime, the brown changed to a soft lacy white with the first snowfall. In spring, rain soaked the soil and the Wasatch Range became a velvety green. All through the seasons, I anticipated a note informing me that Baby Helen had registered in ALMA and wanted to meet me.

I wasn't sure what I wanted from her: most of all I wanted to know she was okay and that I didn't make a mistake giving her up for adoption. I didn't want to be her mother; I knew she had one, and I had my own sweet children, but if I met her and she was okay and healthy and had good parents, then I would be at peace and be able to go on with my life. And if the meeting went okay, maybe we could develop a relationship. I remembered her baby face and how she looked like Mick, with that square jaw and her round brown eyes. I remembered that she looked Italian, with her dark hair and long lashes. Now that she was in her twenties, I wondered how she had changed into a woman. After hoping for a letter every day, my anticipation dampened as weeks and months went by without any news.

In February of 1991, when Baby Helen was twenty-four years old, I sent an inquiry to the Bureau of Health Statistics, Wisconsin Division of Health, using the wording provided from a searching service. I wrote:

February 24, 1991

Dear Registrar:

Please search for and provide a LONG FORM copy of the record of the birth of my daughter.

Name: Helen Liautaud

Born: June 30, 1967

Mother: Judith Ann Liautaud
Father:
Reason for request: Judicial need
A $5 check is enclosed. Sincere appreciation for any endeavor you extend to this request. Thank you, Judy Rodriguez.

I wasn't sure what judicial need meant, but that is what I had found on a template for sending a search request. It sounded important, anyway. About a month later, I received a letter from the Department of Vital Statistics dated March 13, 1991. It was a form letter with two boxes checked.

In regard to your request:

1. No record has been found from the information given. Is it possible the record has been filed with a different name?

2. We have searched our statewide birth/death/marriage/divorce indexes for the years 1965–1969. No record of the event could be located.

Signed: Section of Vital Statistics: Request #M202174-00.

CHAPTER 43
THE NEXT STEP

The following October, I contacted a support group for birthparents called CUB, Concerned United Birthparents. This is when I learned that Wisconsin is a state with sealed adoption records, which means that the original birth certificate with my name as the birthing mother and Helen's name, date, time, and location of birth is kept in a sealed vault. No wonder my request to the Bureau of Health Statistics came back with no evidence of the birth.

At the time of adoption, the original certificate is replaced by the legal certificate naming the adoptive parents. No mention is made of the adoption. In almost every case, the adoptive parents rename the child, so there is no easy way to find out the child's name or whereabouts. In the rare case of a medical emergency, if genetic information might be needed, the original certificate can be extracted from the vault and released by court order. I didn't see how I would ever find my child.

It seemed like another dead end. However, I did find out that there was a form you could fill out and submit to the courthouse, showing your willingness to be contacted in case the child would request it. It was called a mutual consent form.

I was excited to have something new to try. I hand-printed four pages of medical history and submitted the following:

November 27, 1991
Adoption Unit
State of Wisconsin
Dear Sirs:
In June of 1967, I relinquished a child for adoption. Since that

child is now an adult, I would like to file a Waiver of Confidentiality with the proper Court of Jurisdiction in the event that she desires to contact me regarding her biological background or inherited medical problems. Also, please advise the name of the placing agency.

If you would please supply my information to the Proper Court of Jurisdiction for the following relinquished person it would be gratefully appreciated:

    Birth Name: Helen Liautaud
    Date of birth: June 30, 1967
    Place of Birth: [Wauwatosa] Milwaukee, Wisconsin
    Hospital: Salvation Army Home/Booth Memorial Hospital
    Physician: Dr. Wigglesworth
    Agency Caseworker: Catherine Cavanaugh
    Relinquished by: Judy Liautaud DOB May 1, 1950
    Thank you for your assistance.

Now I had two sticks in the fire: the registration with ALMA and the Adoption Unit with the waiver of confidentiality. If Baby Helen, now an adult, contacted either one, she could get my information. My bucket of hope was replenished.

Even though I knew these attempts were shots in the dark, I held on as the months clicked by. I worried that perhaps she had no interest in me. I knew that adopted children were on both ends of the spectrum. Some cared deeply and wanted to meet their birthparents, while others couldn't care less. I had no way of knowing how Baby Helen felt. The lack of response brought recurring doubts. Perhaps I didn't really deserve to meet her. I had given her away, along with my rights to know anything about her. But yet, I couldn't ignore the yearning inside to reconnect with this child.

After another year of no news, in May of 1992, I called the Salvation Army headquarters to see if I could get any clues to help my search, like the name of the adoption placing agency, or details of the birth. I called the New York office and found out that the Booth Memorial Hospital/Home in Wauwatosa, Wisconsin, was closed in 1982. All of the records had been transferred to an office in Des

Plaines, Illinois. I called this number and asked to have the adoption and medical records related to my stay at the Booth Hospital in 1967 released to me.

"No, we don't give out those records," she said. "They are sealed to protect the privacy of the girls who attended the home and the adoptive parents."

"What about the medical records: can I have access to those?" I asked.

"These can only be released by request from a medical doctor."

"If I had the request, where should I send it?"

The lady gave me the address.

I called my doctor, Val Loggsdon, and asked her to send for my records. They arrived two weeks later. Val said that she had to promise that she would not copy these records or give them to me, but I was free to come in and take a look. I hoped there might be something that said the name of the adoption agency or maybe even the people who adopted my baby. The notes pertained strictly to the medical event. This is what I copied it down:

Baby presented posterior. Second stage labor, pushing, two hours. Delivered by forceps. Baby girl born at 3:07 pm. Date: June 30, 1967, in Wauwatosa at Booth Memorial Hospital. Attending physician: Dr. Wigglesworth. Active labor 17 hours. Baby's weight: 8 lb. 4oz. Episiotomy.

There was no mention as to what happened to the baby. It seemed so real to see these words, written on yellowed paper from over twenty years ago. A few tears spilled on the sheet. There it was in black and white. I did not know it then, but the exact time of birth was the clue that would lead to finding Baby Helen.

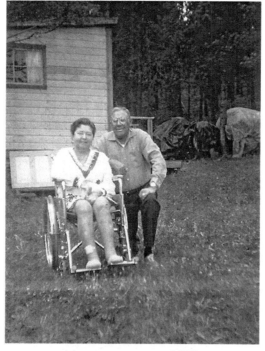

MOM AND DAD 1970

CHAPTER 44
LOSS

While I was living in Colorado, my mom's health continued to decline. She ended up in a nursing home; Jeff would visit her and take her out for an ice-cream cone. On one trip Mom had probably just taken her narcotic pill for pain relief and was talking nonstop. Jeff turned to her and said, "Mom, I'll give you a nickel if you can stop talking for five minutes." Mom said, "You cheapskate, keep your nickel. I'd rather talk."

By the time Kiona was a toddler, Mom suffered serious complications from the steroids she had taken to relieve her arthritic pain. She lingered in the hospital for several days and died peacefully at Passavant Hospital at the young age of sixty-eight. I was thankful that Jeff and my sister-in-law, Mary Ann, were with her. The nurse told them to go out and get some fresh air; when they got back Mom's breath was labored. They prayed and held Mom's hand as she took her last breath.

I regret that, after it was all over, I was never able to talk to Mom about my teen pregnancy. I know she felt responsible because of her illness and absence in the home. I wanted to tell her again that it wasn't her fault and that I made my own choices. But thirty years ago I wasn't ready for such conversations, since I was still protecting the secret. I took comfort in the memories I have of caring for her, answering the buzzer at night, and helping her to the bathroom. I was able to give a bit to atone for the problems I had caused her. In the end, she still called me her blessing in disguise, so I believe that she had forgiven me long before I was able to do that for myself.

It was about eight years after Mom's death and a few winters before Dad died that I went down to visit him in his Florida home.

"The doctor says I have congestive heart failure," Dad said. "That's my ace in the hole." I didn't know what he meant. His ticket to death? An ace in the hole is a good thing. How could congestive heart failure be good? I took it to mean he was ready to die.

He might have been ready, but I wasn't. I longed to get closer to Dad and believed that nursing him or caring for him could be a good way to do that. We had never talked about my teenage pregnancy. It stayed as he wished, like it had never happened. I could feel the wall between us. I knew he was disappointed in me, and it was just another example of my not being able to live up to his expectations. It ran like an underground river in our relationship. The unease hurt me. I longed to be close.

If I could just spend some quiet afternoons with him—maybe tuck the covers around him or bring him a drink of water—it would have been comforting to me. I would then be the person giving, and Dad would be admitting his vulnerable side. It could bring us close. I offered several times to come and stay with him, but he wouldn't have any part of it.

He told me, "Judy, your children should never have to take care of you. It isn't right. It should be the other way around."

"But what if your children want to take care of you?" I asked.

"You don't want to do that. You have your own family. You need to tend to them," he said.

I was angry at him for not understanding that I was the one who needed and wanted to help him. Dad could give and give, but he was very uncomfortable with receiving. He hated depending on others. Getting closer to Dad was something I needed, but I didn't quite know how to get there.

Dad used a heavy dose of hard work as his antidepressant. He often said, "When you get down in the dumps, you just get busy working and before you know it, you feel better."

In his lively years, he spent hours in his tool house by the cabin, cleaning, organizing, or making gadgets out of wood and metal. He cared for his workshop like a baby. Rows of gray cardboard boxes were lined up on his homemade pine shelves, each box numbered with a black Magic Marker. Next to the shelves, tacked to the wall, and protected by a plastic sheath, was an alphabetical list of assorted screws, nails, and hinges, with the box number indexing their location.

As his health began to fail, the muscles in Dad's legs weakened; he couldn't stand long enough to complete a workshop project nor could he get in and out of his fishing boat. Dad's responsibilities at the factory diminished, as my brother John no longer depended on his advice in business matters. By the time Dad was eighty-three, he was often feeling down in the dumps, but he was no longer able to rely on his "get-busy-and-get-to-work" method to help him snap out of it. In his last few years, Dad told me several times, "All my friends are gone. I'm way overdue." Like death would be a relief. I hated it when he said that.

It was mid-September 1986. Fall comes early to the northwoods of Wisconsin. All the families were settled back in Chicago, their cabins closed after Labor Day. It was an unusual circumstance, because Dad had not made his end-of-season plans to have his car driven to Florida nor to purchase his airline ticket. He had worked with my brother Jeff extensively, getting his affairs in order several years earlier. Dad seemed quiet and reflective when I talked to him on the phone a few days earlier.

My dad's youngest brother, Uncle Phil, drove the 450-mile trip from Chicago to visit Dad that lonely day in September. The leaves were starting to change and fall off the trees. Most of the lake people had their piers out of the water in preparation for the winter freeze that would soon cover the lake with several feet of ice. Deer-hunting season was right around the corner.

On September 14, 1986, I got a call from my brother Jeff saying that Dad had died in his sleep. He was eighty-three.

As far as Dad was concerned, the secret of our black heritage was buried with him. When his body failed him with weakness and incontinence, I don't think he could tolerate this loss of control over his own body. As he lived, so he died. It was just like Dad to decide for himself when he was done with it.

When Mom died, I had plenty of warning and knew that her

death finally brought her peace from her suffering. I felt like she had led a full life and was ready to go. But when Dad died, I felt ripped off. I wasn't ready. I was left with a lonely sadness of incompletion. Since his death, I have found ways to commune with him, writing him a letter, doing a role-playing session imagining him talking to me. These days I have peace about his life and death; as an adult, I also have a clearer understanding of his life choices. I love him dearly and Mom, too, and believe they are with me in spirit, guiding me and still loving me as I do them.

CHAPTER 45
THE JOY LUCK CLUB

In November of 1993, Dave and I went to see a movie that propelled me into further action. It was called *The Joy Luck Club*, based on a book written by Amy Tan. The story opens with a woman carrying twins across the countryside in China. She becomes deathly ill and reasons that it will be bad luck for her twin girls to be found next to a dead mother. So she sets them next to a tree, believing they will be found and cared for and continues on her trek, barely able to walk. She ends up living through it all and moving to San Francisco and birthing another child, June. After the mother dies, June receives a letter from the grown twins in China searching for their mother. June goes overseas to meet them and to tell her half-sisters of their mother's death. Their faces fall with sadness and grief as the twins realize they will never be able to meet their mother and wish they had written the letter just a few months sooner. It was a tale of longing and sadness. My throat tightened and I sobbed silently as I thought of how happy this mother would have been to meet her thriving, adult children and to know that they had survived.

The movie brought on a sense of urgency. What if something happened to my child before I was ever able to meet her? I left the theater with a resolve to do whatever it took to move ahead in finding Baby Helen. I was forty-three, and Baby Helen was now twenty-six.

I found the phone number of a professional search artist through an ad in *Mothering Magazine*.

I was nervous as I punched the numbers on the desk phone. It was a late autumn day; dried leaves were blowing against the windows and the wind whistled through the cracks. I took a breath.

I looked at the phone number and dialed.

I hired Mary Sue that day to find my Baby Helen, who was now a woman; she told me it would take four to six months. Mary Sue's fee was $600: I would pay half up front and the rest when Helen was found. I asked how she would go about finding her.

Mary Sue told me that they know her down at the county courthouse, because she does a lot of research. She said that once she had the date, place, and exact time of birth, she goes through all the birth certificates of babies born on that day until she finds the time that matches. This is the identifying clue. Then the baby's given name is available on the certificate.

"Do you have the date and time of birth?" she asked. I was thankful I had the information from my medical records and relayed this to Mary Sue.

I hung up the phone and looked out a nearby window. Light flecks of snow were spinning around the outside corner of the house. Wind whistled through the weather stripping on the glass door. I knew in my gut that I was on the way to finding my child.

Mary Sue had told me that she was only allowed one visit to the courthouse per month and that she was working on several cases. So each month after I hired her, I expected some news. But the waiting trailed on for many months.

CHAPTER 46
BLAST FROM THE PAST

It had been twenty-five years since I spoke to Mick; it was uncanny that he would be calling now, just before I would be making contact with our birth daughter.

My heart thumped as I sat down on the bed with phone in hand and leaned against the pillows. Every shred of attraction and excitement from years ago came down on me. I could hardly think. I didn't know I still cared about him.

He had been thinking of me, he said, was now living in California, happily married with three boys, had his own golf course out back, and his own business as an electrical engineer.

"Geez, it's good to hear your voice," Mick said. Was he throwing me a bone? This time I might sniff, but I wouldn't chomp.

I told Mick that I had just started looking for the child he fathered.

"I always wondered what happened to the baby," he said. "I kind of thought maybe your sister raised it or something."

Mick told me that he wanted to help out, to ease his guilt.

"Why do you feel guilty?" I asked Mick.

"I guess because of how it went down … not cool, on my part. I told my kids about this and they think I'm a real jerk," he said.

I told Mick that if he wanted to, he could pay half of the searching fee. My brother Jim had offered to pay for the other half.

"Sure, I'd love to do that," Mick said. "I'm doing well financially, so it'll be no trouble."

He was doing well financially? My heart sank. I remembered the days when Dave and I lived in the cabin and had to collect coins in a jar to buy milk, the single-wide trailer in Utah, scraping together money for rent when the snow flew and we couldn't teach hang-gliding lessons.

His voice still had that dry wit about it and he still had that contagious laugh. But then I stuffed the fireworks in my gut. It felt disloyal to my husband to linger, even though by now Dave and I were on shaky marital ground.

"I better hang up now, Mick. Do keep in touch. I'll let you know if I hear anything about the search," I said.

I set the phone in its cradle, still pumped with adrenaline. I was shy about showing the silly grin that was plastered to my face.

Dave was in the basement watching TV, so I lit down the stairs to tell him the news.

"That was Mick Romano," I said.

"I know," Dave said as he clicked the remote.

"Are you jealous?"

"No. I don't get jealous."

"Even if I talk to an old boyfriend?" I said.

"No, it doesn't bother me."

Dave was nonchalant and uninterested in the conversation, still staring at the TV.

"He just called me out of the clear blue sky," I said. "I couldn't believe it."

"Why'd he call?" Dave asked.

"I don't know," I said. "He just said he'd been thinking about me. It's so weird that I just started looking for my birth daughter and he called. He said he'd help pay for it."

"That's nice," Dave said and flipped the channel.

I skipped back upstairs to go to bed. Dave had been sleeping in the downstairs bedroom for several years, since he tossed and turned all night and neither of us got much sleep. I fell asleep alone, with sugarplums of Mick dancing in my head.

CHAPTER 47
INTUITION

Why did Mick call me now, after twenty-five years, and right after I started searching for Helen? It was a bit eerie.

I remembered when I was in my first year of college at SIU. I was living in a high-rise dorm when an earthquake rumbled through. As I watched the pictures on the wall rattle and heard the clatter of perfume bottles dancing on my dresser, a shot of panic went through me. But within minutes, the tremors settled down and the phone rang.

"Hi, Judy. Is everything okay? I just had a feeling I should call."

It was my mom. How did she know? Mom's caring love and concern could travel like light.

Mom came to me in spirit during another incident when I needed her. In 1977, Dave was out hang gliding at the Widow Maker Ridge in Utah when he tumbled end over end in the rotor behind the ridge, breaking his back. I was at home when this happened: at that same moment I had an intense feeling that my mother was present. I felt her love wash over me.

About a half hour later, I got the news of Dave's accident. He mended well and suffered no permanent damage except for lingering aches and pains. This incident caused me to suspect that we live on in spirit after our body has been covered in dirt.

So I took Mick's call as another omen that the time was right to find my child. Remembering the story of *The Joy Luck Club*, I had a renewed sense of urgency, and hoped something happened before it was too late. I wondered if this anxious feeling was some kind of motherly instinct like my mom had when she called me after the earthquake.

Four months had passed since I hired Mary Sue. I waited day by day for news. Finally, along about February, we came home from a ski trip in Colorado and the answering machine was blinking. Mary Sue said that she was getting close to wrapping up the investigation, but first—did I want to be on a TV show and have the reunion filmed live in Chicago?

Wrapping it up? Did that mean she had found Helen? I assumed that meant I would hear something soon, but another month passed with no news. I had agreed to appear on the TV show, but since then I had heard nothing. I had the sick feeling that I would be waiting until the talk-show host had an opening or until all the logistics were worked out, so I told Mary Sue that I didn't want to do the show after all. I just wanted to get my information as soon as possible. More weeks passed.

At long last, I received a call from Mary Sue with news.

"I have the contact information for your birth child," she said. "I'll give you the name when I receive the balance owed."

"Do you know anything about her that you can tell me now?" I said.

"She has green eyes, brown hair, and is five feet, five inches tall," said Mary Sue. "I still have to contact the Department of Motor Vehicles to get a current address."

I wired the money to her. Days crept by one after the other while I waited for the final call.

One night that week I had this dream:

I am lying in a blow-up raft and floating at sea. The waves are lapping at the sides. I bounce up and down, afraid to be drifting so far from land. An offshore wind pushes me out in the dark, until the shoreline is gone. Then I hear a baby softly crying in the blackness, somewhere to the right of my raft. I know it was my baby. My lost baby. Then the whimper gets louder, and I reach out to grab her. It seems like I can almost touch the baby, the sound is so close, but I can't see in the blackness. The wind is soft but chilly. I needed to get the baby so I could keep her warm. Then the crying stops.

I hear it again, to my left. The cries are softer and sound like they are farther away. I paddle with my hands to move the raft toward the cries. Then I look up and see someone in a lighthouse. I call out, "Please shine the light. Over here, over here." The lighthouse man walks up a spiral staircase. I think he hears me and is going upstairs to turn on the searchlight. I can still hear the whimpering, faint in the distance. I paddle great dips of water with my bare arms, moving my raft in the direction of the cry. "Please turn on the light," I yell again. Then the man descends the stairs. The wind starts to pick up and the sound of the child vanishes. I hear the waves lapping against my raft.

The man gazes out over the open sea. Wind and spray batter my raft and my body. I hear no further cries. I sob for the loss of the child who was within my grasp. She slipped away. I lay my head down on the raft and let the waves take me farther into the blackness. I am broken with hopeless despair.

Finally the call came with the treasured information.

"Now, Judy," Mary Sue said. "I have your information, but you have to be very careful about contacting her. You can't just barge into her life. She doesn't know you. She might not even want to hear from you."

I swallowed her words like a fish bone. I knew all this. She named my vulnerability. I wasn't a dummy.

"You can't just call her up. One lady who I helped did that; her approach was all wrong and the kid hung up on her and would never talk to her again. She has her life, you know, and she might not want you in it."

"I understand that," I said. "I will put a lot of thought into how I contact her."

"So, do you have my birth daughter's name and information?" I pushed. I'd had enough of the lecturing, enough of the waiting. Finally, the words spilled out of her mouth. I repeated the spelling and wrote it all down.

I hung up the phone and sat in stunned silence until my heartbeat returned to a normal clip. A sense of calm came over me. I was elated to be done with Mary Sue, the phone calls, and the waiting. I looked down at the paper. There it was in black and white:

the information I needed to make contact. Her name was Karen. I ran my hand over the precious words. A shot of electricity pulsed in my veins. I finally had it. Twenty-six years after her birth, I could turn the corner. Perhaps all my questions would be answered very soon.

CHAPTER 48
A CALL TO KAREN

It was one of the wettest Aprils on record in Salt Lake City. Thunderstorms built daily and dumped buckets of rain. After the rivers were full to the brim, the temperature rose to an unseasonably warm 90 degrees. The snow on the high peaks melted all at once and ran from the mountains to the valleys, gaining speed and force. When the water hit the Salt Lake Valley, the rivers couldn't bear the burden and overflowed into basements and roads. State Street turned into a river. Million-dollar homes that sat on the East Bench, overlooking the city, had their yards destroyed by mudslides. Some of them had damaged foundations, and a few slid down the bluff.

Our house, snuggled near the Wasatch Mountain Range, was on the flats and unaffected by the flood. The surrounding ground was crinkled, like a pulled-apart pleated skirt with dips and rises fanning out from the mountain range. Right near our house, where I rode my mountain bike, was a small stream that ran through the gully in the springtime and then dried up by midsummer. This year, as the rain and snow melt came down in torrents, the little gully overflowed with silt, sand, and mud and turned the twenty acres into a lake. At one point, the water was running so fast that you couldn't walk across the gulley—the force would knock you down. When it was all over, the weedy sand fields were just a sea of mud.

Several years later, after the flood was long forgotten, some fancy developer built high-priced luxury homes in that gully. When I walked through the new neighborhood, I noticed that the areas that were once rivers and gooey mud were now lush green lawns with little footbridges nestled among flower gardens and tomato patches. I remembered the destruction and chaos that once ravaged the area.

I wondered if the people who bought those homes knew that they were built on a gully that was once a mud river.

Perhaps it was just a freak of nature, the perfect combination that year of early warm temperatures and heavy thunderstorms in April. Perhaps it would never happen again. But then again, perhaps it would. It reminds me of all the things we try to control, even though the forces of nature are beyond our control. We go on living after a hurricane, tornado, mudslide, or fire, trying to find a sense of safety by forgetting that it ever happened: but deep down we know it could happen again. Our capacity to weather the unimaginable astounds us.

Nature follows its course, regardless of how we try to control it. The best we can do when disaster strikes is go with the flow, forget about wishing it wasn't so, and take note of the blessings brought by wind, rain, fire, or death. Even though I prayed hundreds of rosaries, there was no way to change the course of nature. I asked God to give me a break, make it untrue, make the unwanted pregnancy go away when I was just sixteen. But, of course, once the baby was conceived, the outcome was inevitable and nature took over.

Now, after forty-five years, once in a while I wake and have the awful feeling that disaster is looming, but I take inventory and realize that all is well and I sigh back into peace. But the nagging feeling persists, and perhaps it is the reason I am writing this story. The unease has lessened at an accelerated pace in the past years. I suppose that is because of the writing and listening to the feelings that are asking to be heard and felt. I never will forget the chaos and fright that colored the nine months of my junior year of high school, yet facing those memories directly as an adult has reduced the threat that these strong emotions will knock me flat.

Now that I had Karen's name and address and was done with the search, I could turn the corner—but how to approach her?

"Uh, hi, I'm your mother. No, not your mother, but I gave birth to you. Wanna meet me?" Oh, geez. How could I? What would I say? I decided to find someone to help me with this, a consultant. I found an ad posted by Charlene in the publication for MANA:

Midwives Alliance of North America.

The rain of that wet spring kept coming until it gave way to the white daffodils and yellow hyacinths in our back yard. I called Charlene.

"Charlene, I have the contact information for my adopted child," I said. "I wondered if you could coach me on how to make contact?"

"Oh, how exciting for you!" said Charlene. "You know, I do searches myself and often make the first phone call on behalf of the client. Would you like me to do that?"

"That'd be a godsend," I said. "I don't think I could do it myself."

"I've done this many times and would be honored to help out."

Charlene's voice was deliberate and sweet. I didn't meet her in person, but I loved her soft demeanor. I needed her. I wished I could reach through the telephone wire and hug her.

"What will you say when you call?" I asked.

"I'll say something like this, 'I'm calling on behalf of someone you don't know, but she has been thinking about you since the day you were born.'"

"That's a nice way to put it," I said. "I wouldn't have thought of that."

"I'll say that you wanted to make contact so that you could know she was okay and ask if she is willing to meet sometime."

"Ah, that's good," I said. "Will you call and let me know as soon as you reach her?"

"Of course. I'll call you right after I make contact."

The targeted date was set. I couldn't believe that I might soon hear what Baby Helen's life had been like. Karen, her name was Karen. I wanted to hear that her life was good. It could go either way. I knew nothing, but soon I would have some answers. I hoped she was receptive to hearing from me.

Charlene called me at about 9:30 on Wednesday night. She said that she was able to talk to my birth daughter. My heart flitted with the news.

Charlene said that Karen was shocked and totally stunned to hear that her birth mother had found her. She had been curious about me, but didn't know how to go about finding anything out. She wanted to know about our family's medical history, and she asked how I was able to locate her. She wanted to know what I looked like and how old I was.

Karen, now twenty-six years old, told Charlene that she couldn't have asked for better parents. She was a nurse living in Madison, Wisconsin, and had been married for a year and a half. She was a cheerleader during school and played many sports. Karen has always known she was adopted and has an adopted brother and sister. At the end of the twenty-minute conversation, Charlene asked Karen how she would like to proceed.

"Can Judy contact you, or would you like to make the first move?" said Charlene.

Karen said she would contact me. Charlene then gave her my name, address, and phone number.

I breathed out all the tension and fear I held inside worrying about this child as I listened to Charlene's summary of the call. What a blessing and rush of good fortune. I now had a vague but real picture of my birth child. I felt at peace and that the fruits of my labor were not in vain. My child was healthy, alive, and had gone to good parents. My insides sparkled like fireflies. I hoped she would contact me soon. I was dying to talk to her and meet her.

But Karen was in no hurry to contact me. With every ring of the telephone, I hoped it might be her. I checked the mailbox daily, hoping for a letter or a picture. I waited three months, until I didn't think I would ever hear from her. So in June, I wrote her this letter:

June 21, 1994
Dear Karen,
I recently wrote this story about my teenage pregnancy twenty-seven years ago. I wanted you to read it so you could understand why I gave you up for adoption and what it was like being pregnant and single in the 60s. I wanted to wait until I heard from you because you had asked to make the first move in contacting me. As time goes on, I wonder if perhaps it is difficult for you to write a letter to a total stranger. Our relationship is strictly genetic at this point. I can imagine that you may

have some apprehension about contacting me.

My reasons for searching for you are many. I wanted to know if you'd had good parents. I was elated to hear that you couldn't have asked for better parents and that your life has been full and good. Please know that I do not need to or want to be a parent to you. I would like to get to know you, though. I would like to meet you. I am curious to see who you look like and to see how genetics has influenced you. I am sure that my needs are different from yours. As my story tells, there was a great loss at giving you up to adoption in 1967. I have healed from that loss through the years. My search for you and finding the answers to some of my questions have helped me along.

Now should our relationship be the start of a friendship—or a mere exchange of information—that is up to you. I do hope I hear from you soon, but I entirely respect your feelings and wishes. My family will be going to Wisconsin over the 4th of July. If you'd like to meet a bunch of relatives, we'd love to have you come visit. It is in the Spooner-Hayward area. Until I hear from you, kind wishes, and happy 27th birthday on Thursday.

Judy

Still, there was no word from Karen. Three months later, I called her home. I talked to her husband, Brian, and said that I was sorry to be calling, but I had written a letter and hadn't heard from Karen and wondered if she had received it.

"Yes," he said. "Karen was happy to get your letter and read your story."

Relief gushed through me. "But why hadn't she contacted me?" I wondered.

"Brian, I know she must be apprehensive to meet me, but we're going to my nephew's wedding next month and will be in the Madison area. I was wondering if we could possibly meet, if she is willing."

"I think that would be a great idea," Brian said. "I have been encouraging Karen to follow up on the contact. I think it'll be good for you two to meet. I'll ask her. I'll have her call you."

The next day, I got a call from someone who sounded like Mick's sister. It was Karen.

"Brian told me you called, and I think it would be okay to meet," she said.

"That's wonderful," I said. "Where should we meet?"

"You could come to my house."

Karen's voice sounded sweet and kind, yet skeptical. I hung up the phone and couldn't believe I finally talked to her and would meet her soon. I was jumpy with delight, anticipation, and fright.

Since we were all going to the wedding in Madison, it was planned that Kiona, Tessie, Dave, and I would go together to meet Karen and Brian at their home.

As we drove through the neighborhood, I asked Dave to pull over so I could comb my hair, put on some lipstick. My heart was thumping in my throat. We were equipped with photos of our family and the extended family. Karen and Brian lived in a newer subdivision with modest homes. The yard was spiffy clean and the grass green. I walked up to the house with my family and pressed the bell. I heard the Ding-aling ring through the house, then barking. Brian answered the door.

JUDY AND KAREN REUNION DAY 1993

CHAPTER 49
LOST AND FOUND

I was warmed and relieved when Karen walked up to me and opened her arms for a welcoming hug.

"Hi, Karen," I said. "I'm so happy to meet you finally."

"Me too. Come in," she said.

When I walked into her living room, I had to control myself. I wanted to hug her and swallow her up in my arms. I wanted to say, "Karen, oh, Karen is it really you?" If I had let my heart go, I would have made a bubbling, idiotic fool of myself. But I couldn't. I had to respect her feelings. And besides, I couldn't feel any of that coming from her. She looked at me with guarded reserve. She wasn't elated, like I had hoped. She hadn't missed me. She hadn't loved me the way I loved her. Perhaps she even resented me. After all, I was this woman who didn't her. I was this birth mother who handed her over and never came back into her life until now. I was but the oven that carried her until she was done. I hadn't even held her. She had her mother. She had her family.

I was like an extra digit. A little freaky, not really needed, yet a part of her.

She could have been my niece. She looked just like Jackie's daughters, so familiar, yet strange, too, and unknown. She had a family resemblance about her that was warm and attractive. My heart sparkled with joy at the sight of her. Oh, how I wanted to squeeze her in my arms and say, "Oh, baby, my lost baby, you live! You are here! You are real! It feels like heaven here with you. I want to be close to you and know all about you. What is your life like? Please let me hold you close."

But I couldn't do any of this. I swallowed my elation and held it tight within. I followed her lead and acted unnaturally reserved. She was stunning. Her smile, all teeth. A true Liautaud. Her eyes—I had seen them before. She still had Mick's square jaw and his Italian lush eyelashes. She was so pretty. I couldn't take my eyes off her, but I forced my eyes away, so as not to stare. Her body was well formed and in perfect shape.

After the introductions, we sat down and we talked, my family and hers. She showed me pictures of her mom and dad, of her brother and sister, pictures of their lake place that they shared as they grew up. She didn't ask too much about me. I was expecting her to ask what genetic diseases might run in our family, or what talents we had. She talked about her career as a nurse and showed us pictures of her high school cheer-leading days. I imagined her popular and athletic. Our visit was a bit clinical and matter-of-fact. I should not have expected anything different; she did not know me, after all.

Still, my insides were vibrating with joy, and I took what I could get. But a few hours after we had left, a wall of sadness hit me. I was able to grasp the reality of all that I had missed that was hers: the years of her growing up, her first tooth, her first step, her first date, her wedding. I was sad that Karen did not seem to want me to be a bigger part of her life. "But I must give her time," I thought. "Maybe some time and distance under our belts will change that."

Much later, Karen told me that her mom always worried that I would come back into her life and steal her away. Her mom was not happy that I had contacted Karen. She was skeptical of my advances and asked, "How do you know this person who contacted you is really your birth mother?" I really was an imposter: I had been gone from the scene and came back into Karen's life when she was a full adult. It is understandable that Karen might have felt disloyal giving me the attention I craved. Then again, maybe she just had no need or desire to do this. I understood that. I so wanted to see her again and get to know her, but I didn't think that is what she wanted, so I doubted it would happen like that. The gap between my desires and reality made me very sad.

My meeting with Karen was bittersweet. Bitter to realize she lived "fine" without me. Sweet to know she lived "fine" without

me. What was it? Bitter or sweet? Adoption is a painful choice for
a birth mother and quite unnatural. Abortion is not a good choice
for a birth mother: it is brutal and inhuman. Keeping the baby is
not a good choice for a birth mother who is only seventeen and
has no husband or baby-raising skills or financial security. There
are no good choices for a teen birth mother. So would it have been
better that the prophylactic did not split in two? Would it have been
better that the conception not occur within my young body, which
was unready for the consequences? If I could have made the choice
when I was sixteen, I would have said, "Please! Let none of this be
happening to me."

Now that I am sixty-one and I see the young, beautiful, bright,
intelligent wife and mother of two who is Karen, I can only know
in my heart that the choice was made for me and bigger than
my little body or mind could fathom. The lesson is in letting go,
giving up, and giving thanks for what is. Life unfolds in mysterious
and beautiful ways; I have very little say in this process. I am
continuously learning to let go, let live, and let love wash over the
beauty that has taken me on this journey of sorrow, joy, and life.

Today I feel that of the options open to me at the time, adoption
was the best choice. Could it have been less painful if it had been
an open adoption and I knew during her growing years that she
was well cared for? And could my pain have been lessened if I had
followed my motherly call to hold her when she was born and then
be conscious in my love and choice to give her away? I will never
know the answers to these questions, but I have often looked back
and been thankful that the pregnancy was not terminated by my
halfhearted punches or my father's wishes. The pain of giving her
away was a fair trade for a child who was able to flourish in the arms
of a loving couple.

Over the years I have met with Karen and her family several
times, and I always enjoy spending time with them. I continue to
wish that Karen and I had a closer relationship, but I am honored by
whatever it is that she is able to give at this time.

JUDY AND JOE 2011

Photo by Jonathan Chapman

CHAPTER 50
CHANGES

Dave and I raised our children together. It was mostly a happy marriage full of adventure, yet laced with struggle and poverty. In the final five years, our values and aspirations pulled us in opposite directions: twenty-eight years after we married in the mountain meadow, we went our separate ways. Although painful, the divorce was the best solution for both of us and we were able to split up our assets without involving lawyers, for which I am grateful. Afterward, some said they were surprised we lasted as long as we did because Dave and I were such opposites. I was humbled by the divorce, because I always thought people who split just gave up too easily. That wasn't true with me. I had tried desperately. In the end I see that it was best, as I am better able to align myself with people who nurture my spirit.

After I found Karen, I told Mick and he wanted to meet her. Karen was also curious to meet her birth father. So the following spring, Mick and I traveled to Milwaukee to meet with Karen and her husband for lunch. Mick, like me, was proud of her beauty and sweet spirit. We all seemed a bit nervous, but Karen asked Mick some questions about his family, and he has kept in touch with her over the years.

After Dave and I split up, I spent eight years longing and looking for a new life partner. It was a good lesson in patience: you can't pluck a tulip before it emerges. The years I spent alone prepared me to recognize the gem I found in Joe, and I give thanks every day that he is in my life. My dear Joseph is solid, true, hardworking, astoundingly intelligent, and the main champion of my writing life; most important, I like who I am when I am with Joe.

When Joe and I married in 2006, Karen and Brian attended our wedding and were able to meet my relatives. Some of them found out on the wedding day for the first time that I had a child when I was seventeen. Everyone was curious and gathered around Karen and Brian like they were the main attraction. I hope they were not overwhelmed. It was an outpouring of love, really. My family wanted to swallow Karen right into the fold. Who wouldn't? She is darling and sweet. We wanted to claim her as ours.

A couple years after the wedding, I sent this e-mail to Karen on her birthday:

June 30, 2008
Dear Karen,
You can't be forty-one, can you? I am so blessed to have met you after all the years of thinking about you and wondering if you were having a good life and if you were okay. The first time I saw you when you were an adult, I wanted to hug you and cry. I felt like my baby had died and God said, "Just kidding." It was so healing to find you happy and healthy.
You know when you were born I wanted to hold you so badly, but I was afraid that if I did I would never be able to give you away. I was in a fog, just following the choices that were made for me. I never imagined I had a choice in your adoption. I figured I had messed up and now I had to atone for my sins.
When we met again, what was it? Twenty-six years later? I was sorry I had not been a part of your life and had missed your childhood. Hardly a day went by that I did not think of you. Now you have your own babies and a successful career in nursing. If I had the right, I would be so proud of you. I still am proud. I hope someday, when it is right for you, that we can have a closer relationship and that I can get to know you and your family and spend time together. I have always loved you so.

Happy Birthday,
Judy

Karen wrote back on the same day:

Hi Judy,

Thanks for the nice thoughts on this day; I don't feel a day over thirty! It was nice to see you. At first I felt an instant connection, like I had known you before. I tell a lot of people about you and how I became me. I tell them about your time with midwifery and making books for kids, and how talented, smart, and in good shape you are—and that you drive a Harley, and how down-to-earth you are and sweet. I also tell them how talented you and your family are, from seeing them at your wedding—there are also a lot of medical people in your family. It was so nice to meet them; I am glad that I went. It helped me to meet you, to fill a void, a hole—of where I came from. I feel privileged to have come from such a lovely family as yours. I wish my mom could be more open to talking about you, but I don't bring it up. Someday there may be a time to see each other more. Time will tell, and I would love for my mom to meet you someday.

My life is so busy and full right now with school, I'm telling everybody that I have to be a hermit this summer to get through school. It is a lot of work, more than I had ever imagined. I just take a day at a time and go forward, I persist, and I won't quit, although I would like to at times. My mom taught me never to quit anything, keep going no matter what.

Judy, you did what you had to do when you were sixteen—it was what you needed to do at that time in your life. I have such a wonderful life, and meeting you helped me to understand where my roots started. So I thank you from the bottom of my heart for letting me in yours.

Love,
Karen

The following Christmas I asked Karen if it was okay if I sent this letter to her mother. She agreed, so I sent it off. It read:

December 22, 2008
Dear Mark and Stella,
When I gave Karen up for adoption, I didn't know much about the family that received her. All I knew was that they were Catholic. I prayed that she had gone to a good family. For many years, I worried about the time when I would find out about her life.

Ten years ago, I was able to find out that you, Mark and Stella, were the parents of Karen. She tells me that she has had a blessed life, full of love and caring, and that she couldn't have asked for better parents. I am so thankful. It was a healing experience for me to learn of her upbringing and the parents who nurtured Karen into the beautiful woman she is today.

Stella, Karen tells me that you are a retired teacher, but still busy with volunteer work. I, too, am in the education field. I write and publish children's educational books that teach times tables and addition with cartoons and stories. I hope that someday I can meet you and tell you in person how grateful I am to you.

When I was sixteen and became pregnant, it was the worst thing that could have happened to me. Now, forty-one years later, I realize it was a blessing and a gift to give birth to Karen. Thank you so much for being the mother that I could never be. I know the sacrifices you have made because of the love you have for your children.

Sometimes I wonder if I got pregnant just because you were meant to be the mother of Karen. Some things are beyond our understanding and control and I just believe in my heart that Karen's life was meant to be just as it is. Thank you both for being the great part of her life and taking such sweet care of her.

Merry Christmas to you,
Judy Liautaud

Although I have not met Karen's parents, I received their family Christmas letter after Stella received my letter. I can tell they have a close family and there is plenty of love and cheer.

CHAPTER 51
SUNLIGHT IN THE SHADOWS

In Sept of 1996, my oldest daughter, Kiona, was accepted to the Medical College of Wisconsin in Milwaukee. We packed up a U-Haul and headed to the Midwest. Her apartment happened to be in the same town as the Martha Washington Home for Unwed Mothers. Twenty-nine years had passed.

Even though I knew that the home had closed in 1982, I wanted to visit the area. I headed off to the store alone, and took a detour over to 6306 Cedar Street. I parked along the side of the street under some tall elm trees, opened the car windows, and sat in the shade. I smelled the air. I remembered sitting out in the yard, talking to the other girls. I remembered walking down the street going to town, and I remembered the bookstore incident when the owner told us to get out.

The familiar smells activated the nerve endings of my memory. I felt it all: the longing, the loneliness, the fear, the isolation, the grief of my baby's disappearance, the free feeling of driving home in Jeff's Mustang when it was all over. The emotions from the past rode in waves that crested with each whiff of the summer air. I sat in the car and wept. It amazed me that I went through all this and had come out the other end, still sane, still hurting.

I became self-conscious sitting in a parked car and worried that a neighbor would wonder why I was hanging around. I started the car and pulled away with a heavy, yet grateful heart that it all was in my past. I felt a yearning to someday write my story.

Being a child of my father's, I wanted to please him and I wanted to follow his rules. I felt I owed him that much, after breaking his trust and doing things my way—look where that got me. But as the years ticked by, I came to know that I could not hold the secret close any longer. It was like a boiling cauldron, the pressure prodding me to take off the lid, air it out. I would come to know that I did not have to hold that sadness, grief, and shame. I could let it go once I had looked closely.

I see now that the cover-up, although a relief and a seemingly perfect solution to my dilemma at the time, ended up causing a cancerous erosion of self-esteem. Even if others believed I was away because I had a serious disease, it had no lessening effect on the shame and grief I harbored. I learned coping mechanisms that pushed down the rising of intense feelings, capturing me behind a wall of fog.

Then the sunlight came. It came in the form of the Cabbage Patch baby lying on the bedroom floor, longing to be picked up. It came in the form of Lana, the midwife who guided me back in time so I could revisit my baby's birth day. It came in finally meeting Karen and seeing the starlight in her eyes. It came in the form of writing the memories from my days at the home for unwed mothers. It came in revisiting my story by talking with family and friends, forty years later.

It came in a renewed sense of spirituality. Once the pain and trauma were released from my body, mostly through writing, I was able to see some spiritual light. In my early twenties, I seriously questioned my Catholic religion, and I was bereft. Although I loved nature and was spiritually lifted after a day playing in the waves on Bond Lake, or smelling the pines while walking through the woods looking for mushrooms, or feeling the mountain breeze at my back as I biked the bluffs of Moab, I still longed for a deeper connection.

Over the years, I attended many different churches; St. Joan of Arc's, an active Catholic church, alive with uplifting guitar and song and members calling themselves recovering Catholics, because they grew up in the church and were putting guilt and the fear of hell into a more healthy perspective. I worshipped with Quakers, who strive to be devoid of ritual and judgment, and believe that God is within each of us. I attended Unitarian and Universalist churches.

Although each spoke to my soul, none filled my longing for a deeper spirituality.

It started as a teen but during my early twenties, I aggressively questioned everything I had been taught. I started to think organized religion was for the weak-minded, evidence of an inability to think on your own. My view was myopic, coming from my own experience. Today, my judgmental attitude has softened. People I love dearly have shown me by example how their religion has brought them deep comfort and strength. These are some of my favorite people on the planet, so how could I think they should choose something different just because it is not what I believe? I honor and cherish them for their beliefs, for that is what makes them who they are.

For myself, I have come to believe that there are many paths to spirituality. I have trudged along to find my own. A few years ago, I visited my daughter, Tessie, who was now married to CJ and living in England with their four children. While driving on the way to catch the train to London, I asked Tessie if she was worried about making the wrong decision. They were buying a home in Omaha, Nebraska, yet lived so far away. Tessie said, "No, I don't worry about it. I pray to the Holy Spirit and ask for guidance, and I have faith it will work out." "How comforting that must be for her," I thought, "and how perfect to have the Holy Spirit guiding her." I asked how she knew what the Holy Spirit was trying to tell her. She said, "There is a still small voice, just a quiet knowing. Nothing like bugle horns or loud speakers, subtle."

I saw the sparkle and light in her eyes as she told me about this, and I knew the comfort it gave her. Sunlight again, as I began to think about her words and thought maybe, just maybe, long ago, I threw out the noodles with the boiling water. If I didn't believe in God as the judging Father that I had disappointed, maybe I could reinvent a new version. I believed in intuition and that we humans have spiritual powers beyond our conscious reason—like the feeling that you should go a certain way, and you later find out what a blessing it was. Like the night I attended that speed-dating session where I met my Joseph. I hadn't planned to go, but was invited at the last minute by the owner of the company. And Joe was going to blow it off, but something told him to give it a try. That was the night we met, and how different and empty my life would have been without that fateful meeting.

So, I stumbled upon the belief that there is a spirit inside of me that knows what is best for me. This could be my Holy Spirit. I don't think of it as outside of me and inaccessible, but always there within me, my spirit that guides me toward the light. So I started to pray. "Holy Spirit, help me find the words to write my story." Or, "Holy Spirit, please show me the path to be nonjudgmental and give love." The minute I started praying like this, I felt a shift and a knowing that my prayers could guide me. It was the spiritual connection I had longed for.

After Karen read this book, she told me that she had watched the same movie that put me in action to search, the movie of the forfeited twins, *The Joy Luck Club*, the night before she received the call from Charlene to tell her that I, her birth mother, had been looking for her. Was this a connection orchestrated by the Holy Spirit within us, preparing her for my contact?

I know my Holy Spirit might not come in the same outward form as Tessie's Holy Spirit, nor is it likely to follow the same arrangement that my brother Jeff has with his God. But for me, this is a matter of semantics. I believe it is the place where we connect as humans. We each may use different words to describe our path: God, spirituality, Holy Spirit, or intuition. But I believe our earthly journey leads to the same destination, enabling a closeness and connection with the spirit.

I am watching the soft morning light coming through the raindrops on the window and reflecting on my past. My lesson is about blowing up the secret: the part inside of me that wants to hide who I really am, the part of me that walks with my head down and my tail between my legs because of all the shame.

No wonder I acted like that, I realized as I wrote. No wonder I didn't hold my baby; I thought I would be protecting myself from lingering hurt and pain. No wonder I was caught in the web of guilt and secrecy; I thought I could undo my sins against the church and my culture with secrets. No wonder I gave my baby away; I made the decision before I knew that the lump in my belly was an exquisite child I could not help loving—and then I believed it was too late to question my decision.

In understanding that young person who was me at fifteen, sixteen, and seventeen years old, I came to love her and forgive her for all the mistakes she made. I put my arms around that me-child and I weep for her and love her.

The fear of rejection, the fear of standing up for my own feelings by simply expressing them: these have been the ghosts in my closet. Writing my story has opened the door to let the ghosts scatter. It has brought sunlight to the shadows.

No dark secret with spider webs and monsters hidden inside, no smoldering leaves that can't get enough air for the fire to burn, just pure light of what is. And this is the honesty, the newfound strength within, the newfound strength of acceptance. There is no longer anything to fear, no longer a secret to keep.

I no longer wish for a better past.

I laid down the shame as I laid down each word of my story.

In the talking and writing, sunlight was brought to the shadows. I have no secret to keep, no shame to hide, no regret to mourn. I am no longer Judy L., a truncated version of myself. I am Judy Liautaud, fifth child of Ethel and John, descendant of the family that passed for white in 1911; my nickname is Pood, Goonsfield, or Jude.

It is a fresh start. We all have our secrets, our sorrows, and our regrets. I tell myself, "Embrace them; love yourself for your humanness."

Let the good light continue to shine on truth and all of who we are. Let there be sunlight in the shadows.

LIAUTAUD FAMILY 1959

ACKNOWLEDGMENTS

I would like to give thanks to the following people who held me up during the four years of collaboration of *Sunlight on My Shadow*:

Thanks to my daughter Kiona, who read innumerable drafts and gave me encouragement and guidance along the way.

To my daughter Tessie, for her empathy and loving acceptance, and her husband CJ, who helped me fill in some important blanks.

To my niece Jacki, and my sister-in-law Mary Ann, for their expertise as readers and well-thought-out suggestions.

To my niece Marian, who gave tears, hugs, and rules of style during the editing process.

To my dear friend Ephia, for her final edits and suggestions.

To my lifetime friends, Annie and Jane, who believed in my writing journey and helped me remember details from our high school days.

To my friends from the St. Croix Writers group, for without their cheerleading qualities I may never have finished this book; especially to Cathy and Bob Swanson, Jan Jenson, and Mary Beth Smith for previewing and editing my manuscript.

To my fellow writers at the Loft Literary Center in Minneapolis: John Evans, Lucy Forster-Smith, Abby Bloom, and especially Debra Palmquist for her relentless feedback and dedicated help.

To my writing mentors: Elizabeth Jarrett Andrew and Paulette Alden, who gave me the direction to hone my drafts. And to my copy editor, Alison Baker, who always knew why.

To my brothers Jeff, John, and Jim, who said they wished they had known the details so they could have been there for me and for offering nothing but love and tender respect for my writing journey.

To my sister Jackie, who often had tears in her eyes when I read at St. Croix Writer's Group and helped me with her edits and suggestions.

To my husband Joe, for his editing expertise, his steady love, and belief in my book, and for asking, "Did you write today? Because I like it when you write; it makes you happy."

About the Author

Judy Liautaud is the author of several children's educational books including *Times Tables the Fun Way, Addition the Fun Way,* and *Story Problems the Fun Way.* Her books teach children to learn the basic math facts with cartoons and stories. She became interested in education when she co-owned a Sylvan Learning Center in Bountiful, Utah.

Judy studied as an apprentice to become a lay midwife and delivered babies at home for seven years. She quit the profession to go back to school and graduated from the University of Utah with a Bachelor of Science degree in Psychology.

Judy backpacked through Mexico, Central, and South America, flew hang gliders, and designed and manufactured hang gliding harnesses for Wasatch Wings, which she co-owned.

Her passion today is writing books and operating City Creek Press, her publishing company which started in 1992.

Judy loves spending time with her grandchildren and their parents, writing at the lake cabin in northern Wisconsin, biking, and tennis. She lives in the Minneapolis area with her husband Joe.

Judy's Blog http://sunlightonmyshadow.com
City Creek Press Website http://citycreek.com

author photo by Jonathan Chapman

SUNLIGHT ON MY SHADOW